The Axman Came from Hell

and Other Southern True Crime Stories

The Axman Came from Hell

and Other Southern True Crime Stories

Keven McQueen

Pelican Publishing Company
Gretna 2011

The word "Pelican" and the depiction of a pelican are
trademarks of Pelican Publishing Company, Inc., and
are registered in the U.S. Patent and Trademark Office.

Library of Congress Cataloging-in-Publication Data

McQueen, Keven.
The axman came from hell and other Southern true crime
stories / Keven McQueen.
    p. cm.
Includes bibliographical references and index.
    ISBN 978-1-58980-898-0 (pbk. : alk. paper) 1. Crime—
Southern States—Case studies. 2. Murder—Southern
States—Case studies. 3. Criminals—Southern States—
Case studies. 4. Murderers—Southern States—Case
studies. I. Title.
    HV6793.A13M37 2011
    364.10975—dc23

                                2011018059

Printed in the United States of America
Published by Pelican Publishing Company, Inc.
1000 Burmaster Street, Gretna, Louisiana 70053

This book is dedicated to Nick Wilson and all of America's military men and women, past, present, and future; and also, once again, to my mother. As the years grow longer, the distance grows shorter.

Contents

Acknowledgments

Without whom it would not have been possible:
Lara Beserock; Blu and Loretta's mom; Sally Boitnott; Nancy Burris; Terry Callaway; Geneta Chumley; Sandee Clemons; Drema Colangelo; Gaile Sheppard Dempsey; John Douglas; Eastern Kentucky University Department of English and Theatre; Eastern Kentucky University Interlibrary Loan Department; Wayne Everard and the New Orleans Public Library; Lisa and Tayler Fox; Rosie Garcia-Grimm; Ken Grimm; Nina Kooij and everyone at Pelican Publishing; the *Louisville Courier-Journal;* Kyle and Bonnie McQueen; Darrell and Swecia McQueen; Michael, Lori, and Blaine McQueen and Evan Holbrook; Darren and Alison McQueen; Lee Mitchum; Pat New; John Newman; the *New Orleans Times-Picayune;* Karen Ortolano; Suzanne Pfefferle; Bill Stafford; Mark Taflinger; Mia Temple; University of Florida Interlibrary Loan Department; Ashley Wray; Chris Youngblood. Also: the Author, to use Benjamin Franklin's phrase. This book was edited by Lee Mitchum.

The Axman Came from Hell

On the night of August 13, 1910, a malevolent figure skulked through the streets of New Orleans, avoiding the streetlights' glare. The tropical heat that afflicted the city even past midnight would be no deterrent to his plan. It is easy to picture him inspecting all the corner groceries he passed, trying not to look suspicious, until he found one that met his expectations: August Crutti's store at Lesseps and Royal Streets. Around 3:00 A.M., he carefully removed a pane of glass from the store's rear door, reached in, unlatched the door, and committed a crime so bizarre that the police concluded "he was either drunk or crazy."

As was common practice at the time, the front of the building was the grocery and the rear section was living quarters for the Crutti family. After making his way into the kitchen, the intruder walked barefoot through the house until he found the master bedroom. Mrs. Crutti awoke to see a man bending over the bed, holding up the mosquito bar with his left hand and grasping a meat cleaver with his right. She would be one of only three witnesses to hear the killer speak and live to tell about it. "Give me all you've got," he said in a rough voice. "Come on! Give it to me."

The terrified woman suddenly became aware of two things: she felt a spreading dampness and Mr. Crutti was stretched out along the foot of the bed. "You must have killed my husband. He don't hear you," she said to the stranger.

"Come on, give your money to me. Hurry up," he replied. She handed him a box containing eight dollars. There was more hidden in the room, but she was not about to tell him that. Mrs. Crutti shook her husband and heard him groan.

He rolled over and fell out of the bed. She then realized that he was bleeding from a head wound. The "burglar," as she and the police naïvely took him to be, stepped over and gave the unconscious Mr. Crutti a parting whack on the back of the head with his cleaver. But instead of taking advantage of this opportunity to search for valuables, the attacker took only a cage containing the Cruttis' pet mockingbird and walked back into the kitchen. He left the same way he came in.

Mrs. Schultz, a neighbor who lived across the street, said that she saw the "short, heavyset" man exiting the Cruttis' grocery/residence. In the dim light, she could see him walking across the yard, carrying the bird in one hand and the cleaver and his shoes in the other. At the end of the yard, he tossed the weapon, scaled the fence, and then walked nonchalantly on bare feet to Dauphine Street. Mrs. Schultz saw him sit on a doorstep, release the mockingbird, roll a cigarette, and enjoy a nice leisurely smoke. All the while, Mrs. Crutti was screaming for help and trying to rouse the neighbors, but the man paid no attention. At length, he put on his shoes and sauntered away into the darkness.

Neighbors arrived and lifted the injured Mr. Crutti onto his bed. He had taken at least two blows from the cleaver to the back of his head. Though he had been badly cut and knocked unconscious, he sustained no serious injuries and fully recovered. He was unable to describe his attacker to the police, but Mrs. Crutti described the man as about 5'6", broad-shouldered and clean shaven, and in his mid to late thirties. He had dark hair, a broad nose, and "turned-up, thick lips." Despite the heat, he wore a blue jumper, dark trousers, and a black derby.

The New Orleans Police Department admitted that it was baffled by the case. The Cruttis had lived in the neighborhood for only two months; the neighbors all liked them; Mr. Crutti said he had only one real enemy, who did not match the description of the attacker. In addition to his other unaccountable acts, the would-be killer had broken a cardinal rule of criminality by leaving the weapon behind. The police determined that the cleaver had been stolen from Louis Wagner, a butcher who had a shop six blocks away from the Cruttis' store. The best the police could do was arrest a man named John Flannery on suspicion; of him, we hear nothing more.

Perhaps the attempt on Crutti's life reminded some New Orleanians of the gruesome murder of Alphonse Durel, a misanthropic and stingy hairdresser who had been hacked to death in his house at 219 Bourbon Street on July 8, 1908, while his wife was out of town. Due to his grouchiness, he had few visitors; by the time someone found his body on the kitchen floor, it was stiffened with rigor mortis. "A hatchet and a knife were used," wrote a helpful *New Orleans Daily Picayune* reporter who knew exactly what his customers wanted to read. "There was a terrible wound on the left side of the head, completely fracturing the skull, and most probably inflicted with the hatchet. This wound was just behind the left ear, and the brain oozed out through the large orifice in the skull." Durel's head bore ten other cuts, and the reporter described the exact location and nature of each. Among other things, Durel's left ear was cut in half, his skull bore a two-inch-deep chasm and was fractured in several places, his scalp was opened, and the base of his skull was cracked "as though it was but glass" by two heavy blows. Durel had quarreled with the help so often that the police thought his killer was an enraged servant, in particular a maid named Sarah whom he had fired the day before his murder. But the Durel case was never solved. Some shared circumstances make it seem plausible that the man who killed Durel in 1908 may have attacked the Cruttis in 1910 and future victims as well: he focused his violence on his prey's heads; Durel was wounded with his own hatchet and knives, as were later victims of the killer to become known as the Axman; Durel, like the Cruttis and several later victims, was self-employed and lived in his place of business. And in the cases of Durel, the Cruttis, and many others to come, the invader had little interest in robbery. He appears to have taken Durel's watch, which never turned up, but he left behind seventy dollars' worth of gold and a few hundred dollars in other currency. He didn't even bother looking for the money since Durel's apartment was in strangely—one might even say terrifyingly, considering the violence that took place in it—neat condition.

Perhaps the Alphonse Durel murder and the August Crutti assault were unrelated. Perhaps New Orleanians thought the strange attack on Crutti was a unique incident, never to be repeated. But not even a full month later, on the morning of September 20 came word that another married pair of Italian grocers, Joseph and Vincetta Rissetto, had been beaten nearly to death by a burglar wielding a cleaver. Just before 2:00 A.M., he broke into their store at the corner of London Avenue and Tonti by climbing through an open kitchen window. In the previous attack, the intruder had attacked the man but left the woman alone. This time, as Mr. Rissetto slept, he struck Mrs. Rissetto three times with the cleaver, splitting her cheekbone, cutting her left ear, and making a deep gash just under her left ear. Then he went for Mr. Rissetto, cutting him across the bridge of the nose. Either the blow was not all that forceful or Mr. Rissetto was an unusually sound sleeper, for at first he thought his wife had struck him with her arm. "What's the matter with you? Are you going crazy?" he asked crossly.

"No, darling, I'm cut and dying," she cried. Mr. Rissetto was then struck in the eye with the cleaver. Blinded by blood, he fell out of bed and crawled on the floor, groping until he found a match. After lighting a lamp, he took his revolver and fired three shots into the ceiling. During this commotion, the prowler made his escape.

Neighbors heard the shots and came to the Rissettos' aid. A policeman called for an ambulance; detectives arrived and found a crime scene that was, if anything, even stranger than the one left at the Cruttis' store. The perpetrator had stolen nothing. The grocery's cash register contained twenty-three dollars and Mr. Rissetto's gold watch and chain were found in a drawer. It was difficult to escape the conclusion that the so-called burglar had attacked not for profit but simply for the fun of it. Again, he left his weapon behind: the cleaver was tangled in the bed's mosquito bar at a height that suggested the attacker was taller than average. A butcher in the McCue market, Frank Caruso, identified the cleaver as one that had been stolen from his store three weeks previously. Knives and other implements stolen from Caruso turned up in the shed of another grocer, C. F. Liemann, left there by someone who had robbed his store on the night of August 23. The Rissetto store yielded only one dubious clue: a wee shoe print, size four, with high heels, leading some romantic souls to believe that a woman had attacked the grocers.

A *Picayune* reporter interviewed the Rissettos in the hospital. Since the Cruttis and Rissettos were Italians, many detectives and journalists assumed the involvement of the Black Hand, a terroristic underground society associated

Mr. and Mrs. Rissetto. From the *Daily Picayune*, September 21, 1910. Reprinted by courtesy of the *New Orleans Times-Picayune*.

with the Mafia, but with a greater emphasis on the black-mail and extortion of shopkeepers. Mr. Rissetto stoutly denied that he had been threatened by either organization: "I never got any letter demanding money or threatening me, and I am sure my wife did not either." His wife, barely alive, believed they had been chloroformed before being hacked and plaintively stated, "Oh, we went to bed in such a happy frame of mind, and were very pleasant to one another."

Doctors were certain the couple's injuries would prove fatal, but both survived. Mr. Rissetto was scarred from the tip of his nose to his right cheek and permanently blinded in his right eye; his wife was paralyzed on the left side of her face. On September 26, they were allowed to see each other in the hospital. A journalist wrote, "The meeting between the two was touching, but Rissetto was instructed not to talk much to his wife, as her condition is so serious that any break in her present frame of mind would be injurious to her." Mr. Rissetto died "as a result of a long illness" on November 23, 1912, according to the *Picayune*, but there was no mention whether the illness resulted from his injuries.

The police held six unnamed suspects, but all were released due to insufficient evidence. The Rissetto case became a source of frustration for the New Orleans police. However, newer, more pressing crimes demanded the detectives' attention. As the months passed, the assaults on the Cruttis and the Rissettos faded from memory.

Then the shadow-man came back. Around 1:30 in the morning of June 27, 1911, he invaded a grocery/saloon/home located at the corner of Arts and Galvez streets, owned by twenty-six-year-old Joseph Davi and Marie, his sixteen-year-old "child wife," as the press called her. The killer broke off a couple of window slats, raised the sash, and climbed inside the saloon area. He found the door leading to the Davis' bedroom locked, but he pried it open with a railroad shoe pin. Once inside, he rained blows upon the head of the sleeping Joseph Davi with a heavy-bladed implement that investigators took to be a meat cleaver. Oddly, Mrs. Davi slept through the violence and the intruder did not harm her at first. She awoke when she heard someone rummaging through her clothes. By the dim light of an oil lamp, she saw a young, stout, clean-shaven man of average height in the room. He moved so quickly that she didn't get a good look at him. When he realized she was watching him, he rushed to the bed with a weighty glass mug intended for holding toothbrushes and smashed it into her face. Mrs. Davi heard a voice in the darkness:

"Where is your money?"

He spoke in English and had no noticeable accent. Before she could answer, he chopped at her head and hands with his blade, an action indicating that robbery was not his motive. Mrs. Davi played dead and her attacker left. He did not search for money or valuables, overlooking a money bag containing sixty-four dollars under the Davis' bloody

Mr. and Mrs. Davi. From the *Daily Picayune*, June 28, 1911. Reprinted by courtesy of the *New Orleans Times-Picayune*.

pillows, jewelry, and two revolvers located in a drawer and on a mantelpiece. Mrs. Davi, fearful that the stranger was still on the premises, was too terrified to scream or tend to herself or her dying husband.

Around 5:00 A.M., a local painter, E. M. Boyer, thought it strange that the grocery had not opened at the usual hour. He knocked on the window. The blinds parted from within, and a second later, he was staring into the gashed and bloody face of Mrs. Davi. In a daze, she told Boyer that she could not sell him any bread since her husband was still asleep. Boyer ran to the home of Benjamin Gallin to summon help, and the police arrived to marvel at the bloody scene. Mr. Davi was rushed to the hospital, where he died of a fractured skull on the afternoon of June 28. The police waited until July 5, when Mrs. Davi had recovered, before giving her the bad news that her husband had died and was already buried. The couple had been married only five months.

Mrs. Davi swore that she would devote the rest of her life to finding her husband's slayer. She described the attack to detectives as well as she could remember it. Unlike the two previous occasions, the murderer took his weapon with him instead of leaving it behind for all to see. Detectives Scheffler and Gorman were convinced the intruder had been an ordinary burglar; after all, he had ransacked the Davis' trunks and drawers, though he did not actually take anything. However, Superintendent Frank Mooney instinctively realized this criminal was unlike any other he had encountered and told the *Picayune,* "He is a strange man, for he seems to be without a thought of stealing. . . . Even if he had taken one of the [Davis'] weapons, only to throw it away after getting a safe distance, one could regard him as somewhat common, but he goes away perhaps only with his sharp-edged weapon, when one of the pistols would have been a better protection for him if he had met someone who would try to capture him." Another detective told the newspaper, "This fiend simply revels at the sight of human blood. The pretense at burglary is to confuse pursuit."

The Davis' home and grocery. From the *Daily Picayune,* June 29, 1911. Reprinted by courtesy of the *New Orleans Times-Picayune.*

An editorial in the *Picayune* after the attack on the Davis was not calculated to calm the fears of the populace: "[T]he nature of the crime . . . makes it imperative that no effort be spared to solve the problem and apprehend the guilty party or parties. . . . [I]t is a menace to the entire community that such a dangerous lunatic, if the lunatic theory be the correct one, should be at large." The paper also gave a nickname to the killer—"the Cleaver"—which would later be replaced by a lasting sobriquet when he settled on a weapon of choice.

By early July, the New Orleans police had dropped the idea that the Cleaver was a garden-variety burglar. Several detectives were convinced that the marauder was a sadist and rounded up local "perverts." Inspector of Police Reynolds told the press that the case had top priority: "I want the mystery solved, and every man connected with the police is inclined in that direction, and I am sure that I will hear something tangible soon which will assist in the unraveling of this terrible mystery." Inspector Reynolds had two good reasons to be hopeful: Gov. Jared Y. Sanders offered a five-hundred-dollar reward for information leading to the Cleaver's arrest, and for the first (and only) time, the killer had left an excellent clue at the crime scene. Assistant District Attorney Doyle found the imprint of his left hand on a wall in the Davis' bedroom.

Soon the police arrested two Sicilian truck farmers, Sam Pitzo (aka Pizzo and Parieno) and Philip Daguanno, both of whom were suspected of being members of the Black Hand. The two men had reputations for being extortionists, blackmailers, and homegrown terrorists and were leading suspects in the arson of a grocery store owned by an Italian named George Musacchia only three days before the Davi attack. Perhaps they had been extorting Davi, then murdered him when he refused to pay up? In fact, Joseph Davi had received two anonymous letters from the Black Hand, peculiar amalgamations of politeness and barely veiled threats; his widow showed them to the police in early August. But the letters were a year old and appeared to have no relevance to Joseph Davi's murder. Black Hand members were not noted for their patience when it came to carrying out threats. While the police were able to prove that Pitzo had extorted various Italians in New Orleans, none of the survivors of the Cleaver attacks—the Cruttis, the Rissettos, Mrs. Davi—could identify either Pitzo or Daguanno. On July 14, the *Picayune* all but admitted the detectives had been defeated by the killer: "The police are deeply chagrined at their ill success, but did everything possible in the mysterious affair and are still working the case."

New Orleans's most mysterious assassin resurfaced less than a year later. Tony Sciambra, a well-liked, popular twenty-seven-year-old Italian, closed his grocery located at the corners of France and Villere streets at 10:00 on the night of May 15, 1912. Sciambra had every reason to feel content with life that night. He was happily married to his wife of two years, Johanna. They were the archetypical

The Sciambra family. From the *Daily Picayune,* May 17, 1912.
Reprinted by courtesy of the *New Orleans Times-Picayune.*

couple "who never had a quarrel." Their infant son, Tony
Jr., was almost a year old, and the grocery was turning a
profit. But the family's idyllic life ended in unexpected tragedy. At 2:00 A.M., the neighbors were awakened by Johanna
Sciambra's screams. Rushing to the house, they found Mr.
Sciambra in bed with three bullet holes in his back, one
in the right side of his body and one in his right arm. The
killer had placed the barrel of his gun firmly against the
sleeping Mr. Sciambra, as was proven by the powder burns
on his back. One bullet had passed entirely through Mr.
Sciambra and wounded his wife in the left hip. The baby,
who had been sleeping beside his mother, was unhurt. The
neighbors rushed Mrs. Sciambra to Charity Hospital, but it
was too late for her husband.

The killer had entered by stacking two boxes in the alley and climbing through an open kitchen window. Puzzles
abounded for the police: There was no apparent motive, for
the intruder had stolen nothing. The store's cash register
contained $4.60; fifteen dollars and several blank checks
were found under Mr. Sciambra's pillow. The family's gun
was untouched. Mr. Sciambra had worn underclothes when
he went to bed, yet his corpse was naked. Mrs. Sciambra was
unable to explain the discrepancy, nor could she provide a

description of the shooter. No one could explain why the Sciambras' surly watchdog had not barked that night. Perhaps the dog was acquainted with the killer, who had left behind no clue except for a large shoeprint in mud between the cistern and a shed. Two men were at work near the murder scene that night—a milkman at a dairy and a night watchman at a stable owned by Barber Asphalt Company— but neither heard shots being fired.

Journalists and the police realized that the attacks on the Cruttis, the Rissettos, the Davis, and the Sciambras had probably all been done by the same person. Again, the theory was floated that a Black Hand hit man had assassinated Sciambra out of revenge, but this idea seems to have been based only on the fact that sinister-looking characters had sometimes entered the store. (A neighbor remembered that one of them was a big Italian who addressed Sciambra's wife as "Mrs. Tony," a fact that may prove significant later in the narrative. Within a few days, he was identified as a fellow grocer named Philip Lavello, questioned by the police and released.) Mrs. Sciambra insisted that her husband had never received any Black Hand letters.

Detectives soon found that the killer had attempted to break into another grocery the previous Sunday, May 12, just two blocks away from the Sciambras' store. George Musacchia awoke to discover that a barrel had been placed under his dining room window and that the slat had been broken, as in the Davi case. Why the intruder had abandoned his dark plan, no one could say.

The papers predicted that Mrs. Sciambra would survive her bullet wound, but she died on May 26. The murderer had claimed his second victim—his third, if Joseph Rissetto's death resulted belatedly from his wounds. The orphaned Tony Sciambra, Jr., probably was adopted by one of his father's three sisters.

The Sciambras' killer stifled his instincts for five years. Early on the morning of Saturday, December 22, 1917, an intruder made his way into the home of Mr. and Mrs.

The Sciambras' bedroom. From the *Daily Picayune,* May 17, 1912. Reprinted by courtesy of the *New Orleans Times-Picayune.*

Epifania Andollina, who kept a grocery and saloon at 8301 Apple Street. Mrs. Andollina was awakened by the sound of heavy breathing and saw a man standing by the bed occupied by herself and her husband. The man held a pistol in his right hand and a hatchet in his left. He gave a two-word order: "Shut up." When Mrs. Andollina screamed, he struck her husband several times with the hatchet. The attacker ran into an adjoining bedroom occupied by the grocers' two sons, John and Salvadore. He struck John on the head with the hatchet and hit Salvadore's right arm with the pistol butt. The man escaped through the kitchen. After he left, the Andollinas' sixteen-year-old daughter Mary ran into her parents' bedroom and found her father groaning on the floor in a pool of blood. The police arrived within minutes and Mr. Andollina was sent to Charity Hospital with severe wounds. He was unable to remember anything about the attack. Both father and son survived, according to a *Times-Picayune* story from March 1919. Detectives found that the intruder had gained entrance by chiseling out a panel of the kitchen door. He had also paused during his flight to leave the hatchet near the door. The chiseled door and the planted ax would become the killer's calling cards.

Again, nervous New Orleanians theorized that it might be the work of the Black Hand. Perhaps the grocers were attacked for refusing to be extorted. But before such speculation could bear fruit, the hatchet wielder disappeared once more. All was quiet for six months.

Joseph and Katherine Maggio owned a small grocery located, according to the papers, at 4638 Magnolia Street. (The official police report gives the address as 4901 Magnolia.) The rear section of the building served as living quarters for the couple and Joseph's brothers Andrew and Jake, a cobbler. The house was like virtually every other in the long series of murders: it was located on a corner and had a high board fence around the back side, allowing the murderer to break in without being seen.

Around 4:45 A.M. on the morning of May 23, 1918, Jake Maggio was awakened by loud groans coming from his brother Joseph's bedroom. Instinctively, he knew the sounds were made by someone in distress. He awakened Andrew, not without difficulty; Andrew had just received his draft notice and spent the evening drinking to celebrate his last days of freedom before joining the military. In fact, Andrew had only made it home an hour or two before Jake was awakened by the strange noises behind the wafer-thin wall. The two brothers cautiously entered their married brother's bedroom; what they saw sobered Andrew quickly. A stranger had struck both Mr. and Mrs. Maggio in the head with an ax and cut their throats with a razor. Mr. Maggio lay on the bed with his legs hanging over the side and his feet resting on the floor. He bore ax wounds on the back of the head, the forehead, and the left cheek. He seemed to be dead, but suddenly his eyes fluttered open. Seeing Jake and Andrew, he struggled to get out of bed. Mrs. Maggio was lying dead on the floor, nearly decapitated. The police report informs us that she had been cut in the right cheek, on the right hand over her thumb, and that the left side of her face was split from the forehead to her mouth. The horrified brothers called the police, who took the somewhat illogical step of arresting Jake and Andrew. An ambulance from Charity Hospital came for Joseph Maggio, but he died moments after its arrival.

Further exploration of the crime scene revealed details that would be of considerable interest to a modern FBI profiler. A safe had been opened but contained a box full of money. One hundred dollars was found under Mr. Maggio's pillow and some of Mrs. Maggio's jewelry was in plain sight on a dresser. Beneath the safe was a box containing several hundred dollars' worth of jewelry. The police felt that the attacker had wanted to mislead them into thinking robbery had been the motive. As in the Andollina attack, the killer had chiseled out a panel on the back door and had left his murderous implements behind. The razor was on the bedroom floor and the bloody ax had been abandoned in the bathroom. According to the local press, detectives found it half-hidden under the bathtub. The police report states that the weapon was actually in the tub. In either case, it appears the intruder wanted to taunt investigators by leaving it where it could not possibly be overlooked. The ax had belonged to the victims; therefore, the killer had not brought the weapon with him. The razor may have belonged to Andrew Maggio, a barber by trade. As we shall see, the serial killer often "made do" with whatever weapons happened to be at the scene.

In the Maggios' bedroom, the police found bloodstained clothing, socks, and a black coat with blood on the inside, leading police to believe the killer might have discarded his clothes and put on clean clothing before he left the scene. Authorities found an unfired revolver near the clothes. Attempts to trace the ownership of the gun

came to nothing. Another possible clue was found a block
away from the Maggios' store. Someone with crude, childlike penmanship had chalked a message on the sidewalk
at Upperline and Robertson streets: "Mrs. Joseph Maggio
is going to sit up tonight just like Mrs. Toney." The identity of "Mrs. Toney" was never discovered, but detectives
remembered that in 1912 the Italian grocers Mr. and Mrs.
Tony Sciambra had been shot to death. Was the message a
reference to Mrs. Sciambra?

Jake and Andrew Maggio, manifestly innocent, were freed
within two days of the murders. New Orleanians barely had
time to recover from the unease caused by the bizarre murders when the killer struck again. At 7:00 A.M. on June 27,
a baker named John Zanca went to the back door of Louis
Besumer's grocery at 1514 Dorgenois Street to deliver his
wares (the grocer's name is sometimes given as Besemer).
Zanca noticed that one panel was missing. He knocked with
considerable trepidation. Besumer answered even though he
was bleeding profusely from an enormous head wound. All he
could say was "My God! My God!" Mrs. Besumer was alive,
barely, lying on a bed with deep wounds over her left ear and
on top of her head. According to some accounts, the perpetrator left the bloody weapon behind in the Besumers' bathroom,
but the official police report states that the ax was found (along
with a swatch of Mrs. Besumer's hair) in a pool of blood on the
house's gallery. She had made it to the bedroom and collapsed
where she was found by the police. Again, the ax had belonged
to the victims. Besumer's cash was still in a safe in the grocery
section of the building. Detectives found no fingerprints, for
the assailant had worn rubber gloves that he left behind as if
to enjoy a private joke at the police's expense.

Upon finding the victims, John Zanca immediately sum-
moned Charity Hospital and the police. The latter did not
arrest Zanca as they had the Maggio brothers, but they did
later arrest the fifty-nine-year-old Mr. Besumer once he
had recovered sufficiently from his injury. They suspected
he was a German secret agent, perhaps even the leader

of a spy ring, because he had lived in New Orleans only three months, spoke several languages, received mail from abroad, and the neighbors thought he might be a spy and a drug addict. These flimsy reasons seemed good enough during the Great War. Besumer protested that he was Polish, not German, and that he was not a spy. He confessed that the woman the police assumed to be his wife was actually his live-in girlfriend, Harriet Lowe, age twenty-nine, of Jacksonville, Florida. The real Mrs. Besumer was ill and staying with relatives in Cincinnati. Besumer claimed that he had been hit on the head with an ax while asleep. The invader must have believed him dead since he dealt no additional blows. When Besumer revived, he found Harriet Lowe unconscious on the gallery floor. He carried her to the bed, and then the baker knocked on the door. The story seemed reasonable, but federal authorities were not willing to take any chances. They searched Besumer's home/grocery store and even tore apart a bathrobe he tried to give to Lowe at the hospital. They found nothing incriminating. Besumer told the *Times-Picayune,* "[T]here is $5,000 in good money I would give willingly to know who attacked us. There would hardly be any need for the services of Superintendent Mooney if I could find the party."

On July 5, Harriet Lowe regained consciousness. Doctors expected her to recover, though the right side of her face was partially paralyzed. She told the police just what they wanted to hear: "I've long suspected that Mr. Besumer was a German spy." But the next day she contradicted herself: "I did not say Mr. Besumer is a German spy. That is perfectly ridiculous." The authorities had no choice but to release the hapless Pole a few days later. As she became more lucid, Lowe told police about the night she and Mr. Besumer were attacked. Around midnight, she had gone to the kitchen to check on her stewing prunes. Then all went black: "I don't even know what made me wake up, but I opened my eyes and in the light from outside I saw a man standing over me, making some sort of motions with his hands. I saw the ax [in his hands]. I recall screaming, 'Go away! Don't push me that way!' He was rather a tall man, and heavyset. He was a white man and he wore no hat or cap. I remember his hair was dark brown and almost stood on end. He wore a white shirt, opened at the neck. He just stood there, making motions with the ax, but not hitting me. The next thing I remember is lying out on the gallery with my face in a pool of blood."

However, on July 15 she provided a contradictory version, claiming she had been initially attacked on the gallery rather than in the kitchen. This was probably correct, given the tremendous amount of blood that had been spilled on the gallery. The police questioned the neighbors and found that Besumer and Lowe were given to violent arguments over money and his jealousy. Some detectives plausibly theorized that Besumer had attacked his girlfriend in imitation of the highly publicized ax murders but less plausibly theorized that Besumer had demolished his own head with an ax to divert suspicion. Lowe must have been struck awfully hard by her assailant's blow, or else she simply wanted to make trouble for her boyfriend, for as she lay dying in Charity Hospital on August 5, two days after an operation intended to remove a stray piece of bone, she claimed once again that Besumer had been her attacker. The police rearrested Besumer the day Lowe died. Fortunately for Besumer, if for no one else, that very night came proof positive that he was not the murderer.

Edward Schneider, twenty-eight years old and recently married, left work late at night and returned to his home at 1320 Elmira Street. When he entered his house, all was chaos. Around 2:00 A.M., the next door neighbor, Mrs. Mary Gonzales, had heard Mrs. Rosie Schneider screaming. (The two women were sisters.) Mr. and Mrs. Gonzales hurried over and found the nine-months-pregnant Mrs. Schneider hysterical in her blood-soaked bed, with several of her teeth knocked out and her scalp lacerated. She said that she did not know who had attacked her.

Some aspects of the assault matched earlier cases. Others did not. For the first time, the prowler stole something: approximately seven dollars. On the other hand, as he had done before, he left behind a hatchet in the yard, which Mr. Schneider identified as his own. Mrs. Schneider was the first victim who did not run a grocery. According to the 1920 Louisiana Census, she was a weaver at a cotton mill and her husband was a laborer at a lumber mill. The intruder appeared to have entered via a convenient open window, so there was no need for him to remove a door panel. A broken lamp lay on the floor of the bedroom and the bed was soaked with oil as well as blood. Police theorized that Mrs. Schneider's attacker had hit her with the lamp, just as Mrs. Davi's assailant had struck her with a glass mug. The *Times-Picayune* made its contribution to the legend by giving the marauder his permanent nickname in a headline: "Police Believe an Ax-Man May Be Active in City."

Mrs. Schneider survived the attack—repeatedly, the Axman case bears eloquent testimony as to the durability of the human head—and she gave birth to a healthy daughter a day later. Mrs. Schneider was unable to give the police anything but the blurriest description of her ordeal. She had awakened in the night to see a dark form with an ax standing over her and had just enough time to scream before the blow came.

(Despite this convincing evidence that Louis Besumer was not the maniac who was terrifying the city, he was held in jail for almost *nine months* without a trial, finally getting his day in court on April 30, 1919. The jury found him not guilty the next morning.)

Five days after the Schneider incident, on August 10, a thirty-year-old bachelor barber named Joseph Romano was attacked in his home at the corner of Tonti and Gravier streets. His nieces Pauline and Mary Bruno, aged eighteen and thirteen, respectively, were awakened at 3:00 A.M. by a disturbance in their Uncle Joseph's room. Pauline, who had been fearful of meeting the Axman, had her worst fears realized when the girls opened Romano's bedroom door. A "dark, tall, heavyset [stranger], wearing a dark suit and a dark slouch hat" stood by Romano's bed. (She described the hat to the *Times-Picayune* as a "black slouch Alpine hat.") When the girls screamed, the man seemed to disappear— "almost as if he had wings," Pauline told the *New Orleans Item*—and the terrified witnesses were never able to explain how the man vanished so quickly. Their uncle rose from the bed with two large ax wounds in his head. He staggered a few feet, then collapsed through a door leading to the parlor. He managed to say "I don't know who did it" before forever losing consciousness. A patrolman arrived immediately, having been only two blocks away when he heard Pauline Bruno's screams. But he found no trace of the fleet-footed Axman. The impudent ease with which he came and went added to his terrifying mystique. Joseph Romano died at Charity Hospital a half-hour after arrival. The coroner noted that the ax blade had been so sharp that it cut cleanly into Romano's brain without fracturing his skull.

Detectives found some of the Axman's usual trademarks at the murder scene. Mysteriously, he had brought an ax with him this time but left it clean, pristine, and unused in Joseph Romano's bedroom. He attacked Romano with a second ax he had taken from the rear shed and he left the gory weapon behind in the backyard. As in other cases going all the way back to the attack on the Cruttis, the intruder had ritualistically rearranged his victim's clothing and possessions. He had rummaged through Romano's suit and pockets and left his wallet on a chair in the kitchen, but nothing had been stolen. Rather than chiseling out a rear door panel, the killer had entered via a window after removing a slat, as he had in the Davi incident. However, chisel marks were found on the door, indicating that the Axman had attempted to enter in his usual way before trying the window.

(About those chiseled doors: at the time, some police expressed the belief that the killer must be a small man if he could squeeze through those holes left by the missing door panels. Superintendent Mooney, for instance, theorized that the killer "crawls through the panel of the door. After going into the house he opens the door." But the *Times-Picayune* of March 16, 1919, includes a photo montage showing some doors that had been worked on by the Axman, and it is evident that no one larger than a child, a circus midget, or a homicidally minded cat could have squeezed through most of the holes. Obviously, the Axman's technique was to remove a door panel, then reach through the hole and unlock the door. After a certain point, New Orleanians were so afraid to leave their windows unlocked that the Axman had no choice but to laboriously cut through doors. As for the reason he insisted on leaving behind his murderous weapons, FBI profilers would probably say he did it as a way of mocking the police and making sure that he got proper credit for his "work.")

By now it was all too clear that a diabolical—some thought supernatural—killer was preying on the small business owners of the city. New Orleans author Robert Tallant recounted the terror that gripped the city after the Romano slaying,

New Orleans residences with door panels chiseled out. From the *New Orleans Times-Picayune,* March 16, 1919. Reprinted by courtesy of the *New Orleans Times-Picayune.*

especially among Italians who thought, with good cause, that the murderer was singling them out. Every strange-looking character on the street was good for a call to the police. On August 15, the authorities received several calls claiming the Axman was walking around Tulane Avenue and Broad Street dressed as a woman. On August 21, a woman started a panic when she claimed she saw a graceful, though foolhardy, stranger jumping a fence at Gravier and South White streets while brandishing an ax in one hand. As with UFO sightings in later years, mass hysteria resulted, and suddenly many of her neighbors thought they also saw the sinister acrobat jumping over their backyard fences. One man claimed to have emptied a shotgun at the fleeing Axman. Family members took turns sleeping so that someone would always be on guard for the bloodcurdling sound of a chisel gently scraping against the door.

Despite the hysteria, some of the reports to the police are believable. Grocer Arthur Recknagel, who lived at 2438 Cleveland Avenue, six blocks from Joseph Romano's home, awoke one morning in June to find a back door panel missing and an ax in his yard. Joseph LeBeouf, another grocer, related that someone had removed a panel from his back door on July 28. Luckily for LeBeouf, he was not home that day. His grocery was located only a block away from the Romanos. Similarly, a grocer named Al Durand found an ax and a chisel at his back door on August 11. These incidents may have been aborted visits from the genuine Axman or they may have been mere tasteless pranks. One man who probably did have a close encounter with the Axman was Nick Asunto, who was awakened on the morning of August 30 by strange noises coming from downstairs. He looked at the bottom of the stairs and saw a dark, heavyset man standing with an ax in his hand. When Asunto shouted, the frightening (and frightened) figure ran out the front door.

On August 13, the *Times-Picayune* published an interview with retired Italian detective John Dantonio, who was convinced the current wave of Axman attacks and the ones from years before had all been perpetrated by the same man: "Students of crime have established that a criminal of the dual personality type may be a respectable, law-abiding citizen when his normal self. Then suddenly the impulse to kill comes upon him, and he must obey it. It has been further proved that such unfortunates remain normal for months, even years, without being seized with the affliction." He included a suggestion still worth taking: "This sort of criminal is easily frightened. He fears a dog more than he does ten watchmen. My advice to the public is to put dogs in their yards." On the other hand, the presence of a guard dog had not saved the Sciambras.

Despite all of the close calls and false alarms, the Romano slaying was the Axman's last confirmed kill for several months. New Orleanians wondered if the killer had died, been arrested for some other crime, or simply moved away from the area. Whatever the reason, they were glad he was gone. But he was away only temporarily. When he returned, he struck not in New Orleans proper but in the suburbs, perhaps thinking no one would expect him there.

Around March 7, 1919, the Axman broke into a corner grocery store and residence owned by an Italian named Santo Vicari in Marrero, on the outskirts of New Orleans. He gained entrance to the store by removing a back door panel. The Axman stole an overcoat and a negligible amount of money. He also took two boxes of candy, for even serial killers have a sweet tooth. But for some reason the sleeping Vicari family was not harmed, other than having the living daylights scared out of them when they realized who had been their midnight visitor. He would not be so merciful when he struck again forty-eight hours later in Gretna, another New Orleans suburb a mile and a half away from Marrero.

The Axman had already attacked a pregnant woman, but the new slaying was his most heartless to date. Around 7:00 A.M. on March 9, 1919, a small black girl named Hazel Johnson came to buy groceries at a store owned by Charles and Rosie Cortimiglia, located on the corner of Second and

Jefferson streets. Hazel found the store closed though it was usually open by 5:00 A.M. Curious, she went behind the store and saw that the rear kitchen door was missing a panel. Another passer-by, Aaron Clay, encouraged her to go inside and see if the Cortimiglias were okay, an act that rather casts aspersions on Clay's bravery. Little Hazel cautiously entered the store and came out screaming.

The commotion alerted a fellow grocer who lived across the street, B. Iorlando Guagliardo, who also went by the surname Jordano, probably because it was easier to pronounce. Jordano ran to the Cortimiglia residence, where he found the man of the house lying unconscious on the floor with an ax wound in his head. Mrs. Cortimiglia had five ax wounds in her head and sat on the floor screaming, holding her dead two-year-old daughter, Mary. Jordano tried to comfort the hysterical mother while his son Frank called for help. The Cortimiglias were taken to Charity Hospital on an express wagon. When police inspected the scene, they found Mr. Cortimiglia's bloody ax under the back steps. As at the Maggio residence, the ax was only partially hidden, as if the killer took special joy in making certain that it would be found.

Blood had soaked the bed and splattered all over the walls. Trunks and drawers had been rifled and all the furniture in the room moved about. The killer even troubled to rearrange the victims' shoes and open the face of a clock on the mantel as if searching for valuables. But as nothing was stolen, the Axman likely had been trying to make it look like a routine burglary gone bad. He left untouched a box containing money and jewelry, $129 in cash hidden under the mattress, and a .38-caliber revolver. Despite all of the frenzied activity, he left neither footprints nor fingerprints.

Charles and Rosie Cortimiglia survived, notwithstanding having fractured skulls. Rosie told the police that she had awoken to see her husband fighting a large white man. The attacker took a swing with an ax, and Mr. Cortimiglia hit the floor. Despite Rosie's cries of "Not my baby," the Axman swung again and killed the child instantly with a single blow

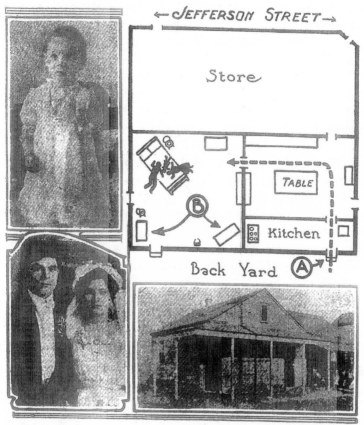

THREE GRETNA VICTIMS OF AX MURDERER

←JEFFERSON STREET→

Store

TABLE

Kitchen

Back Yard Ⓐ

The Cortimiglia family, their grocery/residence, and a map showing the killer's route after he gained entrance by chiseling out a
door panel. From the *New Orleans Times-Picayune*, March 10,
1919. Reprinted by courtesy of the *New Orleans Times-Picayune*.

to the back of her head. A third swing of the ax knocked the
mother unconscious. The Axman chopped away in earnest
at the heads of the parents while they were insensible.

After a few days in the hospital, Mrs. Cortimiglia made
a sensational accusation. She claimed Iorlando and Frank
Jordano had attacked her family, something vehemently

denied by her husband: "I saw the man well and he was a stranger. No, it was not Frank Jordano." In what was becoming a distressing pattern, the police arrested the two Jordanos, just as they had arrested the Maggio brothers and Louis Besumer on negligible evidence. The Jordanos made unlikely suspects: the father was sixty-seven years old and in bad health while the son was only seventeen and on the verge of getting married. The only motive that could be discerned was Rosie Cortimiglia's farfetched theory that the Jordanos wanted to get rid of their rivals in the grocery business. Charles Cortimiglia continued to insist that his attacker had been neither of the Jordanos, adding, "My wife must be out of her mind." Police opinion was divided. Sheriff Marrero of Jefferson Parish was certain that the wave of terror was over, telling the press, "I am confident we have the right men and that the Cortimiglias will recover to tell the complete story of the attack made upon them." On the other hand, Police Superintendent Mooney obviously doubted that the Axman was in custody, as he assigned special detectives to continue tracking down the killer.

After the Cortimiglia incident came the most famous event in the Axman saga. On March 14, the *Times-Picayune* published a letter purportedly from the serial killer, datelined "Hell, March 13, 1919."

Esteemed Mortal: They have never caught me and they never will. They have never seen me, for I am invisible, even as the ether that surrounds your earth. I am not a human being, but a spirit and a fell demon from the hottest hell. I am what you Orleanians and your foolish police call the Axeman.

When I see fit, I shall come again and claim other victims. I alone know who they shall be. I shall leave no clue except my bloody axe, besmeared with the blood and brains of him whom I have sent below to keep me company.

If you wish you may tell the police not to rile me. Of course I am a reasonable spirit. I take no offense at the way they have conducted their investigations in the past. In fact, they have been so utterly stupid as to amuse not only me, but

His Satanic Majesty, Francis Josef, etc. [A reference to the recently deceased emperor of Austria.] But tell them to beware. Let them not try to discover what I am, for it were better that they were never born than to incur the wrath of the Axeman. I don't think there is any need of such a warning, for I feel sure the police will always dodge me, as they have in the past. They are wise and know how to keep away from all harm.

Undoubtedly, you Orleanians think of me as a most horrible murderer, which I am, but I could be much worse if I wanted to. If I wished, I could pay a visit to your city every night. At will I could slay thousands of your best citizens, for I am in close relationship to the Angel of Death.

Now, to be exact, at 12:15 (earthly time) on next Tuesday night, I am going to visit New Orleans again. In my infinite mercy, I am going to make a proposition to you people. Here it is:

I am very fond of jazz music, and I swear by all the devils in the nether regions that every person shall be spared in whose home a jazz band is in full swing at the time I have mentioned. If everyone has a jazz band going, well, then, so much the better for you people. One thing is certain and that is that some of those people who do not jazz it on Tuesday night (if there be any) will get the axe.

Well, as I am cold and crave the warmth of my native Tartarus, and as it is about time that I leave your earthly home, I will cease my discourse. Hoping that thou wilt publish this, that it may go well with thee, I have been, am and will be the worst spirit that ever existed either in fact or realm of fancy.

THE AXEMAN

It is doubtful the Axman actually was the author of the well-written and diabolically clever note. I am reminded of FBI profiler John Douglas's opinion about a famous but dubious letter supposedly written by Jack the Ripper: "Psycholinguistically speaking, the 'Dear Boss' letter is a performance, a characterization by a literate, articulate person of what a crazed killer 'should' sound like. It's too organized, too indicative of intelligence and rational thought, and far too 'cutesy.'" I feel Douglas's description also applies to the letter allegedly sent by the Axman to the *Times-Picayune*. A tantalizing nugget briefly mentioned by the contemporary press and then never mentioned again is the fact that Superintendent Mooney believed the real Axman had sent him two letters. Their contents were never divulged.

Whoever wrote it, the letter to the *Times-Picayune* achieved the desired effect. Legend has it that virtually every residence in New Orleans trembled with the sound of jazz records on the night of Tuesday, March 18. Festive residents held "Axman parties." Persons who did not have phonographs flocked to clubs where jazz bands performed live; the musically gifted stayed at home and warded off the killer with their own improvisations. Especially popular was a quickly written and published piano piece entitled "The Mysterious Axman's Jazz, or: Don't Scare Me, Papa!" The *Times-Picayune* of March 19 ran an editorial cartoon showing a nervous family playing musical instruments as one keeps watch at the door. Likely some New Orleanians were looking for an excuse to party while others decided it paid to be on the safe side. There were no killings that night.

Iorlando and Frank Jordano went to trial on May 21. Neighbors testified as to the men's good character. Charles Cortimiglia testified that he had gotten a good look at the Axman while attempting to fight him off and he was neither of the Jordanos. A reporter for the *New Orleans States* testified that Rosie Cortimiglia's accusations could not be taken seriously, for after regaining consciousness she had also blamed the murder on her grotesquely wounded husband. Despite all of this favorable testimony, on May 26 the jury found both Jordanos guilty after deliberating only forty-five minutes. Iorlando Jordano was sentenced to life in prison and his son Frank was given the death penalty.

As though miffed because the Jordanos were stealing his glory, the real Axman got his work in a little over two months later. Early in the morning of Sunday, August 3,

THE WITCHING HOUR—12:15 A. M.

As observed by some New Orleanians.

Editorial cartoon illustrating the noisiest night in the history of New Orleans. From the *New Orleans Times-Picayune*, March 19, 1919. Reprinted by courtesy of the *New Orleans Times-Picayune*.

he entered the Laumann residence at 2123 Second Street. He went to the bedroom of nineteen-year-old Sarah. Her screams awakened her parents, but by the time they made it to her room, the assailant was gone as though he had vaporized. Nevertheless, their arrival undoubtedly saved her from worse injury. Sarah told her parents that she had awakened to see a man bending over her. Amazingly, she was unaware she had been hit in the head with an ax until the next morning, when she felt pain behind her left ear.

No door panels had been chiseled, but the Laumanns had left a window half-open before retiring. As a precaution, they had closed and bolted the shutters, but the intruder simply removed the bolt. Some writers have been reluctant to credit the Axman with incidents that lacked the calling card of the chiseled door panel, such as the assaults on Mrs. Schneider and Sarah Laumann. I theorize that the Axman, like any sensible murderer, initially tried to enter houses through unlocked windows and operated on back doors only when denied easier access. In almost all other respects, the attack was classic Axman: nothing had been stolen, the weapon used had been pilfered from a shed on the Laumanns' property, and the ax was found near the scene, on the lawn of the St. Francis de Sales School beside the family's house. On the other hand, the Laumanns were neither Italian nor grocers.

Despite having sustained a concussion, Sarah Laumann was able to give the police our most detailed description of the assailant. He seemed to be in his mid-twenties, had a dark complexion, was about 5' 8", and weighed about 165 pounds. He wore a dark coat, dark pants, a cap pulled down low, and a white shirt with dark stripes.

The killer went on the prowl again a week later, on Sunday, August 10. Early in the morning, Frank Genusa heard a knock on his door at Elysian Fields Avenue. When he opened it, his grocer friend Steve Boca fell inside, his head cloven. Genusa called for an ambulance. His quick action probably saved his friend's life. Boca survived but could remember nothing except waking up in time to see a figure with an ax standing over his bed. When he recovered consciousness, he staggered down the street to Genusa's house despite his horrific injuries. No doubt he presented a spectacle to people walking to church that morning. The police went to Boca's house and found that the intruder had gained entrance by chiseling out a door panel and had left the ax in the kitchen. Again, nothing had been stolen. The desperate police, who seem to have held a grudge against Good Samaritans, promptly arrested Frank Genusa. Had Boca not survived to inform the police they had arrested the wrong man, Genusa might have been in real trouble.

The Axman himself had a close scrape on the night of September 2. Druggist William Carlson was up late reading when he heard peculiar noises at his back door. He called out a warning to intruders, then took his revolver and fired through the door. When he opened the door, nobody was there, but there were chisel marks on a panel. Had Carlson not sportingly given the prowler a warning, he might have put an abrupt end to the Axman's career and solved the mystery of his identity.

The Axman struck again—maybe—on October 27 at the corner of South Scott and Ulloa streets. Once again, the victim was an Italian grocer, Mike Pepitone, but this time there were significant changes in the *modus operandi,* and there are reasons for suspecting it was not an Axman murder. Around 1:20 in the morning, Esther Pepitone heard her husband struggling with someone in the adjoining bedroom. She clearly heard him say "Oh, Lord." When she looked into the room, she found her husband bleeding and unconscious. Blood had splattered on the bedroom wall to a height of eight feet. Not wishing to take in any more of the scenery, she alerted the authorities.

When the police arrived, eleven-year-old Rosie Pepitone ran outside, shouting that her father's face was covered with blood. Mrs. Pepitone offered an opinion to Deputy Sheriff Ben Corcoran: "It looks like the Axman was here and murdered Mike." But the police found that he had not been axed. Instead, he had been struck eighteen times in the head with a fourteen-inch metal bar that had a three-inch iron nut at the end. The weapon had been left on a chair next to Pepitone's bed. More significantly, Mrs. Pepitone had gotten a fleeting glimpse of her husband's assailants— note plural—as they fled the house by way of a room in which her six children were sleeping. One attacker was tall and slender, the other short and heavy. They had entered the house/grocery not by chiseling out a door panel but by smashing a window, something the Axman had never done. Mrs. Pepitone noticed that although her husband went to bed clad only in his underwear, when found he was wearing pants, suggesting that he had been awakened by some strange noise and got partially dressed to investigate.

Pepitone died at Charity Hospital a few hours after the attack, never having regained consciousness. At the time of his murder, Pepitone himself was something of a criminal, for he was on parole on a charge of having beaten his six-year-old son Vincent six weeks before.

Whether or not he had actually been killed by the Axman, we know, with the advantage of hindsight, that the killings mysteriously and abruptly ceased forever after Pepitone's murder. But there were still two persons whom the Axman had victimized indirectly: Iorlando and Frank Jordano, who languished in the Gretna prison for a crime they did not commit. In the sort of dramatic postscript that novelists would be reluctant to employ, on December 7, 1920, Rosie Cortimiglia at last confessed to a *Times-Picayune* reporter that she had no idea who had actually killed her daughter. Why did she put the Jordanos through such an ordeal? She told contradictory stories, first claiming that Sheriff Marrero of Gretna had forced her to accuse them, but then stating that it was simply because she hated the Jordanos. Father and son were soon released from prison.

The slayer's final tally, as far as we know, was twelve injured and nine killed—if the Pepitone murder was committed by the Axman. An important step in solving any crime is to study the victimology: from what group, if any, did the killer select his victims, and why? Most serial killers choose victims of a certain race, gender, body type, and overall look. The Axman, however, was known to have attacked solo males, solo females, married couples, and entire families. While it is tempting to speculate that he got a sexual charge from the act of killing—outright molestation, like financial gain, was not a motive—his targets were not always women. He seemed to take delight in axing anyone, male or female. Two of his victims were men sleeping alone, Joseph Romano and Steve Boca (three if we count Mike Pepitone as an Axman victim). The conventional wisdom among past writers was that since most of the Axman's victims were Italian grocers, he must have "borne a grudge" against them. Rather than this being evidence of a grudge, however, it may mean that the Axman was himself Italian, as serial killers usually murder within their "comfort zone"—that is, they murder among their own race in neighborhoods near their homes. It is true that the majority of his victims were Italian, but there were exceptions. Louis Besumer was Polish; Mrs. Schneider and Sarah Laumann had German names. I don't know what ethnicity Harriet Lowe was, but judging from her name she was not Italian. However, almost all of the victims have one thing in common, with the exceptions of the Schneiders and Laumann. The majority of the Axman's prey ran small businesses, usually groceries, and their stores made excellent hunting grounds for the serial killer. The Axman likely went into stores, ostensibly to make purchases but secretly fantasizing about making future victims of the shopkeepers while looking around for doors with panels he could chisel open.

One of the mysteries surrounding the Axman is why this vicious early American serial killer remains relatively unknown. Another conundrum, of course, is his identity, for he was never caught. Like an American version of Jack the Ripper, he killed at will, held a city in terror for a while, then vanished like early morning fog. As with the Ripper, those who advocate a particular Axman suspect must explain why he abruptly stopped killing.

From the start, it was suggested that the Mafia or the Black Hand was behind the ax murders, perhaps as a warning to shopkeepers who refused to be extorted. At first glance, it seems the theory easily can be dismissed. While in the course of researching this chapter, I found numerous contemporary accounts of Black Hand slayings in New Orleans. In virtually every case, the murder weapon of choice was a gun, in rare instances a knife. Why would a hit man bent on making an example of a grocer bother to chisel out a door panel at night when he could simply enter the store during business hours, shoot the proprietor, and make his getaway? Also, compared to guns, axes are an unreliable weapon. Of twenty-one Axman victims, twelve survived. (Only in the Sciambra case did the Axman use a gun to fatal effect.) New Orleans detective Arthur Marullo remarked in March 1918 that he had never heard of the Mafia employing axes. Even if it were common, it is reasonable to expect a professional hit man to bring his own ax to the crime scene rather than leaving it to chance that his victims would unwittingly supply one. Also, as detective John Dantonio pointed out at the time, the Mafia never killed women: "I have never known the Black Hand to kill women. In fact, you could not get a Mafia agent to murder a woman under any circumstances."

On the other hand, the idea that the Mafia or Black Hand was behind at least some of the murders should not be dismissed. Perhaps the Axman did not bring his own ax because he was afraid it could be traced back to him. In addition, a man walking down the street would find it difficult to conceal an ax. In 1918, Detective Dantonio noted that the murderer simply used whatever tool he could handily find at his selected victim's home. His preferred weapon was an ax, though in the earliest slayings he used a cleaver and he attacked the Andollina family with a hatchet. Twice he hit victims with a glass object (a mug and an oil lamp). He shot the Sciambras, but on at least two other occasions he brought a gun and did not use it. The Pepitone killing, if one of the Axman's, was accomplished with an iron bar. If all of the murders were committed by the same man, perhaps the perpetrator was a Black Hand enforcer who started off killing as part of his job, then gradually began

committing murder simply because he enjoyed it. One of
the early victims, Joseph Davi, had in fact been extorted by
the Black Hand. It will be remembered, however, that the
threatening letters arrived a full year before the ax attacks.
This exception aside, the record does not reveal any of the
Axman's surviving victims telling the police they were being extorted by the mob. Some flatly declared that they were
not. Another hole in the extortion theory is that two victims,
Rosie Schneider and Sarah Laumann, did not run businesses.

Perhaps the slayings were the result not of blackmail, but
of a Mafia vendetta. This theory was expressed by Ed Reid
in his 1952 book *Mafia*. Reid noted that Pietro Pepitone,
father of the final alleged Axman victim, had assassinated a high-ranking New Orleans Mafioso, Paul Di Cristina,
in 1909. Reid conjectured that the Axman murders were
meant to avenge Di Cristina. It may not be coincidental
that the elder Pepitone was sentenced to twenty years in
prison on August 9, 1910, and the first atrocity attributed
to the Axman occurred only four days later. However, the
theory does not explain why the Axman killed or wounded twenty innocent persons before he got around to murdering Mike Pepitone. Reid's speculation does explain the
Pepitone murder, which did not match the definite Axman
murders in many details. There is a good chance that the
final murder credited to the Axman was in fact completely
unrelated to the series, and that he coincidentally stopped
murdering after Pepitone's death.

Unlike the plethora of Jack the Ripper suspects, there
has been only one seriously considered suspect in the Axman case. Ed Reid in *Mafia* and Robert Tallant in *Ready to
Hang* (also published in 1952) both claimed the suspect
was an Italian named Joseph Mumfre whose life allegedly
came to a sudden, shocking end little more than a year
after the murder of Mike Pepitone. According to Tallant,
on December 2, 1920, Mumfre was fatally shot by a veiled
woman in a black dress on the streets of Los Angeles. The
woman stood by Mumfre's corpse like a hunter posing with

a trophy until the police arrested her and took her to the station. She identified herself as Esther Albano but later admitted she was Mike Pepitone's widow. She claimed that she had recognized her husband's killer as he ran from their bedroom, and she had tracked Mumfre down to take justice into her own hands. In April 1921, Mrs. Pepitone was tried for murder in Los Angeles. She was sentenced to ten years in prison, served only three, then vanished into obscurity. She died in New Orleans on August 23, 1940, at age forty-nine. (One odd fact I discovered is that long before the Axman crimes, Angelo Albano, the man who would eventually become Mrs. Pepitone's second husband, had in March 1908 unsuccessfully tried to pay one Joseph Messina $400 to murder Mumfre.)

Naturally, the New Orleans police wondered if Mrs. Pepitone had killed the right man. It was true that she had seen her husband's murderers, but at the time she gave the police only vague descriptions rather than names. On the other hand, as told by Reid and Tallant, detectives found that Mumfre had been a career criminal. The two authors allege that when the police checked Mumfre's prison record, they noticed an intriguing pattern: Axman attacks ceased when he was in prison but recommenced when he was out. Some crime writers believe the best evidence that Mumfre was the Axman is that after Mrs. Pepitone killed Mumfre, the serial murders ceased.

While writing this chapter, I explored old issues of the *New Orleans Picayune* (later the *Times-Picayune*) from 1908 to 1918, hoping to find new clues to the Axman's identity. I noticed references to a local Italian thug named Joseph Monfre. I wondered if Monfre was actually Mumfre's real name, given that the contemporary press regularly mangled ethnic names. (To give just two examples, the Axman's first victim was dubbed both Crutti and Coutti in the same article, and his France Street victims' surname was given variously as Sciambra, Schiambra, Scambra, Sciambara, and Sciambria.)

Further research made it evident that Mumfre and Monfre were one and the same. Reid wrote that Mumfre was a member of the Black Hand "who had served time in prison for dynamiting a grocery store" and that his nickname was Doc. The *Picayune* of December 7, 1907, reveals that Monfre was a Black Hand enforcer and was called Doc because he had a side business selling patent medicine and pills. Even better, the article specifically states that after being arrested, "Dock Mumfre . . . gave his name as Joseph Manfre." Specifically, his name was P. G. Monfre. (The G no doubt stood for Giuseppe, Italian for Joseph.) With the suspect's real name, I was able to find many more details about his life of crime.

On October 3, 1907, the Black Hand sent a letter to an Italian grocer named Carmello Graffagnini demanding $1,000. Two days later, Joseph Monfre called at the store at 241 South Claiborne Street, dropping broad hints that he was there to pick up the extortion money. Graffagnini, who happened to be a member of an organization dedicated to stamping out the Black Hand called the Italian Vigilance Committee, refused to give Monfre anything more substantial than a cigar. Monfre left peacefully, but a couple of days later Graffagnini received another letter telling him that if he did not cough up the money by November 15, "you will be blown into the air. . . . [Y]ou and your family will suffer. Think therefore, that $1,000 may save your life." The deadline came and went; Graffagnini still declined to pay. Monfre visited the store on December 5 and left empty-handed again.

At 12:20 A.M. on December 6, 1907, Graffagnini's store and residence was rocked by exploding dynamite. Miraculously, Graffagnini, his wife, and their four children were uninjured. Monfre and a partner named Alberto Pumella were arrested within days, for they had been seen fleeing the scene of the crime by witnesses who identified them at the Saratoga Street police station. Monfre and Pumella went to their preliminary examination on January 9, 1908. The judge committed them to Criminal District Court under bail of $1,000 each. Pumella was unable to furnish bail and went straight to the parish prison to await trial. Despite fears that he would jump bail, Monfre paid the $1,000 and temporarily walked New Orleans a free man. Not a bad trick for a man who claimed to earn a salary of fifty cents per week as a labor agent.

Monfre could not stay out of trouble while out on bail, however, and in April he was rearrested on a charge of horse stealing. "Monfre is not at all a stranger to the police, and has figured in several sensational affairs, principally the celebrated Lamana case," remarked the *Times-Picayune*, referring to the Black Hand kidnapping and murder of a seven-year-old New Orleans boy, Walter Lamana, in June 1907. (See Tallant's *Ready to Hang* for further details.) The newspaper confused him with Stefano Monfre, who drove the getaway wagon when the child was abducted. Stefano escaped arrest and fled to the home of his brother Rafael in Pittsburg, Kansas; he was kicked out of the house by his scandalized brother and never apprehended. Stefano Monfre may have been related to Joseph, but clearly they were not the same man. Joseph was not charged with the kidnapping and murder of the Lamana boy, an event that occurred a mere five months before the dynamiting of Graffagnini's store.

Alberto Pumella was tried first for the dynamiting, and on May 21, 1908, he was found guilty and sentenced to twenty years' hard labor. Monfre was in attendance at the trial and the verdict could not have pleased him. He went on trial in July, displaying his "customary air of braggadocio. . . . but as the trial gradually wore on and damaging evidence was brought out against him he lost his air of confidence, and for the first time appeared to realize that the law counted," according to the *Times-Picayune*. Interestingly, one person who testified against Monfre was Nunzio Maggio, who had known the defendant for three years. Perhaps he was related to Joseph Maggio, an Axman victim a decade later? On July 24, the jury found Monfre guilty after fifteen minutes of deliberation, and on August 21, he was sentenced, like

Pumella, to twenty years' hard labor. The verdict was seen as a major victory for the Italian Vigilance Committee.

Now we come to the reason for all this background into Monfre's dynamiting conviction. Joseph Monfre/Mumfre is universally considered the candidate most likely to have been the Axman. Certainly he was an unsavory character. He was a blackmailer, a thief, an extortionist, and a bomber. But if he served his full sentence of twenty years, he could not have been the Axman, for he would have gotten out of prison in 1928, almost a full decade after the last murder.

A *Times-Picayune* article from December 1908 reveals that he and his lawyer, John Q. A. Flynn, tried to fight the sentence. Flynn applied for a writ of habeas corpus from the Louisiana Supreme Court: "[T]he decree of the Supreme Court affirming the judgment and sentence of Judge Baker had not been filed. . . . The attorney affirms that under the laws of the State no one can be tried, convicted and sentenced in the Criminal Court without having been indicted by the grand jury, and in the case of Monfre this was not done." Flynn threatened to take his case to the Supreme Court of the United States if necessary. The legal wrangling kept Monfre out of jail briefly; according to the records in the Louisiana State Archives, he began serving his sentence in the state penitentiary on January 13, 1909. The 1910 Louisiana Census lists him as a thirty-six-year-old widowed convict in prison at West Feliciana Parish.

Circumstantial evidence seems to point to Monfre as the killer, but critical inspection makes it less impressive than one would like. For example, Ed Reid wrote in 1952, "The advent of Mumfre in New Orleans coincided with the first ax murder, and the date of his departure, shortly after [Pepitone's] murder, marked the end of the gruesome killings." However, the *Picayune* of December 7, 1907, mentions that Monfre had been in New Orleans since before 1897: "[He] has lived here for more than ten years, but does not speak English fluently." (It will be remembered that Mrs. Davi said that her attacker had no discernible accent and "did not appear to be an Italian.") Very suspicious—at first glance—is the fact that some of Monfre's relatives lived in the neighborhood where the Sciambras were shot to death. According to the *Picayune* of May 17, 1912, "[W]hen Sciambra knew of those relatives being in the neighborhood he became a bit worried and talked about selling out his business and moving away." All it really shows is that Monfre and his family had a bad reputation.

Also intriguing, but far from damning, is the description of Monfre included in his prison records. His physical appearance compared favorably with the vague descriptions of the Axman provided by surviving victims. Joseph Monfre was 5'8" and had a stocky build at 170 pounds. He had brown eyes, black hair, and a dark complexion. The penitentiary's description matches Sarah Laumann's description except that she thought her attacker was in his twenties.

Obviously, the most important question to be answered by the prison records concerns the length of Monfre's stay in jail. The records are frustratingly messy. Some dates have been written in and later scratched out; other dates were written above the scratchings; some dates were haphazardly entered without further explanation into various columns in the ledger. But the records do make it clear that Monfre did not serve his full twenty years. I have created a timeline using the prison records and other sources:

July 8, 1908: Hatchet slaying of Alphonse Durel, a possible Axman murder.

August 21, 1908: Monfre is sentenced to twenty years at the Louisiana State Penitentiary near Angola.

January 13, 1909: Monfre begins his prison term.

August 13, 1910: Attack on the Cruttis, the first crime attributed to the Axman.

September 20, 1910: Attack on the Rissettos.

June 27, 1911: Attack on the Davis.

May 15, 1912: Attack on the Sciambras.

June 2, 1915: Monfre is discharged from prison.

July 10, 1916: Monfre returns to prison; according to the

Times-Picayune, he had violated his parole by possessing a revolver and committing "other offenses." The prison ledger states that he "ow[ed] one year, one month and eight days." This would mean that he was scheduled to be released around August 18, 1917, but a couple of lines in the ledger indicate that he was pardoned on April 21, 1918. Perhaps he received extra time in jail for minor infractions. He spent most of his term in the Walls unit and working at the prison's sugar refinery.

December 22, 1917: Attack on the Andollinas.

April 21, 1918: Monfre is released from prison (see above).

May 23, 1918: Attack on the Maggios.

June 27, 1918: Attack on Louis Besumer and Harriet Lowe.

August 5, 1918: Attack on Rosie Schneider.

August 10, 1918: Attack on Joseph Romano.

March 9, 1919: Attack on the Cortimiglias.

August 3, 1919: Attack on Sarah Laumann.

August 10, 1919: Attack on Steve Boca.

October 27, 1919: Attack on Mike Pepitone.

Further muddled dates in the prison log seem to indicate that Monfre spent a short stretch in jail from August 21, 1923, to December 21, 1923. For some reason, the dates September 13, 1922, and November 12, 1922 (both scratched out) and February 21, 1930, are entered in one column.

Joseph Monfre is a good suspect, but only for the 1918-19 crimes. If all of the Axman attacks between 1910 and 1919—with the possible exception of the Pepitone murder—were all committed by the same person, the Axman could not have been Monfre, for the records prove he was in jail during the assaults on the Cruttis, the Rissettos, the Davis, the Sciambras, and the Andollinas. (The Andollina case from 1917 is especially significant, since this attack was the first we can definitely claim to be the work of the Axman. For the first time, his three major trademarks were in evidence: he chiseled out a door panel, used a hatchet, and left the weapon at the scene of the crime.) Monfre was

Joseph Monfre. Was he the Axman? From the *New Orleans Daily Picayune,* August 22, 1908. Reprinted by courtesy of the *New Orleans Times-Picayune.*

released from prison only a month before the attack on the Maggios in May 1918 commenced the Axman's real reign of terror. Perhaps there were two Axmen: an unknown man killing with a gun and a cleaver before 1915, and Monfre using the canonical ax starting in 1918. But if so, who attacked the Andollinas using the Axman's classic *modus operandi* in 1917, while Monfre was in jail?

If we assume that Monfre was the Axman, a mystery remains. Why did he abruptly stop killing in the fall of 1919? The question is neatly answered in the legend related in the books by Robert Tallant and Ed Reid: Mrs. Mike Pepitone, by then known as Esther Albano, killed him on the streets of Los Angeles after her husband's murder. Tallant wrote that the incident occurred in December 1920; according to Reid, it was October 1921. I searched the *New Orleans Times-Picayune,* the *Los Angeles Times,* the *Louisville Courier-Journal,* and the *New York Times* for both dates, and none of the papers reported the shooting. While at first glance it would seem that the event never actually happened, I have confirmed it in a roundabout manner. On February 1, 1922, film director William Desmond Taylor was found shot to death in his house, resulting in one of Hollywood's most infamous unsolved mysteries. According to an Associated Press story datelined Los Angeles February 8:

A final search through William Desmond Taylor's apartments by the public administrator disclosed, hidden in a leather case, a newspaper clipping of the slaying here within the last few months of Leon J. Manfre, also known as Mumfrie, by Mrs. Esther Albano.

This is not to say the murders of Monfre and Taylor were somehow related; perhaps Taylor thought the dramatic revenge slaying might make a basis for a movie script. But it does verify that Mrs. Albano killed a man named "Manfre" in L.A. a few months before February 1922. However, this Leon Monfre could not have been Joseph Monfre, the Black Hand dynamiter from New Orleans and Reid and Tallant's number one suspect. Monfre's prison records indicate that he was alive in 1923 and as late as 1930. In addition, Axman authority William Kingman searched the California vital records in vain for a death certificate for "Joseph Mumfre."

For what it's worth, there is a California death certificate for a man named Joseph Monfre. He is the only Joseph

Monfre who turns up in the entire collection of California vital records. I cannot say with certainty that he is the same Monfre who is the leading Axman suspect, but the document contains grist for speculation. According to the Mafia legend retold by Reid and Tallant, the New Orleans Monfre moved to Los Angeles around 1919-20; the California Monfre moved to Long Beach, Los Angeles County, in 1940. The 1910 Louisiana Census states that the prisoner Monfre was born in 1873 or 1874; the death certificate for the California Monfre reveals that he was born on August 7, 1878. (The three- or four-year discrepancy is par for the course in old records, as any genealogist will attest, and does not in itself rule out the possibility that both Joseph Monfres are the same man.) According to his prison records, the New Orleans Monfre was born in Italy, as were his parents; the death records show that the same is true of the California Monfre. One inconsistency is that the New Orleans man made his living ostensibly as a labor agent, while the California man had been a shoemaker since 1915 (in fact, his last job had been working for a local Sears and Roebuck department store). Needless to say, the California Monfre was not murdered in the street, as legend claims. He died of a generalized marasmus and encephalopathy on January 6, 1975.

While it would make a great story if the Axman got away and died peacefully at the ripe old age of ninety-six, there is evidence that the two Joseph Monfres were different men. The 1920 census of the United States includes an Oil City, Pennsylvania, shoemaker named Joseph Monfre. He was born in Italy around 1878, as was the California Monfre. He moved to the U.S. in 1906, while the thuggish New Orleans Monfre had lived in America since at least 1897. It is not unreasonable to theorize that the Pennsylvania shoemaker moved to California at some point and somehow got mistaken for his iniquitous namesake. If the man who died in 1975 was an innocuous cobbler, whatever happened to the Joseph Monfre from New Orleans?

If we assume Monfre was *not* the Axman, it is worth taking a close look at a series of atrocities that took place in Birmingham, Alabama, and its suburbs. Between 1919 and 1923, that city was terrorized by a wave of murders and assaults committed with axes and meat cleavers (though the killer appears to have behaved himself throughout 1920). The Birmingham attacks commenced soon after the final New Orleans murder, if indeed Mike Pepitone was a victim of the authentic Axman. Even more intriguing, in true Axman fashion, the victims included men, women, and children without regard to ethnicity—and virtually all were grocers or shopkeepers, some Italian. A list of victims provokes an eerie sense of déjà vu. (I have included all name spelling variants from newspaper accounts.)

1. November 28, 1919: A grocer named G. T. Ary was attacked and robbed in his store at 801 South Thirteenth Street. He died the next day without regaining consciousness.

2. December 24, 1919: John H. Belser was bound and gagged and beaten to death with a shovel in his store at 1801 Fifth Avenue. Although Belser was reputedly wealthy, only a small amount was stolen, leading the *Birmingham News* (and the police) to ask, "Was there another motive besides robbery? . . . [Were] the jumbled up merchandise and the broken cash register . . . only a blind to throw sand into the eyes of the officers?"

3. March 5, 1921: C. C. Pipkins was attacked in his shop at 500 Walker Street by two men but survived. According to the *News,* "Seven dollars on the person of the storekeeper was not touched . . . and the investigating officers did not believe that the cash box had been robbed." It was thought that the robbers simply got scared and fled before taking anything.

4. June 18, 1921: J. J. Whittle was clubbed and robbed in his store at Eighth Avenue and Weaver Streets. He recovered.

5. July 13, 1921: Charles and Mary Baldone [Baldona; Bardono; Baldenna; Belladonna] and their eleven-year-old daughter, Virginia, were attacked in their sleep at their store at 4510 Tenth Avenue. The family's three younger

children were left unharmed; the Baldones survived despite having crushed skulls. Three-year-old Frank told police that he saw a black man striking his father. As with the New Orleans Axman's crimes, the bloody ax was left at the scene, beside Mr. Baldone's bed. According to a February 1922 news account, "[T]he case puzzled [police] extremely because it was apparent that the motive was neither robbery nor ordinary attack." Forty dollars were left in the till and the store was not ransacked. Equally mysterious was the method of the attacker's entrance and escape, since all of the doors and windows were locked.

6. August 17, 1921: Hyman I. Borsky [Dorsky] was beaten with a hammer in his store at 217 North Eighteenth Street but survived. His assailant(s) left the weapon behind and stole a gold watch, forty dollars in cash, and two checks.

7. September 6, 1921: Mrs. Sam Zideman was clubbed by two blacks in her store at 1700 Ninth Avenue. She was robbed of sixty dollars but survived.

8. December 21, 1921: Joseph and Susie Mantione were murdered with a homemade ax at their three-room grocery/residence at 3224 Church Street in Collegeville. The murderer left the weapon beneath the kitchen stove and doused the building's floor with gasoline to burn down the store; the blaze was extinguished by a neighbor, Thomas Price. The Mantiones' baby, Pete, was unhurt. The residence was ransacked, but it was not determined whether the attacker had stolen anything.

9. December 21, 1921: Mose Parker, black and middle-aged, was murdered with an ax in his backyard in Tittisville [Titusville] on the same day the Mantiones were slain. His shoes and hat were missing, but otherwise there was no sign of robbery. He appears not to have been a shopkeeper, so there is some doubt as to whether his murder was connected with the others in the series.

10. January 10, 1922: Mr. and Mrs. Clem S. Crawford were attacked in their grocery and home at 1501 Fourth Avenue. The assailant struck Mrs. Crawford from behind

with a hammer or an ax and cut her throat with a knife, killing her instantly. Her husband's head was crushed when he came to her aid. Their three-year-old daughter, Josephine, was untouched. Mr. Crawford died on January 17, having never regained consciousness. The house had been looted and the cash register drawer was open; the killer took a pouch containing an estimated $100 but threw jewelry in a corner. He left behind many bloody fingerprints, which were used to exonerate four early suspects.

11. January 25, 1922: Tony and Rosa Lareno [Larino; Larono; Lomio] were attacked by a black assailant with a short-handled ax or a hammer in their store at 337 South Twelfth Street—just three blocks from the Crawfords' store. Their skulls were pulverized, but they survived. Their three children, Frances, Vincent, and baby Mike, were unharmed. After being struck, Mr. Lareno rallied enough to fire a revolver and a shotgun at the fleeing intruder; had the merchant not been armed, he and his wife almost certainly would have been murdered.

12. June 3, 1922: Joe Lucia and his wife Lena, grocers residing at 2005 Jasper Street, Acipco, were brained by a black customer with a heavy instrument, probably a hammer. Mrs. Lucia's screams scared away the attacker; both grocers survived. Their two children, Jake and Galena, were not harmed.

13. September 30, 1922: J. H. Seay was clubbed in his grocery at Thirty-Ninth Street and Thirty-Fifth Avenue. His pockets, cash register, and personal items were ransacked. Seay survived.

14. November 6, 1922: A black assailant crushed grocer Abraham Levine's skull with a blunt object—probably an ax—in his potato garden and robbed him of fifty dollars, then walked to the store at 1600 Fourth Avenue and lured the merchant's wife, Sarah, to the back porch. He struck her as well but was scared away by the couple's teenage daughter, Emma. Mrs. Levine survived, but her husband died on November 7.

15. January 10, 1923: Grain merchant Joseph Klein and his teenage daughter Ethel, Russian immigrants, were attacked with an ax in his store at 1406 Eighth Avenue by someone posing as a customer. Ethel, who survived, claimed their assailants were three white men.

16. January 23, 1923: Luig [Luigi] and Josephine Vitellaro's skulls were crushed with a sharp ax in their store at 2431 Eighth Avenue. They lay unconscious on the floor all night in a pool of blood. Mrs. Vitellaro died on January 24; her husband died on the thirtieth. The killers left the short-handled ax and a gory knife behind. Robbery was the obvious motive: the store and the Vitellaros' living quarters had been rummaged through and the shopkeeper's pockets were turned inside out.

17. May 28, 1923: Charles Graffeo's throat was cut and his skull crushed with a short-handled ax in his store at 1500 Seventh Avenue. His pockets were picked, the store and residence looted, and the cash register emptied. Like the Axman, the killer left the weapon behind a door.

18. October 22, 1923: Someone entered the grocery/home of Bernard Vigilant [Vigilante] at 201 South Twenty-First Street and struck his wife Juliet in the back of the head with a meat cleaver and cut her throat with a pocket knife. Then he slashed Mr. Vigilant's mother-in-law, Elizabeth Romeo. The Vigilants' three-year-old daughter, Caroline, was untouched. Mrs. Romeo died several hours later; Mrs. Vigilant died on October 24. The killer stole money from the till, but he left behind a pile of Mrs. Vigilant's valuable jewelry—as well as bloody fingerprints on a light bulb.

A February 1922 *Louisville Courier-Journal* article gives an impression of the panic that gripped the city:

Psychologists, criminologists, hard-headed detectives, experienced policemen, Ku Klux Klansmen, soldiers of the World War and even the Ouija board are attempting to ferret out the causes of a series of ax murders and attacks that have set the Birmingham district's nerves on edge. . . . In each case the woman was young and pretty, leading to the conclusion that the crime was the work of a sadist, one of the most dangerous of all perverts and maniacs.

The press mentioned that victims were "mutilated" but provided few details. Dr. William Bohannon, head of the psychology department at Howard College, determined the killer was a "sadist" on the dubious grounds that "the sadist does not molest children. The sadist . . . delights in seeing women, especially young and pretty ones suffer. He rejoices in breaking their bones and watching them welter in their own blood." As the above list demonstrates, however, the Birmingham maniac twice harmed children when the opportunity arose.

In January 1924, the police arrested five blacks suspected of being members of a murder and robbery gang: Peyton Johnson, O'Delle Jackson, John Reed, Fred Glover, and Pearl Jackson. They confessed under the influence of scopolamine, a primitive type of truth serum. Later the suspects signed confessions while not under the influence. They claimed that they drew straws to determine which got to perpetrate murders. With their conviction, the Birmingham ax attacks came to a stop.

Some New Orleans detectives had suspected from the beginning that the "Axman" murders were the work of more than one person. Had they been correct all along? This hypothesis would explain the varying descriptions of the Axman's height and complexion. It would also explain the abrupt ending of the series of murders in both New Orleans and Birmingham, and the fact that Mike Pepitone was slain by two men.

However, the case is far from closed. Unlike the New Orleans Axman, the Birmingham Axmen admitted that their chief motivating factor was robbery; the former murderer seldom took anything of value—and when he did, the police felt he was only trying to make his crimes appear to be robberies since he left items of far greater value behind— but the Alabama killers usually carried away money and merchandise. (On the other hand, according to the *New York Times,* "In some cases robbery appeared the motive . . . while in others there was no sign of robbery.") The Birmingham gang attacked grocers with blunt objects— frequently axes—and left a weapon behind on at least five occasions (the attacks on the Baldones, Borsky, the Mantiones, the Vitellaros, and Graffeo), but I have found no evidence that they chiseled out door panels, the original Axman's other consistent trait. Only once did they attack sleeping victims (the Baldones), contrary to the Axman's inevitable method; almost always, they simply walked into stores during business hours, pretending to be customers, and bludgeoned everyone present.

While the "Birmingham axmen" are interesting suspects, in the final analysis, the New Orleans murders seem to be the work of a single, very idiosyncratic, ritualistically minded killer rather than five men who between them somehow formed a consistent method. In addition, it is difficult to believe that five individual gang members could perpetrate so many violent attacks between 1908 and 1923—fifteen years!—and somehow never be suspected by detectives or police informers or commit a fatal slip of the tongue. As a general rule, the more people who are involved in an activity, the harder it is to keep it secret.

Winston Churchill might have considered Russia "a riddle wrapped in a mystery inside an enigma," but if he wanted to experience real frustration, he should have investigated the Axman murders.

A Sharp Retort for Professor Turner

The bright summer morning of Sunday, June 7, 1925, was a hectic time at Louisiana State University at Baton Rouge because it was finals week. At 8:00 A.M., Raymon G. Markham, a graduate student, approached the south door of the Arsenal, a poorly lit, crumbling red brick building with iron-barred windows that seemed the ideal setting for a murder. The dour and reputedly haunted building of 1835 originally had been built for storing army weapons, but almost a century later, it was used for LSU's chemistry and agronomy (scientific agriculture) classes. Markham peered through a broken window in the door before entering. As he looked into the gloom, he noticed something at the bottom of a stairway that he took to be a pile of papers. When his eyes adjusted to the dim light, he realized it was a man lying on his side in a substantial pool of blood. In terror, Markham accosted the first person he saw, a vocational student named Emile J. Raffo who was walking across campus in the innocuous pursuit of milk and doughnuts.

The injured, barely conscious man was a well-liked professor of agronomy, Oscar Byrd Turner. He had been hit in the head repeatedly with a dull, rusty hatchet: struck once on top of the head, once in the back of the neck, and twice in the chin. One wound extended from the lip to the forehead. Despite the dullness of the weapon, Turner's assailant had struck him with such force that the professor had nearly been decapitated by one of the three hatchet blows to his throat. Turner was unable to speak to Raffo and Markham. The latter, who happened to be Turner's graduate assistant, remembered later that the dying professor could

MURDERED

Professor Turner and the hatchet that ended his life. From the *Baton Rouge State Times,* June 15, 1925.

only make "a funny sort of bubbling, whistling noise" through his cut throat and weakly pulled fragments of broken teeth out of his mouth.

(Even the most horrific murders often are leavened with darkly comic touches. The same hatchet that dealt death to the professor had been used only a week before as a paddle with which upperclassmen spanked freshmen during initiation rites.)

Robbery was not the motive: eleven dollars was in Turner's pocket and his gold watch had not been stolen. He was taken to Our Lady of the Lake Sanitarium, where he died two hours later. The *Baton Rouge State Times* interviewed dozens of students and reported that "not an unkind word was said of him."

Detectives tried to learn as much as they could about the victim. This proved difficult, for despite his popularity with students the known facts of Turner's life were sparse. He was the least likely murder victim that one could imagine. He was fifty-six years old and from Plymouth, Illinois. He had been a successful farmer in his home state but decided to move south for the warmer climate. He had come to LSU to get a master's degree in agronomy and joined the faculty in 1923. Quiet and personable, he was a famously thrifty bachelor who saved money by rooming at 714 College Avenue (now North Fifth Street) with Norman Allen, an entomologist and LSU graduate who worked at the university's experiment station. Despite his parsimony, Turner was no miser. During the Great War, he had given the army a pig every day and a cow every week; in the academic sphere, he had been known to finance students' education with his own money.

As far as anyone knew, Professor Turner's personal life was squeaky clean: he did not drink, did not attend parties, did not consort with women, and was a member of First Baptist Church. Despite his sociability, he had no close friends who could offer insight into the mystery. Two of his three brothers came to Baton Rouge and told the press that Turner had no known enemies; after an elaborate funeral with student cadets forming a military guard of honor, they took his body home to Plymouth for burial. Turner's funeral in Illinois was held in a stucco chapel he had built himself at an estimated cost of $50,000.

A student named W. H. Stracener reported that he saw a man enter the Arsenal via its south door around 6:00 A.M. on the last morning of Turner's life. The victim's roommate, Norman Allen, told the police that Professor Turner had left the apartment at 7:00 A.M. Within an hour, he would be attacked in the Arsenal; within three, he would be dead. Based on bloodstains in the agronomy building, police deduced that Turner had initially been struck with a fist or the hatchet on the stairway, possibly, as he walked away from his assailant. He fell to the bottom of the stairs and then was hacked where he lay, the same fate of the hapless detective in Alfred Hitchcock's *Psycho*. The attack was as silent as it was brutal. Only fifty yards from the Arsenal stood the home of LSU's president, Thomas D. Boyd; his wife had been sitting in a rocking chair on the porch at the time of the murder and had heard nothing out of the ordinary.

Blood drippings in the building indicated that the killer had left the gory hatchet on a dusty shelf and fled by running through a chemistry classroom laboratory, where he paused to wash his hands in a sink. He exited through the Arsenal's east door. Investigator Maurice O'Neill found a seemingly first-rate clue left by the professor's murderer: a bloody fingerprint on the east door facing. Prints were found on the hatchet's handle, but they were too smeared to photograph. Nevertheless, the mere presence of finger-prints at the crime scene was a valuable clue in itself, for they suggested the murder had not been premeditated. Only a novice killer would have failed to wear gloves.

Another intriguing clue was discovered when police searched the chemistry lab. O'Neill looked into an elec-tric oven and found a package containing some of Profes-sor Turner's papers and two of his textbooks, including one with the enthralling title *The Nature and Properties of the Soil*. If the books and papers were incriminating, why did the murderer not simply take them with him? If they were not incriminating, why did he stop in his flight to conceal them? The items were examined by O'Neill, a fingerprint expert from New Orleans Police Department, but to no avail. Detectives eventually learned that Turner sometimes used the oven as a temporary repository for his books, so the placement of the items may have had no significance.

Citizens of Baton Rouge panicked at hearing about Turn-er's grisly death, thinking a homicidal maniac was in their midst. Given their fresh memories of the New Orleans Ax-man's dark deeds, the alarm can be understood—especially since, like the Axman, the professor's murderer had left the bloody hatchet behind at the crime scene. But as no one else was harmed in the ensuing days, Turner's murderer clearly had been interested in killing only him. The citizens' ter-ror was replaced with curiosity and several popular conjec-tures were launched, some of which sound as if they came from people who had been spending too much time taking in melodramas at the silent-movie palaces. Some thought Turner had been murdered by an envious rival teacher. For adherents to this theory, the number-one suspect was Nor-man Allen, Turner's roommate, for a handkerchief bearing

Allen's laundry mark was found near the dying professor. Allen was able to prove he had been elsewhere at the time of the murder. Most likely, Turner had accidentally carried away one of Allen's handkerchiefs. Idle folk, and not a few detectives, wondered whether Raymon Markham, Turner's graduate assistant, had murdered him to get his job. Markham explained to the press that he had already received offers to teach at colleges in Huntsville, Texas, and in South Carolina: "I had never had the least idea of staying here at LSU after I got my master's degree." The belief that the murderer envied Turner's job lost traction when the press revealed that it paid only $125 a month, a shabby salary for a college professor even by 1925 standards. (The equivalent in modern currency would be a little over $1,500 per month.)

Others thought there had been a financial motive after it came out that the frugal instructor had been worth as much as $100,000 at the time of his death. Turner had sometimes lent money to people and kept copies of their outstanding notes in a black briefcase, which disappeared and never was found. Perhaps a debtor had killed Turner and stolen the briefcase, erroneously believing that it contained the original notes?

Since a hatchet was the murder weapon, those inclined to put stock in racial stereotypes believed the killer must have been a "Chinaman" bent on revenge. A quick check of the professor's class roster revealed that he had three Asian students, two from China and one from the Philippines. The exultation some felt in this discovery was short lived, for the three Asian students made some of the highest grades in the class and had no discernible motive for butchering their teacher. Detectives also questioned George Porter, a custodian with a cut hand, but released him when he provided an alibi. Porter told the investigators that he thought Professor Turner was a fine fellow and poignantly recalled the time Turner gave him a dime so he could buy a cup of coffee.

Another red herring swam to the surface of the case when

detectives checking out a professional laundry uncovered a pair of pants with bloodstains in the pockets. When they found that the pants belonged to one of Turner's agronomy students, they tracked him down and apprehended him while he was taking a final. He claimed that the gory pants were the result of a nosebleed, but not his own. A friend of his had punched a woman in the nose. The unlucky student had helped her clean up, then absentmindedly stuck his bloody hands in his pockets. The unlikely story was confirmed when police ascertained that the fight had in fact occurred and interviewed the doctor who had treated the poor woman's nosebleed. The student was dismissed as a suspect and generously allowed to retake the final.

There was talk of a mystery woman, an inevitable feature of any self-respecting unsolved homicide. But the victim's brother claimed that there had been only one true love in Professor Turner's life, and she had been living as a missionary in India since around 1895. Rumor held that the professor had advanced a large sum of money to a woman in Baton Rouge, who decided to play the Mohawk rather than pay back the loan. Detectives investigated the story and found it groundless.

The mystery car is another staple element of baffling murders; the Turner case yielded a bounty of three. On the afternoon before the murder, a woman who worked in the school cafeteria had seen Turner riding in the back seat of a dusty touring car with three other men. The three men stepped forward and identified themselves as Turner's students. The professor had gone on a ride with them that day but only to inspect the site of LSU's new campus then being constructed.

A student saw mystery car number two at 1:00 A.M. on June 7, six hours before Turner was murdered. He noticed that the open car was full of men, two of whom climbed out of the vehicle and skulked away in the darkness. The car then reversed its direction and drove away. The student thought the behavior of the car's occupants was so suspicious that he wrote down its license plate number in case they were up to no good. The auto was traced to a Mississippi man who had simply dropped off friends after a dance.

While these less than rousing events transpired, LSU president Thomas Boyd decided he would spare no expense to find the professor's slayer. Boyd hired an undercover agent from the Pendleton Detective Agency of New Orleans to investigate; his identity was so successfully kept secret that the sleuth is known to the ages only as Agent Number 405. He arrived at LSU on June 9 and soon uncovered the third mystery car. The auto was spotted on campus the morning of the murder and it had a license from Turner's home state, Illinois. Agent 405 traveled seven hundred miles to the Land of Lincoln and found to his excitement that the driver of the third mystery car shared the surname Turner and lived only forty-five miles from the victim's family. A new theory formed: the professor may have been killed by a relative. However, the detective found that it was all an amazing coincidence. The two Turners were not related. Agent 405 reported back to LSU's president with Napoleonic understatement: "I was a little disappointed."

In early July, President Boyd hired a second detective from the New Orleans firm, a man called Agent 303, who posed as a door-to-door magazine salesman. At night, he blended in with LSU students at a favorite haunt, the Square and Compass Club. He observed students shooting craps and partaking of alcohol—these were the days of Prohibition—but heard nothing of any use in solving the murder of Professor Turner. When he asked one underclassman whether he had heard any rumors about police discoveries, the student sneered that the police couldn't track an elephant in the snow. Agent 303 dutifully noted the unwitting student's insult in his daily report.

The whole affair took on a ludicrous tone at the end of the month, when Agent 303 realized that he himself was being shadowed as he pretended to sell magazine subscriptions. His follower was a woman selling corsets, and Agent 303 suspected she had been hired by someone interested in thwarting the course of justice. According to his daily reports, whenever he skipped a street, she did the same; if he paused anywhere, she was sure to pause nearby. At one point, she boldly asked 303 how his business was doing. The undercover man investigated the corset seller and discovered only two facts: she lived in the Palms Hotel and had a fondness for yellow hats. Soon, Agents 303 and 405 threw in the towel and went home to New Orleans, probably after presenting President Boyd with an itemized list of their expenses.

Meanwhile, the head of LSU's psychology department, Prof. C. H. Bean, expressed the opinion that the murderer was a "moron, an imbecile or a pervert." He thought he knew who the culprit was, too: a grubby-looking "man of low mentality" who had been lurking around the campus for the past two months. The man spent most of his time in the campus library. He would wash in the public restroom, a fact suggesting that he was homeless, and often could be seen smoking cigarette stubs he found on the sidewalk. Dr. Bean was informed that the sinister hobo "did not work, and no one could get him to work," and had been on campus as recently as two days after the murder. The man was not named by the press and apparently was cleared by the authorities.

An LSU agriculture professor, whom the police declined to name, stated that he had "had trouble with persons not connected with the university" and believed that he had been the murderer's intended victim. Professor Turner worked in the same building as Professor X and had been attacked in a dimly lit hallway. Had it been a case of mistaken identity? The theory was not as farfetched as others, but when the dust of the investigation settled, the best and most logical hypothesis was that the professor's killer was one of his own students. The reader will recall that the murder occurred during finals week. Raymon Markham, Turner's graduate assistant, told police that on Saturday, June 6, the professor had written the questions for the agronomy final, which was to be held on Monday. Turner had left the exam in his desk in the Arsenal and went to supper with the intention of mimeographing the final after his meal, but when he returned, the first four pages of the five-page test were missing. Markham and Turner spent the evening searching the office for the missing questions; in fact, the desire to resume the search was the reason why the graduate student had been at the Arsenal so early on Sunday morning, and it is probably why Professor Turner also had been there. The day after the professor's murder, Markham unlocked Turner's desk and found that the four missing pages mysteriously had been returned.

The police believed that when Turner arrived at the agronomy building on the morning of June 7, he had surprised one of his students in the act of returning the test questions. After Turner had locked the papers in his desk, the student followed him to the stairs, begging not to be reported, expelled, and disgraced. When Turner refused, the student found a handy weapon on a shelf—the hatchet used to chop kindling wood for the building—and murdered the professor in a fit of anger. The student then returned the hatchet to its usual place and ran from the building, generously coated with spattered blood and lucky that he managed to avoid being seen. If this theory is correct, the mysterious man that W. H. Stracener saw entering the building at 6:00 A.M. on the morning of the murder was not the killer, for it is improbable that he would return the missing test pages and then loiter in the building for more than an hour until Professor Turner showed up.

On the other hand, Markham admitted that the professor had been very absentminded and perhaps had locked the test questions in the drawer to begin with and then forgotten about it. But if Turner thought on Saturday night that the exam was missing, his desk drawer is surely the first place he would have looked. It is safe to assume that the exam was indeed temporarily stolen, and its disappearance the day before the murder and its reappearance the day after was not a coincidence. Almost certainly, the missing test played a critical role in the murder.

It would seem a simple matter to find the guilty party among such a narrow list of suspects. There were only twenty-seven students in Professor Turner's Agronomy 33 section and the killer left a bloody fingerprint. Students were fingerprinted as well as Raymon Markham and Emile Raffo, who had tried to comfort the dying man. But the badly smudged fingerprint could not be matched to anyone. Perhaps the blurry print was left by a student who to his secret relief was dropped as a suspect when his fingerprints did not appear to match it. According to the *State Times,* as of June 12, 1925, five members of the Agronomy 33 class had not been fingerprinted: "Two of them have gone to their homes and will return for commencement. One more will probably not return, while two others are in Baton Rouge. . . . [Police Captain] Woolfley said some of the boys in that class had left before he had obtained definite instructions when to have them fingerprinted." Did a guilty student slip through the investigators' dragnet?

An inspection of the professor's grade book did not shed much light, for none of his students was in danger of failing. The student doing most poorly in the class had an average of 77, a passing grade. The members of the Agronomy 33 class were given Professor Turner's final on Monday, June 8, as scheduled. Their answers were scrutinized by the coroner, who no doubt looked for a student who answered questions a little too flawlessly.

"Surely someone saw the murderer leave the building after the attack," pleaded the *Baton Rouge State Times.* "Surely, if a student is guilty, someone missed him from his room or place of work at the time of the crime. Surely, someone saw someone on the campus around the hours mentioned." However, nobody stepped forward with information that would solve the case. As time passed, it became evident that the murder of Professor Turner was destined to be an unsolved mystery. It remains so

The Agronomy Building on the old LSU campus. Turner was murdered inside on June 7, 1925. From the LSU *Daily Reveille,* June 9, 1970. Reprinted by courtesy of the *Daily Reveille.*

to this day unless some very elderly LSU alumnus chooses to unburden his conscience with a deathbed confession.

Progress has little respect for sites stained by the blood of the murdered. The year after the Turner slaying, LSU moved to a new location three miles south of the old campus. In 1931, the Arsenal was torn down; in 1932, Louisiana's State Capitol Building was constructed near the location where the old agronomy building once stood. Three years later, Sen. Huey Long would be shot to death within a stone's throw of the spot where Professor Turner met his untimely end.

The Servant Girl Annihilator

Three years before Jack the Ripper waged his one-man campaign against London prostitutes, becoming the first world-renowned sexually motivated serial killer, an equally anonymous and vicious murderer set to work ridding Austin, Texas, of its servant girls. Within a year, the killer's toll stood at five black women, one black man, and two white women. The repetition of a certain method reveals that the same person committed the rape-murders. In the beginning, the killer's taste in victims ran to servant girls, hence the nickname bestowed upon him by the press: the Servant Girl Annihilator. The case provides us with a fascinating glimpse at the bewildered reactions of one of the first cities ever to be terrorized by a serial killer, long before the concept of the serial killer was recognized and understood.

Austin's nightmare began at the end of 1884, though one general press account mentions that similar attacks took place in Dallas earlier that year. At 901 West Pecan Street (now Sixth Street) lived W. K. Hall, an insurance salesman. His servant was a twenty-five-year-old mulatto woman, Mollie Smith, who lived in a small indoor apartment behind the Halls' kitchen. She had been the family's cook for only a month but already had a live-in boyfriend named Walter Spencer. Around 3:00 A.M. on the morning of December 31, Mrs. Hall's brother, Thomas Chalmers, was awakened by a figure lurching into his bedroom. It was Walter Spencer, bleeding from five deep head wounds. He groaned, "Mr. Tom, for God's sake do something to help me. Somebody has nearly killed me." Spencer was unable to say who had struck him but was aware that he had been hit with an ax. He remarked with puzzlement that Mollie was missing. Chalmers advised him to see a doctor immediately and Spencer left. Investigators who inspected the room occupied by Mollie and Walter found the bed soaked in blood, furniture in disarray, a smashed mirror, and bloody finger marks on the door. Even this was not the worst part of what the man from the *Austin Daily Statesman* called "one of the most horrible murders that ever a reporter was called on to chronicle—a deed almost unparalleled in the atrocity of its execution."

Mollie was still missing at dawn, but at 9:00 A.M., a neighbor found her by following a bloody trail leading from the house. Like her boyfriend Walter Spencer, Mollie Smith had been struck with a sharp object, but the attacker had dragged her body outside. She was found in the backyard a hundred feet from the house, almost nude and chopped into pieces with an ax. Since the bloodstained ax was found at the foot of her bed, we may deduce that after hacking his victim, the killer had the nerve to return to the scene of the crime to leave the weapon where it would be found. The papers mentioned that Smith was so cut asunder that her body would not hold together in her coffin.

There are plenty of suspects to consider in the Austin servant girl slayings; the police seemingly arrested every other man on the street, some of whom were demonstrably innocent. The first in the long line was William "Lem" Brooks, a black bartender who was a former suitor of Mollie's. He proved that he had been at a ball until 4:00 A.M. the night of the murder. Many witnesses had seen him, as he held a conspicuous role by "calling the figures"—that is, calling out instructions to the dancers. Three attendees at the celebration affirmed that they had accompanied Brooks home afterward. Despite this, jurors at the inquest opined that Brooks was the most likely suspect. (At the end of March 1885, a grand jury found the evidence against Brooks too meager to justify the finding of a true bill of murder. The authorities quietly released him.)

Around January 2, 1885, police arrested Lee Baxter, a married black man, for the murder of Mollie Smith. "[I]t is not believed that he had any hand in the killing," remarked the *Statesman*. Nothing more is heard of Baxter in the press, giving credence to the *Statesman*'s assessment. In the meanwhile, Walter Spencer recovered from his injuries and spent the rest of his life wondering who had attacked him and murdered his girlfriend.

In the ensuing weeks, Austin was the scene of much violence, almost all of it directed at servant girls. Whether all (or any) of this mayhem was authored by the killer of Mollie Smith, no one can say. Some of the attacks involved a sole perpetrator, others more than one. Perhaps some of the acts were committed by the Annihilator and others by copycats. On the night of February 22, a young white woman who worked as a nurse for a wealthy citizen was seized near the bridge over Shoal Creek, only a block from the Pecan Street site where Mollie Smith had been murdered. She struggled free and escaped. At 3:00 A.M. on the morning of March 9, a German girl who worked in a house on East Hickory Street awoke in her room to see a white man demanding "her money or her life," the obligatory phrase on such occasions. She screamed; he struck her several times in the head with a rock. An occupant of the house came to the rescue with a gun, but before he could put it to good use, the intruder fled. As he ran, the villain defiantly threw the rock against the side of the house.

The night of March 13 yielded four separate incidents. A black cook who worked for Dr. W. A. Morris was awakened by a violent shaking of her door. Her husband fired a gun at the intruders outside, who threw rocks at the door and wall as they left. Later, two black servant girls who resided at Maj. Joe Stewart's house were terrified by a man who knocked on their door and tried to enter by raising a window. The girls fled the room in terror with the man in hot pursuit. He threw one to the ground, but her screams attracted a crowd and he escaped. Eerily, when the girls returned to their room the next morning, they found their clothes and furniture piled in the center of the room and a previously unlit lamp burning. In a third incident, a man tried to break into a woman's room in a house located near city hall, but her screams frightened him away. The *Statesman* reported that black "toughs" were behind these activities; perhaps they were cruel practical jokes. But a fourth occurrence that night was most serious. A black servant staying at the home of a Mrs. Parish on Pecan Street was raped by two black men. One of them she recognized as a mulatto barber named Abe Pearson, who was arrested the next day. He was not the Annihilator, for on April 30 Pearson was sentenced to two years in the penitentiary for burglary (and was tried for rape later). Pearson was safely locked away during the Annihilator's future activities.

The disturbances continued. On the night of March 15, a young Swedish girl who worked for clothier Abe Williams was alarmed by the sound of someone trying to enter the door and then the window of her separate living quarters. In terror, she bolted through the door and ran for the main house, the intruder hot on her heels. Her screams drew the curiosity of Mrs. Williams and the man ran away. The *Statesman* remarked, "[T]he reporter has a right to 'kick' when he is called to chronicle the same sad story of the 'Servant girl' night after night." Police arrested a mulatto named Gus Johnson on March 18 for having broken into the apartment of a black servant girl who lived on Charles Street. On March 19, an incident occurred at J. H. Pope's residence at the corner of College Avenue and Guadalupe. His two Swedish servants, Clara and Christine, lived in an apartment detached from the main house. They heard a knock on their door at 1:00 A.M. As Clara lit a lamp, someone shot at her through a window, grazing her neck. Clara ran outside in panic and was captured as she reached the doorknob leading to the Pope family's dining room. The man tried to drag her away, but she kept a desperate grip on the knob. The family was awakened by the noise and the man appeared to leave the scene, but minutes later, someone fired at Christine through the same broken window, wounding her near the spine. Mrs. Pope was in the room with Christine at the time but was left untouched; the shooter was interested only in harming the servant. A few hours later, there was an assault on a black cook working for Ella Rust, who, like the Swedish victims, lived on College Avenue. Her attacker broke a window and tore out a wire screen. The cook fired a gun at him and missed, but as it was a self-cocking pistol, she did not know how to fire a second time. A woman in Rust's family came outside to investigate and, standing only a few feet from the man, ordered him to vacate the premises. He did, but not before throwing rocks at her. The Swedish girls and Ms. Rust's cook all claimed that their attacker was black. The *Statesman* reported that several other houses were visited by a marauder that night—though no one could say with certainty that the marauder was the same man in each case.

The attacks had become so rampant that on March 20 the *Statesman* advocated lynch law should the miscreant or miscreants be caught and published a poem called "Song of the Servant Girl:"

> Oh! I've gone and bought me a gun
> And I mean to learn how to shoot,
> I'm going to have a barrel of fun,
> By plugging a prowling galoot.

The writer remarked, "It is said that out of 1,357 servant girls in Austin, 942 have left service because of terror, and the rest are sleeping in the same apartments with their mistresses." The absurdly precise statistics were intended as a joke, but the point is clear that the city's domestics knew they were being singled out for violence and were afraid. On March 20, Mayor Robertson called a special meeting of the city council to discuss the crime wave. Members discussed implementing a midnight curfew; Alderman Platt facetiously remarked that he would give $500 to the first servant girl who shot her assailant. In the end, the council voted to authorize the mayor and the aldermen "to take such action as they may deem advisable to detect, punish, and suppress lawlessness in the city." The council approved hiring fifty special policemen—a force badly needed by Austin, which had only five policemen performing street duty at any given time during the night, and two had to guard the business district. These forlorn men were expected to keep a city with a population of 17,000 safe from crime. But as of the beginning of June, the fifty extra men had not been hired. Marshal Grooms Lee detailed the scandalous understaffing of the police department: "[T]here are only twelve policemen, including the clerk at the station, and one the boss of the street gang. This leaves ten men for active duty, five of whom serve half of the twenty-four hours and the other five the remainder. Now how can so small a force guard a city the size of Austin?"

All was quiet for a few days after the city council's meeting. On March 27, the *Statesman* waxed prideful: "[T]he fiends have ceased their nocturnal assaults on the girls. . . . Austin has once more subsided into its customary state as one of the most orderly and peaceful cities in the South." But a month later the attacks began again. At 1:00 A.M. on the morning of April 29, the black cook who lived at the residence of Mrs. John Calloway at 302 Mulberry Street was awakened by a black man wearing a dress he had stolen from Mrs. Calloway's clothesline. The cross-dressing maniac seized the cook by the throat and threatened her with a razor. Luckily for her, two women passing by noticed her apartment door was open and called out to her. The rattled intruder ran outside, still clad in the stolen dress, and made parting jabs at the two women with his razor as he passed. The man also slashed at his dress with the razor in a novel attempt at removing it on the fly. A neighbor, Orlando Caldwell, gave chase but the man leaped over a fence. The next morning, the discarded dress was found; bloodstains indicated that the wearer had injured himself while cutting it off. The police thought the intruder was "Old John," a character who recently had been discharged from an insane asylum.

In the early morning hours of May 1, a black man invaded the room of R. W. Finlay's cook—located just north of the governor's mansion. Finlay scared the man away before he could wreak any havoc, but he returned that night and again tried to enter the cook's room. That same night, somebody shot out the windows of the buildings occupied by the black female servants of J. H. Robinson, near Pecan Street. A similar disturbance was reported at the home of a Mr. Lawrence on West Mulberry. In addition, J. M. Breckinridge of 405 West Mesquite was awakened by a noise in his yard. He looked outside and saw his elderly cook struggling with a large black man. When Breckinridge approached, the man fled with such alacrity that he left his hat and coat still in the cook's hands. He returned that night and threw rocks at Breckinridge's house and the cook's quarters. The coat and hat were found to have been stolen from a bartender named Dock Tobin. The next day, two blacks were arrested: Andrew Jackson and Henry Wallace, names that will amuse students of American history who are familiar with presidents and vice presidents. The belief was expressed in the local press that Jackson and Wallace were minor thugs, and "the main perpetrator is still at large"—a belief proved correct by what happened next.

The Servant Girl Annihilator may have been responsible for some of the rapes and acts of terrorism that plagued Austin in February, March, and April 1885, but no women were murdered in those three months. On May 7 came the second murder we may definitely attribute to the serial killer. Dr. L. B. Johnson—another figure in the case who shared a name with a president, at least as long as we refer to him by his initials—lived on the corner of San Jacinto and Cypress streets. Behind his house stood a cabin in which lived his black cook, Eliza Shelly, "an excellent woman . . . [of] good character," and her three children. At 6:00 A.M. on the day in question, Dr. Johnson went to market. While he was absent, his wife heard screams issuing from Eliza's cabin. She sent her niece to investigate. After the girl peered into the window, she dared not enter. The physician was apprised of the situation when he returned.

Stepping into the cabin, Dr. Johnson saw the body of his cook on the floor. She bore a deep cut over her right eye, made with an ax or hatchet. The wound must have caused instantaneous death, but the killer inflicted other mutilations. Shelly had a deep, round hole over her ear and another between her eyes; it was speculated that the killer had stabbed her with an iron bar. He had taken the trouble to break open a couple of trunks and scatter their contents about the room. He also wrapped Shelly's body in a bloody bedspread and laid her down on patchwork he found in one of the trunks. Unlike in the Mollie Smith case, Shelly's body had not been dragged outside nor was the murder weapon (or weapons) left behind. Dr. Johnson found bare footprints in the soil outside the cabin.

There was an eyewitness. All three of Eliza Shelly's little boys were present during the attack, and the oldest, an eight-year-old, was able to tell a *Statesman* reporter what he had seen. Several odd features in the boy's story render it not entirely believable. Still in a state of shock, he said, "A man came in the room and asked me where my mother kept her money. I told him I didn't know. He told me to cover up my head; if I didn't he would kill me. The man said he was going to St. Louis the next morning." The boy could not see whether the invader was white or black as he wore a rag over his face, but the man made a point of telling the boy that he was white; if this detail in the boy's story was true, it is likely that the attacker was black and was clumsily attempting to divert suspicion. Afterward, the boy went back to sleep and was unaware that anything dire had happened to his mother until daylight. I assume it was his screaming that attracted the attention of Mrs. Johnson in the morning and that the murderer had performed his brutal acts against Shelly in eerie silence, so as not to awaken her sons.

Whoever the Annihilator was, we may rule out as suspects several blacks who were already in jail on charges of raping or threatening servant girls at the time of Shelly's murder: Gus Johnson, Andrew Jackson, Henry Wallace, and the crazy dress-wearing "Old John." The police first theorized that the murder was the result of a domestic dispute, but it turned out that Eliza Shelly's husband was in prison. Almost entirely without clues, the police were reduced to arresting a "half-witted" black teenager, Andrew Williams, simply because he was barefooted. His feet must not have matched the footprints found by Dr. Johnson at the murder scene, for the press ceased all mention of Williams.

Although it has sometimes been claimed that only Austin's black community was upset by the crimes against the city's domestics, the *Statesman* noted just after Shelly's murder, "It is not putting it too strong to say that the dissatisfaction [with the police] is wide-spread and confined to no particular class of citizen." The paper called for Gov. John Ireland to offer a reward for the killer of Shelly: "It does not matter that the victim is an obscure colored woman. Her life was as dear to her, and should have been held as sacred, as that of the proudest lady in the land." The residents of Austin considered forming a vigilance committee.

Days after Shelly's murder, the police arrested a black vagrant named Ike Plummer. His examining trial was held on May 13, at which he came across as simple-minded rather than malevolent. The chief witness against him, Andrew Rogers, claimed that Plummer and Eliza Shelly had lived together on Red River Street before Shelly went to live with Dr. L. B. Johnson's family, although the Johnsons told the press that Shelly had worked for them for years. Rogers testified that he had overheard a vicious argument between Plummer and Shelly the day before the murder. Plummer threatened her and stalked away; as he left, the keen-eyed Rogers observed a hammer or hatchet protruding from

Plummer's pocket. It so happened that Rogers lived near Plummer, and at 1:00 A.M. on the morning of the murder, Plummer dropped by just for the sheer pleasure of saying hello. This hardly credible yarn was good enough for the police, and Plummer was bound over. While Plummer was in the lockup, another black servant girl, Mattie Johnson, was assaulted in the early morning hours of May 14. The police arrested a man named Mabry, but no explanation was provided by the papers.

Around May 19, another black, Newt Harper, was put on trial for the abuse of J. M. Breckinridge's servant girl, which had occurred a couple of weeks before. Even if he were guilty of that crime, he could not have been the Annihilator, for the villain struck again while Harper was still in jail. Harper was stabbed in a fight, probably fatally, on July 19; the Annihilator's crimes continued for months afterward. Harper was yet another red herring in a teeming ocean.

The Annihilator claimed his third victim on May 23. In Mrs. Whittman's backyard on East Linden Street was a house containing two apartments. In one lived her black servant, Irene Cross, and her adult son; in the other, Cross's young nephew. Her son had the distressing habit of leaving the doors unlocked when he came home late. Shortly after midnight, a stranger tested the unlocked door and walked into the apartment occupied by the nephew. The boy later described him as a large, barefooted black man, with his pants rolled up and wearing a brown hat and ragged coat. The boy started to scream. The man said that he had no intention of harming him and ordered him to keep quiet. He then walked into Irene Cross's room. A few minutes later, he emerged, pocket knife in hand. Cross reeled outside; her cries alerted the Whittmans, who telephoned for a doctor. A reporter from the *Statesman* arrived at the scene even before the doctor. He described the woman's injuries:

> Familiar as he was with repulsive sights, the reporter could not help being horrified at the ghastly object that met his

view. The woman's right arm was nearly cut in two, from a gash over six inches long. A cruel cut extended over half-way around her head, commencing just above the right eye. It looked as if the intention had been to scalp her. She was moaning and writhing in pain.

She had no idea who had attacked her, and after con-siderable suffering, she breathed her last on the morning of May 25. Although it was obvious that her slayer was the same person who had killed Eliza Shelly, Ike Plummer re-mained in jail. A wave of fear swept the city and some de-manded that "every loafer and vagabond, white and black," be run out of the city. The latter solution, of course, was predicated on the idea that the killer *must* be a stranger, for no true Austinian was thought to be capable of committing such atrocities.

Around 4:00 a.m. on June 2, someone shot through the slightly raised window of an apartment where lived Jane Coleman, black servant of Professor Tallichet of the State University in North Austin. The bullet entered Coleman's left arm and her chest; while painful, the wounds were not fatal. The man shot at the armed professor when he came running, but missed. Coleman's assailant was long gone by the time a policeman arrived. If it was the Annihilator, he was experimenting with a new method of murder.

Two months of relative quiet came and went. "Austin is once more serene," printed the *Statesman* on June 11. The paper spoke too soon, for in a few weeks the Servant Girl Annihilator grew bolder and meaner.

On the East Cedar Street property of V. O. Weed, neph-ew of the famous politician and journalist Thurlow Weed, stood a servants' cabin occupied by forty-year-old Rebecca Ramey and her eleven-year-old daughter, Mary. Around 5:00 A.M. on August 30, Weed heard agonized groans com-ing from the cabin. He went inside and found Rebecca unconscious. Her skull had been fractured; she had been struck in the left temple with a sharp object such as an ax. Young Mary had been hit in the head with a sandbag and dragged outside into a washhouse. She had been raped and then hacked with an ax; at the inquest later, a doctor described her as "considerably torn." As in the Eliza Shelly murder, her attacker had driven an iron pin through her ears, which, horribly, appears to have been the cause of death. Weed called in the services of two physicians, but it was too late. Mary Ramey died a little more than an hour after Weed found her. Rebecca Ramey could remember no details of the assault and, in fact, did not even know she had been hurt until she woke up in the doctors' care. Her recovery was slow and painful, but by September 15, she was reported to be "almost well," though unable to tell who had so cruelly treated her and her daughter.

As if the Austin Police Department had not been embarrassed enough lately, Marshal Lee did not show up at the scene until seven hours after the crime occurred. The attack on the Rameys was so outrageous that the police unleashed their most state-of-the-art method of criminal detection: bloodhounds. Bare footprints were found at the scene and the dogs set out on the hunt. They followed a trail from Weed's yard to a neighbor's stable, where the police found a barefoot black youth named Tom Allen. His feet perfectly fit the footprints and he could not give a satisfactory account of his movements on the morning of the murder. The police thought they had their man at last. But when a physician named Dr. Burt examined Allen, his "examination proved very conclusively in his mind that Allen was not the man who raped the girl." The papers did not explain his conclusion in further detail, but despite the suspicious circumstances under which he was caught, Tom Allen joined the parade of men who were briefly held as Annihilator suspects, then unceremoniously released.

In the wake of the latest unsolved murder, local blacks organized. On September 1, they met at the court house and formed a committee resolving "[t]hat we, the colored citizens of Austin, pledge ourselves to use every lawful means to aid the civil authorities in arresting and punishing these villains to the fullest extent of the law." The committee asked the mayor, city council, and Governor Ireland to offer a reward for Mary Ramey's murderer. The authorities declined to do so, prompting the *Statesman* to ask on September 16, "Is it customary for Texas to offer rewards for the apprehension of murderers? If so, why is it that none has been offered by the Governor for the apprehension of the Ramie assassin? Is it because there are no available funds to offer?" The citizens of Austin took the initiative to raise reward money.

The Annihilator provided Austinians with a dreadful spectacle on a roughly monthly basis. On the night of Sunday, September 27, someone pried a window in the servant's room at one Mr. Robinson's house. Fortunately for the Swedish servant girl who usually slept in the room, her mistress had insisted that she sleep in safer quarters, and the Annihilator found himself in an empty room. In frustration, he stole an inscribed watch given to the girl by her father and left the premises. Later the same night, he found more potential victims at 2310 San Marcos Street: the black servants who lived in a wooden shanty in the backyard of Maj. W. B. Dunham, editor of the *Texas Court Reporter*. Just before 1:00 A.M. on September 28, the Annihilator sneaked into the servants' quarters through an open window. Four people were sleeping in a single room: Patsy Gibson, Lucinda Boddy, Gracie Vance, and Vance's husband (some accounts say live-in boyfriend), the intriguingly named Orange Washington. Gibson and Boddy were not servants of the Dunhams; they were visitors who had chosen a very bad night to call on Vance and Washington. The Annihilator took stock of the situation, then commenced striking Gibson and Boddy on their heads with a sandbag, fracturing both women's skulls. For the other two, he reserved use of an ax, which was later found under bedclothes. Within moments, all four were unconscious and Vance and Washington were dying.

The killer picked up the battered Gracie Vance. Rather than simply exit the house via the door, he shoved her through the open window, as proven by the presence of blood on the sill. He then threw Vance over a fence and dragged her through a weedy vacant lot to a stable owned by a neighbor named W. H. Hotchkiss, seventy-five yards from the cabin. Investigators realized that Vance must have recovered consciousness at the stable. There were signs of a fierce struggle. The Annihilator finished his work by battering her head with a handy brick. As in two earlier incidents, the victim had been wounded above or near both ears and in the temple. Investigators found signs that the woman had been raped while dead or dying. The killer left a watch with a broken crystal on her body, the chain wrapped around her arm. It was positively identified as the watch that had been stolen from the Swedish servant girl's room earlier that night.

As the murderer finished his evil deeds, back in the servants' quarters Lucinda Boddy shook off her injuries and stumbled about in the darkness until she found a lamp. The Annihilator, seeing the glow of a light in the servants' house, was concerned enough to abandon the stable, run to the servants' window, and angrily demand that she turn off the lamp. Boddy screamed and ran out of the building. The Annihilator—who apparently preferred windows to doors—took the trouble to climb through the window again and extinguish the light. Then he tried to catch up with Boddy, at last overtaking her at the front gate. Things might have gone even worse for her had Mr. Dunham not been awakened by all the noise outside. When he stepped outside with a gun, Lucinda Boddy threw her arms around him. Within moments, Dunham sounded the alarm. Mrs. Hotchkiss shouted that she had just seen a man running from her stable. A crowd of neighbors pursued the killer in vain through a nearby thicket. The group included an ex-alderman named Duff and a police officer, both of whom ineffectually fired several shots at the retreating form. The slayer left tethered to a tree a stolen horse that he had ridden to the Weed residence. Had the Annihilator been less fleet of foot, his career would have ended that night, since the crowd was in a lynching disposition.

Orange Washington died from his injuries after a few hours. Patsy Gibson and Lucinda Boddy were taken to the hospital. Doctors were certain Gibson would die, but she appears to have recovered. (When a *Statesman* reporter visited her in the hospital at the end of the month, he noted, "[Her] brain is oozing from the wounds in her skull every few moments.") Boddy claimed that she recognized the man who had stuck his head in the window and ordered her to blow out the lamp. Within minutes of the fierce attack, Boddy had told both Major Dunham and Mr. Duff that her attacker was a black named Dock Woods, who happened to be the owner of the horse abandoned by the Annihilator.

Woods was arrested as soon as the police could find him. It was later claimed that when taken to jail he was divested of bloody garments. While they were at it, the police arrested a couple of other blacks on suspicion: Oliver Townsend, whose frequent brushes with the law on minor charges were mentioned often in the *Statesman* in the months leading up to the murders, and Netherly Overton, who had come to claim the horse for Dock Woods. Overton was soon released when it became obvious that he had only been trying to do Woods a favor.

The imprisoned Dock Woods protested that he was innocent, claiming that his bloody clothes were the result of a venereal disease. But Lucinda Boddy was brought before him, and she declared that he was the man who had entered the shanty on the night of the massacre. The fates of Woods and Townsend seemed sealed when a couple of undercover men from Houston's Noble Detective Agency announced that they had proof positive against the two suspects: a witness named Johnson Trigg, who overheard them plotting the murders of Gracie Vance and Orange Washington. No one seems to have wondered why the eavesdropper did not warn Vance and Washington of their impending doom even though, according to Trigg's story, he followed Townsend right to the threshold of the servants' cabin on the bloody night. (Trigg even claimed that when he heard the sounds of the women being attacked he ran away without alerting anyone.) Nor did anyone realize that Lucinda Boddy's severe head trauma made her identification of Woods less than ironclad. Nor could anyone establish a motive. But none of these details mattered to Austinians, who were relieved that the nightmare seemed to be over at last. Police had to be ever wary of lynch mobs in the wake of the arrests; on a less malevolent note, for several days the *Statesman* ran complacent, congratulatory items about the Houston detectives' brilliant work. Despite the fact that the police were now quite sure that they had the right men in custody, several men arrested previously for the crimes remained in jail.

With autumn 1885 came the slow realization that neither the Houston detectives nor the local ones were so brilliant after all. Dock Woods and Oliver Townsend languished in jail with no solid evidence against them. Both confidently told a reporter that they had alibis for the night of the murders. It was proved that Woods' clothing had been saturated with his own blood, as he had claimed when arrested. The talkative and fanciful eavesdropper, Johnson Trigg, embellished his already strained story at the inquest, claiming under oath that by happy coincidence he had also overheard Oliver Townsend vowing that he would murder Rebecca and Mary Ramey on the night they were attacked. (In mid-October came news that Trigg had confessed to lying and was charged with perjury.) At the inquest, Patsy Gibson was mentally competent, despite her injuries, to testify that a few nights before the murder, Dock Woods had come to the cabin while Orange Washington was away and demanded to be allowed to spend the night, but she and Gracie had successfully chased him away. This did not in itself prove that Woods had murder in his heart.

The police department turned its attention to a new suspect, a black man named Aleck Mack who was arrested at a saloon on October 3. After his release from jail a week later, Mack went to the office of the *Austin Daily Dispatch* and told reporters that Marshal Grooms Lee and four others—including three of those admired Houston detectives—had threatened him, choked him with a rope, and attempted to beat a confession out of him. As proof of his story, Mack showed the reporters his bruises and scars. Marshal Lee denied it all and swore that Mack was a good suspect in the murder of Mary Ramey but said he could not give the press any details because the evidence was still before the grand jury. Lee explained that he had taken so many men with him when making the arrest because Mack was a notoriously violent drunk. In order to keep Mack calm, Lee had arrested him on a fictitious charge of hitting someone with a beer glass. The arrestee was docile at first, according to Lee, but on the way to the jailhouse, Mack suddenly became "boisterous" and struggled to get away. So violent did he become at the jail that it was necessary to throw a rope around his neck and drag him into his cell. Marshal Lee told the *Statesman,* "He was not maltreated in any way, and only such force [was] used as was absolutely necessary to conquer him. . . . If Mack has any bruises or scars on his person, they are the result of his own desperate efforts to resist arrest and incarceration."

The other officers who had participated in Mack's arrest corroborated the marshal's story, but the city council was not satisfied and formed a committee to meet November 9 in order to probe the alleged outrages. Marshal Lee did not improve his standing by his high-handed attempts to control the investigation. In disgust, the members requested on November 10 that the city council discharge the committee: "We are induced to make this declaration from the fact that the city marshal has attempted to create the impression that we were going to act partially in the investigation." The police protested that they had heard about the committee's meeting "only by hearsay, and not by any formal or legal notice or summons." Marshal Lee claimed that he had the right to confront his accusers in the presence of his attorney, like any other citizen. Whether or not Mack's charges were legitimate, on December 21 Marshal Lee stepped down from his position. The new city marshal, James E. Lucy, found himself facing the case of a lifetime only days after being sworn in.

Dock Woods and Oliver Townsend were still in jail on suspicion of having murdered Gracie Vance and Orange Washington, and in November, a month before he left office, Marshal Lee arrested a man named James Thompson for the attack on the Rameys. But none of the three men was the killer, for while they were in prison the Servant Girl Annihilator made a final, spectacular attack in Austin. The *Statesman* had remarked in an editorial on September 30, "It seems to be very generally understood that there is no danger of attempts of this kind being made on the white population, but it may be safely stated that Austin is the best armed city in the United States today." The killer seemed determined to prove the newspaper wrong, for he was a respecter of neither race nor weaponry. It often has been stated that the white citizens of Austin showed little concern about the marauder who was killing off the city's black servants, though a glance through the pages of the *Statesman* reveals considerable fear, interest, and sympathy. However, it is fair to say that when the Annihilator killed two white women—not servants, but women from the upper-middle class—the level of hysteria in the city reached hitherto unprecedented levels.

The Servant Girl Annihilator's assault on Austin ended as it had begun: at Christmastime. Moses H. Hancock was a middle-aged carpenter (or mechanic or painter, depending on the account) who lived at 203 East Water Street with his two teenage daughters and his wife, Susan, described in a contemporary report as "a beautiful woman, about forty years of age. She was born and educated in the Eastern states, and had much literary ability." Around midnight on December 24, he was awakened by the sound of groans. Alarmed, he hurried to his wife's room only to find an empty, blood-spattered bed. Hancock followed a trail of blood drippings out the front door, around the side of the house, and into the backyard, where he thought he saw two men jumping a fence. He found Susan barely alive, lying in a pool of blood a hundred feet from her bedroom. A modern FBI profiler would try to figure out why the Annihilator attacked most of his victims in relative safety indoors, then ran the risk of carrying their bodies outside to an open yard or to distant outbuildings to perform postmortem rape and/or butchery.

Susan Hancock had been smashed in the head and face with an ax, which the killer had left behind. Her left ear was cut through, she had a wound just above the left eye, her cheekbone was cut, and her skull was fractured in two places. The fiend again injured a victim's ear: he had stabbed Mrs. Hancock in the right ear with a long, sharp instrument with enough force to pierce the auditory canal, her skull, and even her brain to a depth of two inches. A *Statesman* reporter arrived on the scene shortly after the attack and mentioned in his account that "blood was oozing from both ears. Her groans of agony were piercing, and with what seemed to be her expiring breath, cupfuls of blood were emitted from her mouth." Doctors refused to state whether or not she had been sexually assaulted.

Perhaps the Annihilator had been frustrated by Mr. Hancock's appearance, since an hour later he struck again a dozen blocks away at 302 West Hickory Street, the residence of James Phillips, a well-known local architect. At 1:00 A.M., Grandmother Phillips awoke to hear her infant grandson crying. When she entered the bedroom, she found her son, James, lying unconscious with ax wounds in his head and neck, including a deep cut over the ear. The baby, unharmed but upset, was standing upright in his parents' blood-soaked bed and holding a piece of an apple.

The grandmother fainted at the sight—the wounds and the blood, not the apple—but soon revived. She then realized that James's wife, Eula, was missing.

A neighbor heard the commotion and came to investigate. Just as Mr. Hancock had done an hour before, the neighbor followed a bloody trail outside. At the end of the trail lay Mrs. Phillips dead and naked in a neighbor's backyard. She had been killed by a savage blow with the butt end of an ax to the forehead, which was crushed in to a depth of an inch and a half. The murderer had enigmatically placed a heavy rail across her chest and arms. She appeared to have been raped. Bloody handprints on a nearby fence indicated that the killer had escaped by jumping over it. The ax had been left on the victims' bed, forcing us to draw two conclusions: the weapons used to attack Mrs. Hancock and the Phillips belonged to the victims—both axes were left at the scenes of the crimes and it is unlikely that the Annihilator had wandered the city that evening carrying a pair of axes— and also that after hacking Mr. Phillips, then dragging Mrs. Phillips outside and killing her, the slayer had had the gall to return to the bedroom to plant the ax, as he had in the Mollie Smith case.

On Christmas morning, the police brought in two blood-hounds. The dogs followed a westward trail up Blanco Street until they had traveled two miles outside the city, then could not follow the scent any further.

Susan Hancock lingered on the brink a few days after the attack. She died at home on the night of December 28, in the same bloodstained bed on which she had been struck by the man with the ax. Her funeral was held in her own dining room. As if the Hancocks had not suffered enough, the man from the *Statesman* related his disgust at seeing a newly married couple making out "just like it was the beginning of a honeymoon" a few feet from the coffin during the wake; the murdered woman's family hastened to assure the public that the impolite ones were uninvited guests, not relatives.

The murders of the two women took place in the heart of

the city, indeed almost within sight of Texas's capitol building. The reaction to the latest round of murders was pure,
undiluted terror. "Walkabout," a columnist for the *Statesman* sternly advocated vigilante justice. The same paper
editorialized on December 26:

> We are totally in the dark. The murderers have so com-
> pletely concealed their trail that the very bloodhounds are
> at fault in tracing and establishing their identity. In fact, so
> mysterious has been the accomplishment of these horrible
> murders that the superstitious are beginning to attribute
> them to supernatural agencies.

The *Statesman* took back its earlier flattering remarks
about the Houston detectives, calling them "complete
failures."

Mayor Robertson called an emergency meeting at the
Hall of Representatives in the capitol, which was attended
by more than a thousand citizens—perhaps including the
gloating murderer, if our modern understanding of serial
killers can provide insight into the mentality of this killer
from long ago. A Citizens' Committee on Safety was formed,
and one of the first items of business was to figure out a way
to prevent a lynching should the perpetrator be arrested.
Private citizens and businesses raised several thousand dollars to aid police investigations. The Citizens' Committee
offered a $1,000 reward for information leading to the ar-
rest and conviction of the murderer. Detectives were im-
ported from other states and Marshal Lucy enforced a strict
curfew. Much too late, an additional thirty policemen were
hired to patrol Austin and Governor Ireland finally saw the
wisdom in offering a $300 reward for information leading
to the killer's arrest. By January 3, 1886, the reward had
grown tenfold. Perhaps this activity scared the Annihilator
into lying low, for as far as is known he never struck in the
city again.

James, husband of Eula Phillips, slowly recovered from

what doctors opined was certain impending death. As he recuperated, there were the inevitable whispers about town that he had attacked his own wife. The evidence consisted of nothing but rumors, but that had never stopped the police before, and James Phillips was arrested on New Year's Day on a charge sworn out by a detective. A *Statesman* reporter described the prisoner as "in such a physical condition from the effects of the wounds received on his head . . . that he cannot give any intelligent account of the affair." The injured man's father, James Phillips, Sr., denied the stories in a January 3 interview with the *Statesman*, while admitting that his son had been known to drink on occasion. When the *Statesman* announced that Phillips was to be arraigned, the paper added, "[T]here are few, if any, who believe he has been guilty of perpetrating the bloody crime laid at his door." The examining trial was postponed until February 11, although Phillips was in such bad shape it was feared that he would never live to see his day in court.

Arresting the barely surviving Phillips was an exercise in absurdity, but the dark comedy was augmented when, on January 27, Moses Hancock also was arrested on suspicion of having murdered his own wife. Rumor held that he and Susan had not gotten along and that he had once threatened to kill her—and that appears to have been deemed sufficient grounds for an arrest. Detectives, the district attorney, and Justice William von Rosenberg hinted that they had more solid evidence but refused to discuss it with reporters. They would not even say who swore out the warrant against Mr. Hancock. The reader will observe several problems with the police's theory, not the least of which is that it requires belief in not one astronomical coincidence but several. Perhaps out of desperation, the Austin police chose to accept that two men—and there was no evidence that they were acquainted—who lived several blocks apart had chosen to murder their wives using the same bizarre, bloody method, within an hour of each other. If the theory were correct, it also meant that James Phillips had given himself nearly lethal ax blows to the head and neck in order to make his story convincing.

In the ensuing days, there was talk of forthcoming incriminating evidence from former neighbors in San Antonio concerning Moses Hancock's violent tendencies; there were stories reminiscent of bad mystery fiction about a bloody hatchet found hidden inside a wall in the Hancock house; and a letter from Mrs. Hancock to her sister expressing mortal fear of her husband—and conveniently bearing bloody fingerprints. Mr. Hancock assured the press that he was too poor to afford a lawyer ("and a poor man don't have much showing"). It was his great good fortune that he was able to secure the services of a sympathetic ex-congressman who acted as his attorney *pro bono,* Hon. John Hancock (no relation to the accused, but another figure in the grim tale of the Annihilator who shared a name with a famous person from American history).

The *Statesman* predicted that when Moses Hancock went to trial, his attorney Judge John Hancock would rake the detectives "fore and aft [with] hot logical shot and withering sarcasm. . . . It is going to be a bad day for some of the 'alleged' detectives, and it is more than likely that when the judge [Hancock] gets through with them they will be as limp as rags, with the starch out, and wish they had never been born." Somebody must have had second thoughts about the paltriness of the evidence because on February 4 the case against Moses Hancock was dismissed without so much as an examining trial.

One might think the dismissal of Hancock would bode well for James Phillips, the still-critically wounded widower of Eula Phillips, but his examining trial began as scheduled. Phillips showed up in court leaning on the arm of a friend and with visible ax wounds in his head. Having learned absolutely nothing from the Hancock debacle, the Austin police and other members of the legal system refused to discuss the nature of their evidence against Phillips, leading the *Statesman* to call the proceedings a "Colossal Star

Chamber." "[T]he non-publication of the evidence may be eminently proper, but this inquest business being conducted with closed doors is, to place it mild, an outrage."

Nevertheless, tawdry details did leak out to the press, not the least interesting of which was that the late Eula Phillips had once been employed as a prostitute and was acquainted with two black local madams, Fanny Whipple and May Tobin. There was evidence that she continued to ply her old trade behind her husband's back as recently as the day before she was murdered. May Tobin testified that Eula Phillips had visited her establishment on the night of the murder. Several witnesses declared that the couple did not enjoy a harmonious marriage and that Eula feared her husband when he had been drinking and gone into jealous rages. None of this, of course, proved that James Phillips had chopped up his wife and brained himself with an ax. To explain the murder, the prosecution theorized that Eula faced James' wrath after her visit to May Tobin; she had taken the ax into her bedroom for self-defense; when her husband attacked, she hit him in the head with the ax; he wrested it away and killed her instead, keeping the presence of mind to perfectly imitate the Servant Girl Annihilator's murders. How it came to pass that the real Annihilator had coincidentally chosen that very same hour to perform a nearly identical murder only a dozen blocks away, the attorneys did not trouble to explain. On February 15, Justice von Rosenberg ruled that Phillips was to be remanded to jail and stand trial for murder.

Phillips got out of jail on bond. In late April, rumor incorrectly held that he had abandoned the city—to the *Statesman*'s embarrassment, a cub reporter ran the gossip as a factual item—but the paper reported that Phillips was at home on April 27, for the police had him under surveillance. Phillips went on trial for the murder of his wife on May 24 in a courthouse so packed with spectators that there was hardly standing room. The first day's testimony was largely a recap of that given at the examining trial, only this time "some of the testimony adduced smirched the names of several prominent citizens, two of whom are state officers," according to the *Statesman*, which refused to reveal the identities of those named but did state that "the deponent is engaged in the most meretricious of all callings." Translation: one of the madams who had employed Eula Phillips was naming her establishment's prominent clients.

On the second day of the trial, a worthy named John Abrahams testified that he and two other men had been walking near the Phillips house between midnight and 1:00 A.M. on the night of the murder. They had seen a light come on and heard a woman cry out, "Mercy me, murder!" The detail about the endangered woman's odd choice of words in the face of certain bloody doom leaves the unavoidable impression that Abrahams had been reading too many dime novels. The men ran to get the police, and when the group arrived back at the Phillips house, it was apparent that a murder really had occurred. Eula's sister Alma swore that James Phillips was prone to violent fits of jealousy. The court also heard more testimony from the madams May Tobin and Fanny Whipple. Importantly, a Dr. Litten testified that it was possible, but "highly improbable," that Phillips's head wounds had been self-inflicted.

The third day of the trial included the testimony of George McCutcheon of Williamson County, with whom Mr. and Mrs. Phillips had briefly lived a few weeks before the murder. McCutcheon too had seen Phillips's fits of rage and had heard him state that if he found out his wife was not faithful, he would kill her and then himself. The defense feebly attempted to imply that McCutcheon himself could have been the killer. Four witnesses, including Eula Phillips's father, provided an airtight alibi for McCutcheon: they had been with him in Williamson County, twenty-five miles from Austin, until midnight on the night of the murder. That ended the defense team's efforts to shift the blame.

On the final day of testimony, May 27, the chief witness was Dr. Joseph Cummings, Phillips's personal physician, who testified to the seriousness of his patient's injuries. In his professional opinion, the wounds could not have been self-inflicted. On that day, the jury got to see pieces of wooden panels from the Phillips home, each bearing the killer's bloody bare footprints. The defense had James Phillips coat his bare feet with ink and then step onto a planed board. His footprints were smaller than those left by the killer.

The trial ended on May 28. "The arguments on both sides," said the *Statesman*, "were able and ingenious." But despite the improbability of Phillips's having demolished his own head with an ax, despite the fact that his feet did not match the bloody prints found at the murder site, the jury found him guilty of murder in the second degree and recommended that he serve seven years in the state penitentiary. The *Statesman* pointed out in an editorial that even if the murder of Eula Phillips had been explained, that still left seven other almost identical murders unsolved. (James Phillips's lawyers requested an appeal on the grounds that the jury was "a travesty on law, logic, justice and common sense." Among other things, they argued that the prosecution had not proved that Mr. Phillips knew of his wife's infidelity. He was found not guilty at his second trial.)

Moses Hancock was then rearrested for the murder of his wife Susan. The treatment of Phillips and Hancock proves that well-to-do white men were not always considered the law's darlings in those days. The police also arrested as an accessory Dave C. Hagy, a San Antonio carpenter formerly from Austin and a man of sterling reputation. The press had freewheeling fun with his name, referring to him as Hagga, Haggy, Hegga, and Heggi. He had had the ill fortune to be at a party also attended by Mrs. Hancock on the last night of her life. To shorten a very long and silly subplot in the Servant Girl Annihilator case, the examining trial for Hancock and Hagy commenced on June 17, 1886. After a few days of testimony rightly described by the *Statesman* as "a whirling mass of confused rubbish of no criminating importance," it became clear that Hagy had had nothing whatsoever to do with the murder and he was released from jail on a writ of habeas corpus. The *Statesman* remarked, "Up to the date of [his] arrest, Hagy's character stood without a tarnish; yet, the moment the leprous hand of a hireling detective was laid upon him, its fetid grasp seemed to soil the fair escutcheon of Hagy's name." Evidently the paper's former fondness for detectives had died a wretched death. On June 23, Moses Hancock was released on a bond of $500, a sum so low considering the seriousness of the charge that the *Statesman* considered it "equivalent, almost, to a presumption of innocence." On that note, the inquiry was terminated.

The search for suspects continued despite the distraction caused by the arrests and trials of James Phillips and Moses Hancock. By January 1886, the Austin police had questioned more than four hundred suspects. Working from the theory that the killer was a sexual deviant, "nearly every man in the city, black or white, known to have idiosyncrasies of any kind have been watched by the detectives, but without avail," according to the *New York Times*. Nevertheless, arrests came often in the weeks after the Christmas murders. Two white brothers named Norwood, allegedly from Austin and clad in bloody clothing, were arrested in Temple, Texas, on December 26, 1885. The Norwoods claimed they had been in a fight. It is inconceivable that two killers would walk around in public for days after committing a highly publicized murder with their victims' blood still smeared on their clothes and hands, so it is safe to assume the brothers were questioned and released. Similarly, police received an alarmed call from a citizen who had seen J. Q. Echols, white, washing bloody clothes. Despite the fact that it is much easier for a killer to simply destroy sanguinary garments rather than wash and wear them, Echols was arrested and made to account for his actions.

Another possible candidate for the Annihilator was a Mexican named Anastacio (or Eustacio) Martinez, age approximately forty, whom the police arrested on the night of December 30, 1885. He lived in isolation near the river;

when the police searched the premises, they found women's clothes, including some stained with blood. They uncovered many other interesting items: a Colt six-shooter; seven knives, some bloodstained; a razor; a small ice pick; a long iron spike, which looked like the sort of weapon that had been thrust into some of the Annihilator victims' ears; a prayer book inscribed "Ella R. Rooney" (some news accounts give the even more incriminating inscription "Ella R. Ramey"); and two handkerchiefs bearing the initials "J.R." Authorities also found "[e]vidence . . . connecting the prisoner with the recent murders of Mrs. Hancock and Mrs. Phillips," but the papers did not elaborate. In addition, Martinez admitted he had served two years in the prison at Brownsville for assaulting women. However, a German woman whom Martinez was accused of assaulting the previous summer was unable to identify him. Also, Martinez's footprints did not match the ones found at the Phillips house. He soon disappeared from the headlines.

On January 21, 1886, a black man named Sidney Brown, who had recently lived in Austin, was arrested for beating and attempting to murder Sam Ford, a farmer. The press reported that Brown was "supposed to have been implicated in the Austin murders." We will never know to what extent Brown was involved in the Servant Girl killings, if at all, because a mob lynched him in Rockdale the same day he was imprisoned.

Since the press had little to say about any of these suspects after the initial stories broke, likely there was no solid evidence linking them to the atrocities. Perhaps the real Annihilator was among the four hundred men arrested and/or interrogated but managed to slip through the police's net. (For instance, one is left with the nagging feeling that the Austin police too hastily dismissed Tom Allen, whose feet perfectly fit footprints found at the Mary Ramey murder site and whom police found in a stable close to the scene after the murder.) By mid-1886, no more murders had occurred in Austin, and it was clear that the Servant

Girl Annihilator had left the city for good. He seemed to have vanished with the prairie mist.

Or did he simply move elsewhere in Texas after finding it unsafe to remain in Austin? On the morning of January 30, 1886, the residents of San Antonio were terrified by a crime that seemed to be the work of the Annihilator. Patty Scott, a twenty-eight-year-old mulatto servant of E. B. Chandler, was murdered in her room in an outbuilding by three hatchet blows to the head. She had also been beaten with a crowbar and her face mutilated. Her body bore the same deep cut on the base of the skull that had been seen on three of the Annihilator's Austin victims and she had received a blow on top of the head, an injury common to the earlier victims. As in the Austin crimes, the weapons had been left behind and the corpse had been sexually violated. The victim's abusive estranged husband William Scott was suspected; a bloody embroidered corset was found in his trunk and the bloodstains on it matched perfectly the location of the stains on the victim's nightgown. Mrs. Chandler testified that she knew the corset had belonged to Patty Scott, for she had given it to her servant. The inquest was held on February 5, and the jury's verdict was that he should stand trial for murder. Two other suspects were arrested: Henry Washburn, who worked as a gardener at the Chandler residence, and Washburn's roommate, a man named Turner. When arrested, Washburn was wearing bloody pants that had been washed and scraped recently; he and Turner told conflicting stories about their whereabouts on the night of Patty Scott's murder. At this point, the newspapers anticlimactically dropped the story.

The Annihilator may have appeared for the last time in Gainesville, Texas, on the morning of July 13, 1887. Captain Bostick was away from home on business, leaving behind his wife, his daughter Mamie, and her friend Genie Watkins, a visitor from Dallas. Mrs. Bostick was awakened by the sound of a scuffle coming from the bedroom where the girls were sleeping. She entered the room to see a man escaping through the east window. The girls had been attacked with a hatchet. Ms. Watkins survived until July 15, despite injuries including a cut that extended completely across the forehead, a deeply lacerated arm, and her right eye knocked out of its socket; one paper remarked that "her suffering was so intense that death was undoubtedly relief to her." Rumor held that she named her killer shortly before her death, but her doctors stated that she "did not pass a perfectly rational moment from the time she was assaulted until she died." The coroner found that she was kept under the influence of opiates and that she answered nearly every question the police asked in the affirmative, rendering useless the long list of suspects read to her by the authorities. Mamie Bostick recovered but could remember nothing but being awakened by her friend's struggle and then being knocked unconscious.

Several promising leads went nowhere. There were the usual reports of a "crazy man" having been seen in town on the fatal Tuesday, but he was never found. The dead girl's father, Capt. J. C. Watkins, stated in an interview that several years before, his daughter's testimony had been essential in convicting a man for robbery. The man had sworn vengeance and his sentence ended just a few days before the murder. Another suspect was Mamie Bostick's epileptic brother. The police soon arrested a black named Allen Ward and a couple of weeks later, a Mexican named George Spaniard. Both of them independently told incoherent and contradictory tales of having witnessed the attack on the girls. Both claimed to have been bystanders while someone else handled the ax. Of Ward, a reporter wrote, "The general impression here is still that having learned of the details of the tragedy in some way he made the confessions in Greenville . . . on account of a weak or disordered mind." The press has little more to say of either Ward or Spaniard, so the police probably let them go due to lack of evidence.

Journalists of the day could not help noticing the similarities between the attack on Bostick and Watkins and the unsolved Austin murders of two years previously. The crime was solved—maybe—the next year. On the day after Christmas, 1887, a white native Mississippian named William L. Beason passed a forged check in Luling, Caldwell County, Texas. Policeman Ben Evans found that Beason had fled to Meridian, Mississippi, and that he "was suffering from some heavy load on his mind, that he could not sleep, and often threatened to kill himself." Questioning Beason's sister-in-law, who lived near Luling, Evans found that Beason had confessed to her that he had attacked Genie Watkins and Mamie Bostick. He told her that his motive had been robbery and that he killed Watkins in a moment of panic with a hatchet he had used to pry open a window. Evans telegraphed the authorities in Meridian, who arrested Beason and clapped him in a prison cell. When Evans arrived, the prisoner confessed. On February 29, 1888, Evans accompanied his prisoner on a Santa Fe Railroad train back to Texas. When the train reached Belleville, however, Beason decided it was time for one more murder. He ran to the back of the train and leaped overboard as the locomotive traveled at forty miles per hour. He died in Fort Worth a few hours later without regaining consciousness. Beason was approximately thirty years old and had been married for only two weeks.

Journalists in 1887 assumed that the Servant Girl Annihilator murdered Genie Watkins. Does this mean W. L. Beason was the Annihilator? On one hand, the motive Beason gave for the murder—that he merely intended to steal jewelry—does not square with the motives of the Annihilator, who raped and murdered but rarely robbed. That he confessed to a relative due to his guilty conscience does not square with our knowledge of the typical serial killer's remorselessness. Also, no evidence has turned up indicating that Beason ever lived in Austin. Many of Beason's relatives and acquaintances did not think him guilty even of Genie Watkins's murder; they thought he had confessed due to temporary insanity. Captain Bostick, father of one of the injured Gainesville girls, believed Beason innocent. On the other hand, it is worth noting that after Beason's suicide there were no more murders that seemed the work of the Annihilator. We are left with three plausible scenarios: 1) Beason was neither the Annihilator nor the murderer of Genie Watkins, but falsely took credit for a murder committed by the genuine psychopath; 2) Beason did kill Watkins but was not the Annihilator; that his crime resembled those of the Annihilator and that the murders ended some months before Beason's death were coincidences; 3) Beason was the Annihilator and killed a number of women in addition to Watkins.

The same year of Beason's death, Jack the Ripper's sordid deeds in Whitechapel, London, electrified the world. Journalists and criminologists had a new question to ponder: were Jack the Ripper and the Servant Girl Annihilator the same person? Was it not possible that the killer traveled to England when it became too risky to stay in Texas and there continued to indulge his twisted obsessions? The idea was taken seriously in the 1880s. For example, the *Atlanta Constitution* suggested a link in late September or early October 1888, and by mid-October, the idea had been discussed in three London papers, the *Daily News,* the *Times,* and the *Star.* In December 1888, Dr. Spitzka of the Society of Medical Jurisprudence in New York opined that "the mysterious Texan and Jack are one and the same."

However, we in the early twenty-first century have had much more experience with serial killers than did the sleuths of the Victorian era. There are four compelling reasons to believe the Servant Girl Annihilator was not Jack the Ripper. First, there is the victimology: the Ripper preyed exclusively on prostitutes while most of the Annihilator's victims were servants. Secondly, there is the choice of weapons: the Ripper used knives but the Annihilator primarily used a hatchet or ax. Thirdly, if we compare the crimes, we find that the Ripper killed all of his victims outside except one, whom he murdered and butchered indoors. The Annihilator, on the other hand, preferred to attack women indoors and then move their bodies outside for further carnage. Lastly—and probably most significantly—the Ripper never raped his victims, but the Annihilator did, whether premortem or postmortem. The only solid comparison we can make between Jack the Ripper and the Servant Girl Annihilator is that neither murderer was ever identified, and likely never will be.

Mr. Flanagan Rings in the New Year

A long time ago, in the year 1896—William McKinley had recently defeated William Jennings Bryan in the bid for the White House, though he would have lived to a ripe old age if Bryan had won, and John Philip Sousa had finished composing "Stars and Stripes Forever"—there was a boarding-house. It was located in Poplar Springs, Georgia, a suburb of Atlanta, and was about to become the most infamous such establishment in the nation.

The proprietor was George W. Allen, and one of his boarders was thirty-eight-year-old Edward C. Flanagan, who claimed to be from Louisville, Kentucky—a claim the city would soon heartily deny—but who actually hailed from Ramer, McNairy County, Tennessee. Flanagan had worked as a warehouse constructor for the Standard Oil Company all over the south for several years and was the kind of fellow who enjoyed hinting at his prosperity by flashing large rolls of bills in public. So successful was he, in fact, that sometime earlier in 1896 he decided to temporarily retire at Poplar Springs.

On the last night of the year, the Allens noted that Mr. Flanagan had not come down from his room to dine with the other boarders. They sent a young girl after him. Flanagan replied that he would join the others if they would send a drink of water up to his room. This was done, and the girl saw him drop some concoction in the water. (Exactly what it was was never determined.) After draining the cup, Flanagan came to the dining-room table, all smiles.

"Good evening, my friends," said he. "The old year is about done, and I think all of us would be happier if we were done with it. I thank you for the drink you sent me."

At this point, Flanagan celebrated the closing of the year not by singing "Auld Lang Syne," but by producing a revolver. "Prepare to meet your God tonight," he announced. Then he started firing randomly at the assembly.

Seconds later, Mrs. Dixon Allen, George's elderly mother, was dead with a bullet in the brain. Another shot killed not a boarder, but a visitor, Ruth Slack of Greensboro, Georgia, aged only eighteen and due to be married in a few days. She had come to Poplar Springs to purchase her wedding gown. Flanagan seriously wounded George and his father; George survived, but his father died later of his injuries. In the pandemonium, most of the Allens' boarders escaped unharmed.

When the carnage was over, Flanagan reloaded his revolver and walked toward the city, threatening to shoot anyone who followed him. He was pursued by a mob that would have treated him to a lynching had he not been rescued at the last moment by a cop who hurried him off to the safety of a jail cell. When the police asked him why he did it, he feigned drunkenness (eyewitnesses to the massacre noted that he had been perfectly sober at the time): "I don't know why I did it. Whisky always does me that way." The feeling was so high against Flanagan that he was moved to the jail at Decatur.

It seemed at first an incomprehensible crime, but the next day—New Year's Day, 1897—Flanagan's motive was uncovered: he was a pervert who had a longstanding habit of falling in love with underage girls—some *very* underage. His technique was described thusly: "He had a mania for making love to and seeking to marry very young girls. His method was to advertise for a nurse for a mythical niece, and when young girls made application he would select the prettiest of the lot and propose marriage." It was in this manner that he ended up boarding with the Allens, for the latest object of his peculiar attentions was Leila Allen, daughter of George. Leila was ten, eleven, twelve, or thirteen years old, depending on which account you believe. Flanagan explained from the jailhouse: "I proposed to Leila and was accepted. Her father and mother told me I must wait until Leila grew older." (The naïve Allens, underestimating the depths of Flanagan's perversion, thought he was only kidding.) But as time went by and nothing more was said of the matter, Flanagan's paranoid brain decided that his beloved Leila must be a victim of incest—why else would she be able to resist such a catch as Edward C. Flanagan? "I saw that Mr. Allen was taking undue liberty with his daughter. . . . I told Dr. Purse of my suspicions and he abused my confidence by telling Mr. Allen." Flanagan was certain that Allen was about to have him arrested, so he elected to go out shooting.

Spending time in the cooler considerably dampened Flanagan's bravado, which was reduced even further by rumors that he was to be lynched. It happened that the official trying the case, Judge Candler, was also a colonel in the Fifth Georgia Regiment. He vowed that he would protect Flanagan at all costs. Candler's mettle was tested on the night of February 17, when a mob of eight hundred men, headed by the brother of victim Ruth Slack, journeyed to Decatur with the purpose of abstracting Flanagan from his cell. Candler and the guards got their prisoner on a train bound for Atlanta just as the mob arrived. Candler ordered the Fifth Regiment to guard the courtroom when Flanagan went on trial February 18, but even this was not deemed sufficient protection. Flanagan was whisked back to Decatur—since Decatur was considered a safer place for him than Atlanta—and Governor Atkinson sent two companies of the Atlanta militia to guard him and ordered five more companies, including a machine-gun battery, to stand by in case they were needed. To say that Edward Flanagan was an unpopular man would be as droll an understatement as calling the Donner party a picnic. At any rate, the prisoner remained unmolested—unlike several young girls of his acquaintance—and the extra soldiers' services were not needed.

The trial went without incident. Not surprisingly, Flanagan was found guilty and sentenced to hang. His attorneys won a second trial for him, which was held in Decatur at the end of July. Colonel Glenn for the defense asked for a change of venue on the grounds that his client was so universally loathed in DeKalb County that he could not get a fair trial there. The motion was denied, but on the other hand, Judge Candler was solicitous of Flanagan's welfare, promising that at the first sign of trouble the courtroom would be cleared and guards called out. No trouble erupted and the proceedings moved with admirable swiftness. Some of the defense witnesses' testimonies about Flanagan's depraved sexual tastes were deemed unfit for publication. As one newspaper account summarized, "It developed this afternoon [July 28], as the result of a dozen or more expert witnesses' testimony, that Flanagan has what is known as paranoia, known to the medical world as an insane passion for little girls." Another account noted, "The testimony on the trial revealed the most remarkable case of sexual perversion on record in the courts of this state."

Despite the defense's best efforts to win a verdict of "not guilty by reason of insanity," on July 31 the jury found Flanagan guilty as charged and recommended the death penalty. Judge Candler decreed that he should be hanged on August 25. But due to the generous American appeals process, Flanagan did not hang. Instead of remaining on his best behavior, however, he escaped from the Decatur jail on the night of September 14.

He was recaptured and tried a third time; again he was found guilty, sentenced to die, and won another trial on appeal. The fourth trial was scheduled for January 1899 but never took place. A medical expert, Dr. J. L. McDaniel, opined that the prisoner was mentally unfit to stand trial. This was weighty indeed, for during the three previous trials Dr. McDaniel had testified the opposite: that in his opinion, Flanagan was sane and faking insanity. If Dr. McDaniel was correct, between his third and fourth trials, Flanagan had gone insane for real. Judge Candler appointed a committee of three other physicians to examine Flanagan to determine his mental state. The doctors said they could not contradict McDaniel, so Judge Candler issued an order continuing the trial indefinitely. Flanagan was sent to the insane asylum at Milledgeville, with the understanding that he would be tried again if he regained his sanity.

This ruling took Flanagan out of the legal spotlight temporarily, but he still had a few nasty surprises awaiting the world. At some point, he must have recovered enough of his sanity to stand trial, since by autumn 1899 he had been removed from the asylum and taken back to jail. On the morning of October 21, he attempted a second jailbreak, this time by grabbing Sheriff Talley's two-year-old child. With a knife in his right hand and the screaming hostage under his left arm, Flanagan descended the jail stairway and made his way down the corridor to what he thought would be freedom. Instead, he ran into a room that happened to be occupied by the sheriff and his wife. The parents did not appreciate the spectacle of a noted child molester brandishing their baby, and they attacked with gusto: Sheriff Talley grabbed Flanagan by the neck while the missus caressed the fiend with a broomstick handle. A guard arrived at this timely juncture, and after rescuing the child, the three adults forced Flanagan back to his cell.

Not long afterward, Flanagan attempted to start a prison insurrection in order to break out a third time. He won a bullet in the leg for his pains. Whether he was insane and whether he deserved to be hanged became moot points on March 6, 1900, when he died in the Decatur jail and went to a very hot place with a very short name.

Blue Floyd's Light Show

In years past, it took a murder of unusual atrocity to outrage and excite the mountaineers of southeastern Kentucky since they were not strangers to frequent and creative violence. Just such a murder occurred in Letcher County, on the Virginia border, more than a century ago.

Ellen Mullins Flanery's husband, Art, had died in spring 1906, leaving her to raise four small children by herself in a cabin on Pert Creek, two miles from Whitesburg. On the morning of May 22, 1907, the respected thirty-year-old widow left her children at home and went to a nearby mountain to pick greens for lunch. But she didn't come home for lunch or for dinner or that night or for breakfast the next morning. The frightened little Flanerys alerted the neighbors, who searched the area and, in short order, had the unenviable task of informing the children that they were now orphans. Searchers found Ellen Flanery's badly beaten body under a pile of stones in a ravine near the family cabin. Her skull was crushed, her throat was cut, and her chest, arms, and hands had been slashed.

That afternoon, Sheriff Crawford became interested in a strange young man who had joined the search party: Floyd Frazier of Little Cowan Creek, eighteen years old and a member of "one of the best families of Letcher County," as a news report had it. Frazier was pressed to explain the fresh bloodstains on his clothes, particularly since he had no injuries on his person. He could not, and before the day was over, Frazier found himself heir to a jail cell. Two days after his confinement, Frazier confessed to a fellow prisoner that he had murdered Ellen Flanery by cutting her throat with a Case knife, an all-purpose implement that no self-respecting Kentucky man of the era would have left home without. He did not explain his motive, which to this very day is known only to God. Frazier had to be moved to the jail in Pineville, Bell County, owing to a large number of excitable citizens who wanted to adorn a tree with his body. Frazier was returned—under heavy guard—to Whitesburg to stand trial for murder on January 15, 1908. It was thought that Letcher Countians were too angry to give him a fair trial, so a jury from Perry County was brought in. The result, on January 27, was a hung jury. Eleven members thought Frazier deserved the death penalty, but the twelfth disagreed and would not change his mind. Frazier was whisked back to Pineville for further safekeeping.

The prisoner faced the Letcher Circuit Court for the second time on April 28. This time, a jury from Floyd County heard the case. On April 30, they sentenced him to be hanged for his brutal, pointless murder. July 23 was named as the date, and again Frazier was taken to the jail at Pineville to thwart an impatient mob. Frazier himself had some very definite opinions on the topic of his hanging, and in November, he and seven other prisoners broke out. He was captured shortly afterward on Bryson Mountain in Claiborne County, Tennessee.

The Letcher County court had denied Frazier an appeal, but the Court of Appeals granted him a retrial in April 1909 on the grounds of a writ of error in the instructions of the trial judge. The jury for the third trial came from Knott and Floyd counties. The appellate court might as well have not bothered, because this jury also found Frazier guilty and richly deserving of the death penalty. He was sentenced to be hanged. Frazier certainly would meet his doom on July 9.

Well, not quite. His attorneys, hoping they would get lucky twice, filed another appeal in June. On January 28, 1910, the Court of Appeals affirmed the judgment of the lower court; unless Governor Willson was in the mood to coddle a murderer—albeit a very young one—Frazier would be

Floyd Frazier. From the *Louisville Courier-Journal*, May 16, 1909. Reprinted by courtesy of the *Louisville Courier-Journal*.

hanged. Upon hearing the bad tidings, the prisoner blamed everyone but himself: "Well, they fixed it just like it already was, have they? I have been alone in this fight. My friends have not done what they could." (One wonders what more Frazier thought his friends and attorneys possibly could have done; they had already filed two appeals on his behalf and saved him from a date with the gallows twice.) "I am going to appeal to the governor," Frazier added. Then he burst into tears.

Frazier's Letcher County relatives pressured Governor Willson to commute the sentence to life in prison. Nannie Adams, the prisoner's mother, went to Frankfort to plead on his behalf. Frazier's well-wishers wrote letters to Willson arguing that he had been convicted on circumstantial evidence—including his own voluntary confession, it would appear. Some added that, by somehow plumbing the depths of the prisoner's subconscious, they could tell that he was "mentally irresponsible." In other words, according to these letter writers, Frazier was innocent, and even if he were guilty, he couldn't help himself. People who favored the "mentally irresponsible" argument claimed that Frazier was "not mentally capable of entertaining criminal intent"— that is, he was incapable of telling right from wrong. Presumably, then, after he beat and slashed a woman to death, he *hid her body in a ravine and covered it with rocks* for the healthful exercise of it.

A petition was circulated for those with less time to write impassioned though nonsensical letters, but it is doubtful that Ellen Flanery's relatives signed it. The governor dropped a none-too-subtle hint about his intentions when he fixed April 7 as the date for the youthful murderer's execution. A desperate Frazier responded by attempting to break out of jail a second time, this time at Whitesburg, but was caught in the act. He was watched more closely than ever before, especially when every day brought him closer to the end.

Floyd Frazier became understandably depressed as the closing of his life drew near, so fans of classic psychedelic rock music might enjoy nicknaming him Blue Floyd. He refused to speak to anyone, not even his closest friends, with the exception of a minister named David Maggard. The scaffold arose piece by piece. Governor Willson reviewed the case and found no reason to interfere with the sentence. On April 7, Letcher County officials requested that the state militia be called into Whitesburg; the governor refused. Rivers of humanity poured into town to see the hanging;

one source believed it was the largest crowd the city had
ever seen. But everyone was to be disappointed—except
possibly Floyd Frazier and his family. Governor Willson
changed his mind at the last moment. He wired the news to
Sheriff Lewis Cook that Frazier had been given a six weeks'
respite at the request of three judges of the Court of
Appeals "until a further investigation of the condition of
Frazier could be made," which meant they wanted to test
his sanity. Should they find Frazier fit to swing, and if the
governor did not have a change of heart, he would positively fulfill his just sentence on May 19.

Popular culture, sentimental historians, and foes of the
death penalty leave us with the impression that the bloodthirsty "hanging judges" of times past were apt to stretch
prisoners' necks for any and all offenses, for no better reason
than to sate their own sadistic impulses, and that hundreds—
nay, thousands!—of innocent men have been executed
whom Father Time might have exonerated. The story of
Floyd Frazier is instructive in that it demonstrates what a
long and difficult process it was to execute someone, even
in those strict "law and order" days, even in southeastern
Kentucky—not exactly a citadel of political correctness.
Frazier had three trials, two appeals, the benefit of a judi-
cial system that saved him from lynching and made certain
that he did not face jurors from his home county, petitions
and pleadings from interested citizens, a last-minute stay of
execution provided by the governor himself, and no fewer
than four dates of execution. These complications delayed
Frazier's hanging interminably—even though there was not
the slightest shadow of doubt about his guilt, even though
he sullenly refused to explain his motive, and even though
his victim was an impoverished widow with four children!

But the inevitable cannot be delayed forever; a little after
noon on May 19, 1910, Frazier took that last walk to the
gallows. At least three thousand people came to Whitesburg
to see it. That was a conservative estimate; others thought
the number closer to five thousand. They came from all

over Letcher County, from surrounding counties, and from Virginia. A thousand sightseers came from Ellen Flanery's original home, Wise County, Virginia. It was speculated that Frazier would be the last man hanged in Kentucky since the state was about to get an electric chair. This proved erroneous; however, Frazier's hanging was the first legal execution in Letcher County. The knowledge that he had made history in his own fashion probably did not cheer him much.

As Frazier stood on the platform, he was accompanied by a stenographer, D. I. Day, who recorded everything the condemned man said. As far as I know, this circumstance is unparalleled, but it allows posterity to know exactly what Frazier said as he gazed into eternity. To Dr. Fitzpatrick he stated, "Where is the picture man [photographer], doctor? They are trying to take my picture and I don't want them to." Fitzpatrick asked all photographers to leave, which they did—but not before taking three photos which still exist, showing what has been described as the "very sober" crowd sitting on the hills surrounding the gallows. When Frazier tested the trapdoor, he remarked, "I cannot think hard of no man. I think hard of none of you. I cannot afford to." The last words he said, as recorded by the stenographer, were bloodcurdling: "Goodbye to everybody, forever and forever! My mother, oh my mother! Oh Lord!"

The rope used to hang Frazier was kept as a souvenir in the county court clerk's office for years; a high school was built on the site where the gallows stood. Frazier was buried in the Steve Adams graveyard on Little Cowan Creek with only a sandstone slab as a grave marker.

The night before his execution, Blue Floyd saw a spectacular light show when Halley's Comet made its journey across the heavens. I wonder if he looked out the window of his cell, saw the comet careening through the cosmos, and contemplated the futility of man and his actions.

Henry Delaney's Half-Hour Marriage

It was an early spring morning—a little after 3:00 A.M. on April 5, 1893, for those who like precision—and Henry Delaney of Union County, Kentucky, appeared to have everything going his way. A number of young women in the vicinity found him attractive; he had a steady job as a clerk at George Henry's drugstore in the town of Sturgis; and he had just married—only a few minutes before—Abbie Oliver, a nineteen-year-old beauty who, like Delaney, was from a wealthy and influential family.

Despite this, joy did not dwell within Henry Delaney. He had gained local renown for being a seducer, a cad, a masher, a lecher, and a rounder, and on this date, his reputation finally caught up with him. A few hours earlier, around 9:00 P.M., Abbie's mother had entered the drugstore where Henry worked and insisted that he go for a buggy ride with the Oliver family. She brandished a revolver as an enticement. Delaney agreed to go, but his heart wasn't in it.

The buggy's contents included Abbie, who was eight months pregnant; her father, Taylor Oliver; her mother; and of course, the unhappy and mortified Henry Delaney, who protested that the child could not be his since he had not seen Abbie in a year. The four traveled fifteen miles to Morganfield, and in the dead of night, the Olivers rousted a preacher who felt his duty to God outweighed his need for sleep.

And now they were married and heading back to Sturgis— Henry Delaney and the girl he had wronged, jostling along under the light of a waning gibbous moon in a carriage with her miffed parents. It is likely that little was said in the way

116

of conversation, and what was said was probably curt and very much to the point.

At Teer Hill, about three miles from Morganfield, several armed men on horseback rode up, surrounded the buggy, and opened fire. Delaney jumped out of the conveyance and ran with a speed that would have provoked admiration under other circumstances. Curiously, he ran not *away* from the shooting party but *toward* it. Abbie was shot through the temple; her father was hit in the face and the right arm. Mrs. Oliver escaped harm and, grabbing the reins, sent the horses galloping to the house of G. A. Robinson. There, Abbie and her unborn baby died two hours later. A bullet damaged the muscle in Taylor Oliver's arm and another mangled his face; a bullet remained lodged in his left cheek. It was thought he could not survive and the Commonwealth's attorney rushed to take his statement in case he should die. But Mr. Oliver, a former Union soldier, slowly recovered.

The assassins had not bothered to disguise themselves, as they had not counted on leaving witnesses. Mrs. Oliver saw

Henry Delaney. From the *Louisville Courier-Journal,* April 9, 1893. Reprinted by courtesy of the *Louisville Courier-Journal.*

them clearly by the light of the moon and swore in an affidavit before County Attorney Davis that three of them were George P. Henry, Frank Holt, and George Delaney. They were rounded up and arrested. It was due to the indulgence of the Almighty, the cleverness of the lawmen, and help from well-armed friends that the trio was not lynched. The Delaneys were a popular family, and their many supporters helped the police stave off mobs.

Naturally, lawmen wondered about Henry Delaney's fleetness of foot when the assassins fired upon the party—especially since one of the killers was Delaney's brother; another, George Henry, was his employer; and the third, Frank Holt, was Delaney's brother-in-law. Had Delaney's flight been a display of cowardice or cleverness? It certainly seemed convenient that the bride Henry did not want had been murdered only minutes after the sad, impromptu wedding. Had the Olivers been deliberately ambushed? Had the shooters allowed the bridegroom to escape? The miraculously unscathed Mrs. Oliver continued to insist that George Delaney had shot Abbie and Frank Holt had shot Mr. Oliver.

It seemed more likely to be a conspiracy than a coincidence. On April 6, the authorities arrested two more men: James Lee Tate and Will Omer, both of Sturgis. They were taken to join Henry Delaney at the Capitol Hotel, where they were watched by armed guards—at the suspects' own expense. Considering that a mob awaited them at the jailhouse, none of them complained. The group did little talking except for George Henry, who protested that he had been at a friend's house in Sturgis on the night of the assassination. Rumor on the street held that one of the arrested men would turn state's evidence and give away the others in exchange for a lighter sentence.

Surely enough, a confession came the very next day—but it was from someone not under arrest. A "quiet young man" and friend of the Oliver family named Lewis Land was overcome with guilt while tending to the dead girl's wounded father. Out of shame, he went to Police Judge A. J. Berry and made a statement implicating all of the men in custody except for George Henry. (Land had feared that if he did not promptly confess, the innocent druggist might be lynched.) He added three hitherto unsuspected persons to the list: Alex Thomason, Will Holt, and himself.

Delaney's buddies had planned a unique method of murder: a preplanned ambush. They were, however, too incompetent to quite pull it off. The reader might be wondering how, in the days before the cell phone, the conspirators knew just where and when to find the wagon containing Delaney and the Oliver family in the wee hours of the night right after the forced wedding. It appears that, rather than the Olivers' visit to Delaney's place of employment being a total surprise, Mr. Delaney and his cohorts were expecting it and had prearranged a signal in case of trouble. In his detailed statement, Land claimed that between 9:00 P.M. and 10:00 P.M. on the night of April 4, Will Omer had come to his room and asked if he was willing to go to town and see if "they had captured Henry"—"they" meaning the Olivers. Wrote Land: "[Omer] said a pistol had been fired and that he thought that it was a signal Henry was captured." Land wasn't interested in taking part in someone else's quarrel and went to sleep, but a few hours later Omer and James Lee Tate came back and insisted he come with them. Again, Land refused and went back to sleep. But Omer returned a third time, and at last, Land joined a party consisting of Frank Holt, Will Holt, George Delaney, James Lee Tate, Will Omer, Alex Thomason, and a stranger. The group was armed with three shotguns and stated that their avowed purpose was to "get [that is, rescue] Henry Delaney if he did not want to marry the woman."

It did not require a hogshead of brains to figure out that the Olivers would most likely take Delaney to Morganfield for discretion's sake, and that after accomplishing their matrimonial purpose the party would return home to Sturgis. It was a simple matter of waiting by the roadside until the right buggy came along—and the bright moonlight made identification of their target easy. Before long, the Olivers' buggy came by. The assassins formed a diagonal line across the highway. A shot rang out from the carriage—from an alarmed Oliver or from Henry Delaney as a signal? The highwaymen opened fire on the carriage and the moonglow assured that Henry had a chance to jump out and dash out of harm's way. When the massacre did not go entirely as planned—Mrs. Oliver took control of the horses and drove away—the group decided the wisest course was to split up, go home, cross their fingers, and hope they would not be identified. When Will Holt heard about Land's confession, he broke down and admitted its truth. One by one, the others confessed as well.

On Sunday, April 9, the prisoners held religious services in the jail corridor. (At some point, they must have been moved from the hotel to the jail; too soon, it would appear, because the palpable fear of lynching hung over the lockup for days.) They sang a hymn with the ironic title "The Half Has Never Yet Been Told"—ironic because the exact identity of the assassins has always been a sealed mystery. It is not even certain how many there were. For example, Mr. and Mrs. Oliver were positive that druggist George Henry was among the number, but Lewis Land exonerated him completely. Although their descriptions of the crime failed to corroborate each other's on several important points, lawmen must have believed Land over the Olivers because the druggist was released and restored to an enthusiastic crowd of friends. Not everyone in Sturgis was convinced of his innocence, however, and some feared that mob violence would result. It could be argued that even if George Henry had not been present at the murder scene, he was at least a conspirator since he knew something of the coming violence. Mr. and Mrs. Oliver continued to state categorically that they had recognized George Henry as one of the shooters.

Even more problematic was that although the imprisoned men confessed, Land modified his confession on April 9. He now claimed that Alex Thomason and Will Holt had followed the little expedition in a buggy but were not present during the actual shooting. Another difficulty was the identity of the alleged eighth gunmen. He was probably Albert Carter, son of a wealthy Crittenden County farmer, who was duly arrested.

Due to the confusion, only five of the eight accused went

to trial. Will Omer was sentenced to twenty-one years in prison but served only a tenth of his sentence. Albert Carter pled guilty to charges of conspiracy and in July 1894 was sentenced to seven years. George Delaney was sentenced to life. Lewis Land, whose guilty conscience had led him to confess and rat out the others, was the last to be tried. He was sentenced to twenty-one years, but Governor Brown commuted the sentence to ten years. (Land served only a fraction of this greatly reduced sentence and was pardoned in June 1897.)

Henry Delaney, who most considered the catalyst of the crime, was tried on a lesser charge than murder and received a brief sentence. Later, his case was reversed and he was freed, but in autumn 1894, he was scheduled to be retried—this time for murdering Abbie Oliver.

One might think that Delaney had learned something

from his experiences, but he was made of sterner stuff. On September 2, 1894, he underwent a second shotgun marriage— this time to a lucky schoolteacher named Fannie Tate. The wedding took place in Shawneetown, Illinois; it was supposed to be kept secret, but word leaked to the press. At the time, the groom was under a $5,000 bond, having not yet been retried. The blushing bride was the sister of James Lee Tate, one of the gang who had been accused of conspiracy to assassinate the Oliver family. Perhaps Mr. Tate, being well

Abbie Oliver. From the *Louisville Courier-Journal,* April 9, 1893. Reprinted by courtesy of the *Louisville Courier-Journal.*

acquainted with Henry Delaney, considered giving his sister a wedding present that was ornamental yet practical—like, say, a bulletproof vest. After the wedding, Henry and Fannie returned to Sturgis. So great was the feeling against him that his bondsmen gave him up, and he was clapped in the slammer, after having been married for only one day. The *Owensboro Messenger* explained to readers in words that may have courted a libel suit had Delaney not had more pressing matters on his mind: "His previous actions with the Tate girl have been so notorious that the people were shocked. She is said to have been in an interesting condition for about five months." A wealthy farmer, Charles Hammock, sympathized with the prisoner and paid his bail. Delaney was free until he went on trial in Morganfield for slaying his first wife.

Delaney was on the stand for an hour and a half on November 21. When asked directly if he had killed Abbie Oliver, he replied, "I did not," but admitted he had gone armed the night of the shooting. He claimed he never so much as took his pistol from his pocket that night—odd behavior if he thought he was being fired upon by strangers. Delaney's attorney, H. D. Allen, requested that the case be thrown out of court, but the evidence against his client was considered strong.

Delaney's two attorneys filled the entire day of November 23 making their closing arguments; the prosecutor, J. H. Powell, spent "only" four hours making his case against Delaney the next day. The jury was officially deadlocked on November 27 and Delaney was released on bail.

His third trial began on March 12, 1895, before a jury especially brought in from another location, Henderson County, in the interests of fairness. The state established beyond doubt that there had been a plot to kill the Oliver family. A Sturgis man named W. P. Dyer testified that he had conspired with Delaney a couple of weeks before the shooting. He must have chickened out at the last moment. Delaney took the stand on his own behalf. "He did not strengthen his case by his own testimony," remarked a court observer. "On the contrary the prosecution got the better of him and tomorrow he will be contradicted by several creditable witnesses. This time the prosecution has had a better chance to develop the conspiracy and beyond question has proved it."

When closing arguments were made, attorney Henry Hughes did a good job defending Delaney, but if a prize for purple oratory had been given that day, it would have gone to prosecutor Howard Davis, who told the jury that Delaney was a liar and that the defense dared not deny it and that Delaney's "blood was so corrupt it would curdle the gastric juices of hell." Despite this lurid display of eloquence, however, the jury acquitted Delaney on March 18—much to the surprise of nearly everyone, the conventional wisdom being that the state had a stronger case against him during the second trial than it had had during the first one. The jury reasoned that although there certainly had been a conspiracy and Delaney had been part of it, he had not fired the shot that killed Abbie Oliver. Therefore, he must be found not guilty! Union Countians were largely embarrassed by the verdict, and the press of Kentucky was not much pleased. A few examples will provide the tenor of editorial comment:

Paducah News: "Since the chief villain in that Union County tragedy has been released why prolong the farce? Why not let the others loose and have an end to the miserable business? [The] red-handed devil implicated in this tragedy deserves to hang on a gibbet as high as the gallows of Haman."

Glasgow Times: "And thus ends one of the darkest, most infamous tragedies ever brought before a Kentucky court for trial."

Owensboro Messenger: "[The jury] may have weighed the evidence fairly, but there will always be an impression in the minds of the people who have heard or read anything of the case that justice has been outraged. . . . [Of] the gang who admittedly took part in the killing of the poor betrayed girl, only one has suffered a short imprisonment in the penitentiary. The crime was a blot on the fair name of Kentucky and it is an outrage to decency and a crime against justice, when somebody is not given punishment commensurate with the offense but rather allowed to go scot free."

Princeton Banner: "If Union County wants her criminals attended to she should send them down here for trial. A Caldwell County jury would have cracked the necks of at least two of the murderers of poor Abbie Oliver."

Stanford Interior-Journal: "Another failure of justice comes to disgust people with the way the courts permit criminals to get the advantage of the law. . . . [T]hey are beginning to ask how long their patience will be abused."

Once Henry Delaney was turned loose, there seemed to be a general air of resignation in Union County. If Delaney didn't pay for the crime, why should anyone else—even those already convicted for conspiracy? There was talk of circulating a petition to free Lewis Land and Albert Carter; the *Uniontown Telegram* remarked, "We haven't yet heard a single man say he would refuse to sign it."

Good luck seemed to run in the Delaney family. Henry's brother George, it will be recalled, had been convicted and sentenced to prison for life, but his case was reversed by the Court of Appeals. He was retried in Morganfield in March 1896. Public sympathy was on his side, as it was widely considered that Henry Delaney was the biggest scoundrel in this real-life soap opera. Therefore, it was deemed wise to import a jury from places other than his home county. "Judging from their appearance," said an observer from the press, "they are fairly intelligent." As had happened at the trial of his brother Henry, prosecutors proved the existence of a conspiracy to kill the Olivers. It took the jury so long to come to a decision that it was thought they would be deadlocked, but the final verdict—rendered on March 21—was that he was guilty, not of murder but manslaughter. He was refused a new trial and was sentenced to six years in the penitentiary.

In short, some conspirators in the Oliver massacre never went to trial; others did go to trial but were acquitted; still others, having been tried and found guilty, served short prison sentences. The sole exceptions were Henry Delaney's brother George and Albert Carter, who seem to have fully served their respective whopping six and seven year sentences. None received a punishment that seemed appropriate, considering the enormity of the crime. On the other hand, Taylor Oliver, innocent father of the murdered girl, had his life ruined. In better days, he had been an agent for the Atchison Machine Company and Moline Plow Company; by April 1896, he had devolved into an object of pity. In that month, the *Owensboro Messenger* noted that he had been to Frankfort to try to secure a pardon for some of the men then (briefly) serving time for his daughter's murder. "He was boozy and dead broke," said the paper.

The crime began with a wedding so it was ironic when, in May 1898, conspirator Will Omer married his girlfriend of long standing, Annie Reasor, who had waited for him while he remained in prison. Considering that he was supposed to serve twenty-one years but served merely two, her sacrifice was not as great as it seemed to some romantic souls.

The final macabre chapter in the celebrated Delaney-Oliver murder came in November 1907, fourteen years after the crime. Abbie Oliver's family had her coffin exhumed so her remains could be moved to another location. When the coffin was opened, it was found that her body had been stolen from the grave long before—by whom and why, nobody knew.

Psychopathia Sexu-Alice

It must have seemed, at first, like a scene from a Currier and Ives lithograph. It was a cold winter's afternoon late in the Victorian era—January 25, 1892—on a street near a levee in Memphis, Tennessee. Two buggies approached; each full of young women from the upper levels of society dressed in the smartest fashions. One carriage, a stylish rig called a turnout, contained Ms. Lillie Johnson and Ms. Alice Mitchell, daughter of retired furniture dealer George Mitchell and niece of Cincinnati millionaire Robert Mitchell. The other carriage held two sisters, Frederica (known as Freda) and Jo Ward, daughters of wealthy planter and merchant John Ward of Gold Dust, Arkansas. The Wards had just placed a third sister aboard the steamboat *Rosa Lee*. The buggies stopped alongside each other and the four women commenced a friendly chat, the topic of which has been lost to the ages.

Well brought-up young ladies of that era were expected to behave with decorum, particularly in the South. Carrying concealed weapons, for example, was definitely frowned upon by polite society. Yet Alice Mitchell sat in her buggy quietly stroking her father's shaving razor—not a wimpy modern disposable, but a large, fearsome thing like the ones brandished by Sweeney Todd. Alice's calm exterior hid an inner hurricane of emotion. When at last she could stand it no longer, she leapt from her carriage and into the other and cut several hideous gashes in Freda Ward's throat. Ms. Ward crumpled to the pavement, blood spraying in jets from a slit jugular vein. Her sister Jo struggled with Alice and received a trivial cut near the ear. Jo unhanded Alice,

126

who leaped back into her buggy. According to witnesses, she cried, "Drive quick! I've done it!" Lillie Johnson lashed the horses and they fled up Madison Street. Alice then disposed of the razor, which was never found.

Passersby gingerly placed Freda Ward in a carriage and took her to Rogers Infirmary. Her blood loss was too great, and she was pronounced DOA, to use modern terminology. (As a unique insight into the race relations of the times, a black man stood nearby during the slicing but had refused to intervene out of the belief that it was not his place to do so—or so he said. Maybe he just had a healthy respect for Alice's skill with a razor.)

The unhappy police officers had to go to the Mitchell residence on Union Street and arrest Alice, who was merely nineteen years old, and charge her with a grotesque—and

very publicly committed—murder. Based on the standards of the era, the slashing was a minor surprise compared to the one Alice was about to spring. She refused to reveal her motive, but gossips had intriguing clues. Freda Ward had been a frequent guest at the Mitchell house— in the past, that is. Lately, she had refused to accept Alice's hospitality and, when encountering her erstwhile dear friend on the streets, had

Alice Mitchell. From the *Louisville Courier-Journal,* July 19, 1892. Reprinted by courtesy of the *Louisville Courier-Journal.*

pretended to not even know her. Several persons had heard Freda making unflattering remarks about Alice as of late; thus, upper-crust Memphis society—naïve souls!—figured that Alice must have butchered Freda for insulting her.

Lillie Johnson, Alice's companion in the buggy, was arrested as an accomplice and placed in the same cell as Alice, though the latter insisted that Lillie had not known of her intention to kill Freda. It did not seem to dawn on the jailhouse authorities, although it certainly did occur to Lillie's protesting family, that it might not be a good idea for a murderess to share a cell with potential prey. Ms. Lillie's father insisted that he be allowed to sleep in a nearby armchair.

Lillie was more willing than Alice to talk to the police. She broke the scandal wide open when she gave away her friend's motive: "As she got back in the buggy, I asked her what was the matter. She replied, 'I have cut Freda's throat. I don't know that I have killed her; I love her so I could not help it.'" Lillie added, "I have known of the infatuation for some time. Alice said she loved Freda and could never give her up. There was an estrangement some time ago, and since that time Alice has not been herself."

In short: Alice Mitchell was a lesbian, and a violent one, in an era when such things were overlooked, excused, unacknowledged, or just plain unknown. One of the more interesting, and darkly amusing, aspects of the newspaper accounts is seeing the writers squirm and strain for polite euphemisms when explaining the crime. Said one: "It is . . . said that Ms. Mitchell had an unusual affection for her victim, and when they were separated by a third person, she became desperate, and was finally worked up to the point of killing her rather than have to pass her as a stranger."

The morning after, two young women—one a murderess and the other her victim—got visits from their relatives. Alice's father, mother, and brother visited her at the jail, accompanied by two attorneys adorned with military titles, Col. George Gantt and Gen. Luke Wright. Freda Ward's father, having arrived from Arkansas overnight, saw his daughter's body—either at the undertaker's or on display at Grace Church—and his grief was so great that it was feared he might lose his mind. On the same day, Judge DuBose and Attorney General Peters questioned the dead girl's sister, Jo, and a young woman named Ms. Christina Parnell, who had witnessed the crime. Jo turned over letters that had been exchanged between Alice and Freda.

January 27 was the day of Freda Ward's funeral. It was attended by what a journalist called a "tremendous throng," composed no doubt of friends, family, well-wishers, and morbidly curious souls who considered funerals of strangers to be entertainment, especially if the guest of honor perished under unseemly or disgraceful circumstances. "The floral offerings were numerous and very beautiful," added the journalist. "A long line of carriages followed the body to Elmwood, where the interment took place." Alice and Lillie spent the day in indifferent and easy conversation as though they were at a spelling bee or taffy pull instead of sitting in the Shelby County Jail.

Alice enjoying jailhouse hospitality. From the *Louisville Courier-Journal,* January 30, 1892. Reprinted by courtesy of the *Louisville Courier-Journal.*

(Despite the fulminations of modern radical feminists about the unequal treatment women received in the bad old days—say, around January 1892—the "unequal treatment" sometimes was to their advantage, especially if they had been charged with a heinous and gory murder. Alice and Lillie were given the best

room in the prison; though it was not exactly a suite at the
Ritz, it had furniture and a charming view of the river. Also,
they were served meals specially brought by relatives, not
the usual jailhouse slop.)

Matters only became more scandalous when Alice started talking to investigators. The prosecutors theorized that
she had killed Freda merely to avenge some personal insult, but they underestimated the depth of the affection the
murderess felt for her victim and vice versa. When one of
Mitchell's attorneys asked her why she had slashed Freda,
the following dialogue ensued:

"I killed Freda because I loved her and she refused to
marry me. I asked her to marry me three times and at last
she consented. We were going to marry here and then go to
St. Louis." (Presumably carrying out this plan would have
called for Alice to don male clothing. She said that she intended to improve the masculinity of her appearance by
shaving the fine hairs under her nose until they coarsened
into a convincing moustache.)

"What did you intend to do in St. Louis?"

"Oh, I do not know, but when Freda promised to marry me
I was so happy. I sent her an engagement ring and she wore it
for a time, but when it was returned I was miserable. I could
not bear to be separated from her, and I resolved to kill her. I
would rather she were dead than away from me." Then—perhaps laying ground for an insanity plea?—she asked where
Freda was. Dead and at the undertaker's, she was told.

"Oh!" exclaimed Alice, sounding like the heroines in contemporary popular novels. "If I could only see her. Please let
me go to see her. If I could only lie down by her side I would
be so happy." When told she would not be permitted to do
so, she burst into tears—not necessarily because Freda was
dead, but because she could not stand the separation.

An examination of the letters that passed between the
two revealed that they were larded with nauseatingly excessive sentimentalities and endearments that were com-
monplace among well-educated young ladies of the late

nineteenth century, and also that Alice and Freda had indeed planned to elope.

The grand jury heard Alice Mitchell's case on January 29. Jo Ward and Christina Parnell were called to testify as was a Mrs. Campbell, who had witnessed the crime and even claimed to have heard Alice say to Lillie, "You wait here while I go and fix her." Also called to the stand were two black girls, Sarah Hulsey and Clara Miller, who claimed to have overheard a woman called "Miss Alice" talking to a man on the street the night before the murder. This Miss Alice swore to the man that she was going to "cut the throat" of someone named Freda. It sounds like a suspiciously convenient story concocted after the fact by creative minds, but Mrs. Lavisa Watson testified that the girls had told her of the conversation seven hours before the murder. Sarah and Clara were led to Alice's cell, where they immediately identified her. The prisoner reportedly did a double take worthy of a vaudeville comedian when she saw her unannounced visitors. (Assuming the girls' story was true, the mystery man to whom Alice confided her dark plan was never identified.) Further testimony revealed that the summer before, Alice had written a menacing letter to Freda Ward's married sister, Mrs. Volkmar, in which she threatened to kill Mrs. Volkmar for separating her and Freda.

Not surprisingly, Alice's attorneys argued that she was insane—how else could her feelings toward Freda be explained? It was said that Mrs. Mitchell had been temporarily insane while pregnant with Alice; therefore, the prisoner must have inherited her mentality. While the defense claimed that Alice Mitchell was insane due to her attraction to another girl, the state contended that she was a crafty stalker rather than a lunatic, albeit unorthodox in her tastes.

The jury returned a verdict on January 30: Alice Mitchell must stand trial for the first-degree murder of Freda Ward. That was expected, but to the astonishment of onlookers, the same verdict was found for Lillie Johnson. The jurors regarded her in the same way a modern jury might consider the driver of a getaway vehicle as an aider and abettor. A reporter noted, "The indictment . . . of Miss Johnson occasioned considerable surprise, as it was thought she had nothing to do with the crime beyond being accidentally present when it was committed." If Alice had in fact said to Lillie, "You wait here while I go and fix her," as the witness Mrs. Campbell had testified, it is difficult to believe that Lillie had had no idea what was about to transpire. Other testimony indicated that a week before the murder, Alice and Lillie had disguised themselves as men and boarded a steamboat on which the Ward sisters were falsely rumored to have booked passage for a trip home to Arkansas. Alice's apparent intention was fulfilled seven days later, when she overtook the sisters as they rode a carriage to the docks.

The verdict was bad news for the girls' families, but their lawyers immediately started earning their high fees. Alice's attorneys requested a sanity hearing, while Lillie's tried to have her released on bail. In the meanwhile, a young express messenger named James Draper, who had erroneously thought he was Alice Mitchell's "sweetheart," fled Memphis out of sheer embarrassment. He wasn't the only putative boyfriend of Alice's due for unwanted public scrutiny. It turned out that she wrote to an undoubtedly dashing young man in Pittsburgh named Thomas Reiger for six months. She signed the notes with the pen name "Freda Ward." Reiger, a West Virginian by birth, had first become acquainted with "Ward" via a matrimonial newspaper. She went so far as to mail him a photograph—a token of serious commitment in 1892—but whether it was actually a photo of herself or of Freda we shall never know, because Reiger got jittery and threw it away when the Mitchell-Ward murder hit the newspapers. Why Alice had carried on a romantic correspondence with a male, and under a pseudonym, when her interest clearly lay elsewhere has never been determined. For a brief time, the police wondered if the unlucky Reiger had been involved in the murder, but it came out that Alice and her pal Lillie sent mash notes to men all over the country after Freda split with Alice. One of the pen names they used, for reasons now known only to God, was "Miss Jesse Freda James."

A few days in jail convinced Alice that this indictment-for-murder business was rather serious after all. She and Lillie were heavily veiled when arraigned in court on February 1. Judge DuBose requested that they remove their facial coverings. The pioneering German psychologist Krafft-Ebing, who wrote about the case some years afterward, described Alice as "not pretty. The face was childlike and 'almost too small for her size,' and asymmetrical." A reporter who was present the day of the unveiling wrote that Alice's eyes were "close together, and [had] but little expression." However, newspaper illustrations based on photographs do not seem to tally with these unflattering descriptions.

After the clerk read the indictment aloud, Lillie Johnson pled innocent. She swooned, as all women were then expected to do in court, and was caught by her father. Alice's attorney Colonel Gantt announced that she would plead insanity. The court agreed a few days later to grant an inquest to determine her state of mind.

It is possible that Alice was genuinely insane, unlike so many criminals who have bamboozled juries by pleading insanity. Nevertheless, her behavior over the next few weeks was so ostentatiously crazy that it is difficult to escape the conclusion that she was putting on a show for bystanders. On one hand, she denied having committed any crime by slaughtering Freda Ward; on the other hand, she wished that the hangman would hurry up and get his work in so she might join her lover in the World That Knows Neither Jealousy Nor Razors. Wrote a reporter: "She regarded the indictment as tantamount to conviction, and when informed by her father of the efforts to be made to save her she became almost frantic from disappointment," after which she made suicide threats that were sufficiently blatant that no one could miss her intended meaning, yet coy enough to have some deniability. It is an art form.

As Alice whiled away dull hours in jail, some details about her forbidden yearnings found their way to the press. She had raised eyebrows when she visited the home of Mr. C. G. Hubbard of Cincinnati in 1889, during which she had made unsubtle moves on Mr. Hubbard's fifteen-year-old niece, Clara Bailey. "[Alice] would hug and kiss her immoderately and say, 'Wouldn't you prefer me to a man for a husband?' In parting she would kiss Miss Bailey and say, 'Take that kiss from your lover.'" Young Clara, who by 1892 was deceased, was not interested and was so annoyed by Alice's entreaties that she told her uncle about them. The Hubbards finally banned Miss Mitchell from the house regardless of her wealth and social status. This episode inspired a mean joke in the *Louisville Courier-Journal:* "There is now no doubt of Alice Mitchell's insanity. She once fell in love with one of those plain Cincinnati girls."

The celebrated French actress Sarah Bernhardt took a strong interest in Alice and Lillie's story. She thought their predicament could be the subject of a great onstage drama; but, she added, "most of it would have to be left to the imagination of the audience." Mlle. Bernhardt received permission from the attorney general to visit the jail, but when she got there Alice and Lillie refused to see her.

The overheated letters that had passed between Alice and Freda were a very touchy subject—and not only those, but also letters written by members of both families who had noticed the excessive closeness between the girls and had disapproved of it. Young women wrote overly sentimental notes to each other in those pre-Freudian days— indeed, they were expected to—but apparently the gushy, mushy correspondence between murderer and victim far outstripped anything then considered socially acceptable. The defense considered the letters proof that their client was insane and wanted to allow alienists—the 1892 term for psychologists—to examine them. The attorney general denied that they had any right to the missives, which seems a trifle high-handed, but he cited legal precedent to support his argument. On the other hand, the defense possessed letters that they did not necessarily want the prosecution to see. If Alice's attorneys won the right to inspect letters in the state's possession, the state could demand to see theirs.

On February 15, Alice made a second appearance in court while her attorneys argued about their right to see those smokin' hot letters. A reporter commented on Alice's appearance as if he were reviewing a fashion show or a debutante's coming-out party: "She was enveloped in a new-market ulster, which revealed the rounded graces of her slender form to advantage, and barely missed concealing a pair of pretty feet in Oxford ties. Her small, shapely hands were neatly gloved and a heavy veil covered her face." Judge DuBose, called "the most noted criminal judge in Tennessee," requested to gaze upon her face. "I want to see who I am trying here," he said. He wasn't the only one; the courtroom overflowed with people who wanted to see the city's renowned murderess. She did as she was told and the same reporter who had described her enchanting ensemble wrote, "She stood revealed a very attractive blonde, with light gray eyes and a wealth of light brown hair inclining to

curl. The defects of her face on a close inspection are a mouth somewhat too large and sensual, and a chin expressing masculine determination." (Whatever that possibly could have meant; people believed the theories of the criminologist Lombroso, whose studies of criminals' physiognomies convinced him that murderers were inclined to share certain degenerate physical features. In other words, killers looked the

Alice in profile. From the *Louisville Courier-Journal*, January 29, 1892. Reprinted by courtesy of the *Louisville Courier-Journal*.

way killers were commonly "supposed" to look, such as having receding foreheads, shaggy brows, and eyes too close together. Observers were likely to see the stamp of criminality on Alice Mitchell's features whether they actually were there or not.)

Judge DuBose announced his decision on February 23: the correspondence between Alice and Freda would not be entered as evidence. ("Thank Goodness!" said the *Louisville Courier-Journal*'s headline.) Most of their contents were never released, so we shall never know exactly what they said unless they turn up someday in a neatly tied bundle in an antique store. On the same day, twenty-three-year-old Jo Ward took the stand and told of the day Alice Mitchell cut her sister to death before her eyes. Jo had understandably protested when Alice carved away at Freda; Alice replied, "I'm doing what I want to do, and I don't care if I hang for it." Jo confirmed that at one time her sister was engaged to be married to Alice, who intended to disguise herself in men's clothing and go by the name "Alvin J. Ward." (Obviously, Alice—who had signed letters as "Freda Ward" and "Jesse Freda James"—had a juvenile fascination for disguises and pseudonyms.) Jo testified that Freda's sister Mrs. Volkmar had been instrumental in ending the relationship in summer 1891.

The next day, it was to be determined whether Lillie Johnson could be bailed out of jail. The twenty-year-old said that she had known Alice Mitchell for five years and the Ward sisters about two. She admitted that she had driven the carriage in which she and Alice pursued the Wards but claimed that she knew nothing of Alice's intentions until the girl returned to the carriage coated in blood and shouting, "I've cut Freda Ward's throat! Tell me the quickest way to kill myself!" Lillie convinced Alice to go home to her family and await her inevitable arrest. Lillie's father and twin brother Jim testified that she had had "head troubles and nervous spells" since childhood. Father Veale of St. Patrick's Church and other witnesses attested to Lillie's good behavior. Her family physician, Dr. Henning, swore that she had always been plagued by bad health and opined that further confinement might result fatally. Lillie shuffled feebly to her seat and was led in and out of the proceedings each day supported by her father. (She was indeed ailing, but just how much nobody yet knew.)

These displays had their effect. On February 27, Judge DuBose ruled that the pale and emaciated Lillie Johnson could leave the cell she shared with Alice Mitchell under $10,000 bail. That would be a hefty sum even today; in 1892, $10,000 was the equivalent of nearly $250,000 in modern currency. The sum was quickly paid and Lillie's father came to take her away. A news account states that Alice gave her former cellmate a slobbery farewell: "Alice became violently agitated by the thought of the loss she was about to sustain. She frantically embraced Lillie and covered her face with kisses and even extended similar caresses to the father of her companion."

Lillie was restored to the loving arms of her friends and family at the Johnsons' Vance Street home. That was the up side. The down side was that, while making his ruling, the judge declared that Lillie would stand trial for being an accessory in the murder of Freda Ward. Observers thought the state had incriminating evidence it had not yet released.

The public's fascination with the case refused to wane. Every courtroom proceeding was packed and, according to a reporter, "Among the young people and pupils of the different schools it is noticeable that the papers are perused with great avidity which threatens to interfere with lessons." This seemed an especially daunting problem at the all-girls' schools so common then in the South; the principal at one Memphis female college forbade students to read any newspaper accounts of the case. Meanwhile, once Lillie was removed from the cell, Alice spent her time drawing pictures and talking to portraits of Freda, which she had cut out of the newspapers. I suspect she made a special note of doing this whenever the guards were nearby. She never expressed regret for having butchered her former bride-to-be.

The next big event in Alice Mitchell's life, her trial/insanity hearing, commenced on July 18. Some of the evidence used to prove Alice's insanity seems laughable today, but in 1892, it was soberly taken into consideration.

On the first day, the defense brought in her father George, who affirmed that Alice's mother had been temporarily crazy and added that Alice herself had been doing strange things lately, such as wanting to be by herself a lot. She shunned the company of men, yet she had corresponded with men who were utter strangers to her. She "had always been more like a boy than a girl." For example, as a child she learned to shoot a rifle, hunted sparrows, rode horses bareback, and—cue dramatic music!—even played marbles. He had noticed her obsession with the Ward girl and once caught her signing the name "Freda Ward" on a receipt for a coal delivery. In addition, he "had noticed a peculiar brightness about her eyes about this time that he had never observed before." No doubt that clinched it for some jurors, but the hearing continued.

As for the murder itself: George Mitchell had noticed that his razor went missing last November—which certainly implied premeditation—and later his daughter confessed that it was the murder weapon. He testified that she still talked about Freda in the present tense, as though she were still alive, yet contradictorily she "was very fond of talking about the killing of Freda Ward." (Some thought this evidence of mental imbalance, but it could just as easily mean that Alice was "acting crazy" and kept forgetting to stay in character.)

Day two of the trial revealed further details about Alice's mother. She had spent two months in summer 1857 in an asylum after the birth of her first child "and was scarcely herself for a good many years thereafter." The court received a written deposition from Dr. Comstock of St. Louis, who had been her attending physician from 1857 to 1860. She fancied herself to be dead, yet displayed ferocious bursts of temper. Heredity is the chief cause of insanity, the doctor wrote, so the inference was obvious: Alice was a natural-born lunatic. (The problem here is that Mrs. Mitchell's symptoms of "madness," which came just after childbirth and were temporary, sound suspiciously like what we now call postpartum depression—which, as nineteenth-century doctors did not realize, is perfectly natural and is neither hereditary nor insanity.)

Lucy Franklin, the family cook, offered evidence that makes Alice sound more like a petulant adolescent than a madwoman. She was often "cranky" and said she was in love with a woman whose family didn't like her. She often said she would rather be dead than alive, once going so far as to place the barrel of a gun to her head. She would spend hours poring over the contents of a cigar box full of love letters and other tokens of love, the most revolting being a thimbleful of Freda's blood. "She would walk around and worry," said the servant. Alice showed her an engagement ring and said she wanted to marry Freda, but "her mother had told her it was not right."

After all the fuss over the admissibility of Alice and Freda's letters, it appears that several were read aloud in court that day, but the newspapers had nothing to say about their content except that they were "disjointed."

The letters were the focus of the third day of the trial—not just the ones exchanged between murderer and victim, but also the ones the duo sent pseudonymously to men. In one, Freda said their plan to elope had been discovered and urged Alice to write to her no more, but she pledged her faithfulness and swore they'd be married someday despite interference from the Volkmars. The last letter from Freda—dated January 18, a week before her throat was cut—expressed love and regret that she had been forbidden to see "Allie" and included a warning to "say nothing about that last summer's business" (an allusion to their failed elopement). By contrast, in a mighty flirtatious letter to Mr. V. J. Ward of Carbon, Texas, Alice—who signed it "Freda

Ward"—expressed delight that he had fallen in love with her description of herself and wondered how long it would be before Mr. Ward fell in love with her personally. Another epistle by Alice, written to the aforementioned Thomas Reiger of Pittsburgh, was dated only three days before the murder. The most sinister letter was written by Alice to Freda on August 1, 1891, in which the writer accused Freda of loving a man named Ashley Rosell and said she would kill Freda before Mr. Rosell would have her. She feared that if they didn't hurry up and elope, Freda would fall in love with "some boy." It appears that Freda was having a hard time making up her mind about certain very personal matters.

After these letters were read—presumably, the *really* scandalous ones were not admitted or were suppressed by the newspapers—Lillie Johnson took the stand to face friendly questioning by the defense. She insisted that she was guiltless and it was only through a stroke of bad luck that she happened to be Alice's companion on the day she committed murder. She told of the longstanding affection between Alice and Freda and described the events leading up to the moment when she and Alice, riding in one carriage, saw the Ward sisters in another heading for the steamboat wharf. Lillie's testimony added little to the record that was new, but she claimed that before jumping out of the buggy, Alice had not said "You wait here while I go and fix her," as the witness Mrs. Campbell had claimed, but only "I must tell her goodbye."

On July 21, day four, Lillie took the stand to face the prosecution's cross-examination. Again, she gave her perspective on the tragedy, claimed innocence, and said she had no idea that Alice was about to use her father's razor in a fashion not recommended by its manufacturer. She added more details about her friend's strange personal life: "[O]nce they [Alice and Lillie] had sent flowers and a note to an actor. [Lillie] denied that Alice cared anything for young men, but on close questioning admitted knowing one or two young men that she and Alice sometimes talked to." As for their hobby of writing letters to gentlemen they had never met, "They had answered the matrimonial advertisements just for fun and amusement." She added that Alice had enjoyed playing baseball while at school. This was thought to mean something significant—exactly what, no one seemed to know, but something. Dr. Comstock's deposition, in which he stated that he thought Alice had been insane at the time of the murder, was re-read.

There was no shortage of witnesses to keep the chair in the dock warm over the next few days. Addie Mitchell attested to her sister's predilection for boyish sports and added that she often had headaches and nosebleeds. What the headaches and nosebleeds had to do with anything does not appear, but perhaps it was hoped that generous jurors would think those were symptoms of insanity. Lillie Johnson's brother James said that as far as he knew, Alice "had always displayed a most decided aversion to the society of gentlemen." Brother-in-law William Volkmar of Gold Dust, Arkansas, said that he considered the relationship between Alice and Freda to be normal until last summer when Alice and Lillie Johnson came to visit. Mr. Volkmar noticed unmistakable clues that Freda was planning to elope; she insisted on sleeping in a different room and keeping the window open. Imagine his surprise when he caught her just before she ran away and realized that the intended "groom" was Alice Mitchell! The visitors were quickly sent packing back to Memphis. On the other hand, Jo Ward said Alice had confessed being in love with some lucky fellow named Harry Bilger, whose name appears in the record on this occasion and never again.

One of the most important witnesses when it came to deciding Alice's fate was Dr. F. L. Sim, who avowed under oath on July 23 his belief that Miss Mitchell was a genuine lunatic: "She made her relations with Freda Ward very clear to me. It was that there was a mutual love between them as between male and female. Such cases are rare, but are on record and are recognized by the profession." He added that this is "a form of mania that is rarely ever cured." Dr. Sim was no quack; he had been a doctor for forty years, held a chair in the local medical college, and was editor of the *Memphis Medical Monthly*. But even he was in thrall to the then-indisputable theories of Lombroso, demonstrating that so-called dispassionate and logical science too has its fads, fashions, and superstitions: he was convinced that Alice had a subpar intellect because her face "did not show the intelligence to be expected in a girl of her years." That is to say, she must be stupid because he thought she *looked* stupid.

Another physician, B. F. Turner, concurred with his colleague. An expert on diseases of the mind, he based his conclusion on two factors: 1) Her mother was insane, so it must be hereditary, and 2) the fact that she wanted to marry another girl was corroborative evidence that she was out of her mind. But if Alice was crazy for falling in love with a girl, did that mean Freda was too? Nobody seemed to answer this question or even ask it.

In addition to Drs. Sim and Turner, every medical expert who testified agreed that Alice Mitchell was insane. Dr. E. B. Sale based his belief on the lack of sympathy on her face. "As to her final cure, witness said defendant might be made a very useful person in an asylum, but he believed she would never be mentally sound." Dr. Campbell, superintendent of the Knoxville insane asylum, opined that Alice was crazy at the time of the murder and remained so. Dr. J. H. Callender, medical superintendent for the Central Insane Asylum at Nashville, had testified when Charles Guiteau shot President Garfield; he said Alice had suffered from an unquenchable impulse to kill the object of her affection and herself. When Dr. Callender asked Alice in an interview why she had not cut her own throat as she allegedly had planned, she replied, "Why, doctor, I forgot all about it"—which sounds to me, at least, more like craftiness than craziness. Callender differed from the other doctors in his belief that Alice might someday recover her sanity. One wonders whether all of these expert witnesses really thought she was insane or if they merely said she was so that, gallant Southerners that they were, they might save a woman from jail or the gallows.

Plenty more evidence of Alice's insanity was offered at the trial, or at least what passed for such evidence back in 1892. Not only had her mother spent time in the goof-works, but so had an aunt and a great-uncle. Several cousins were alleged to be insane. One of her brothers had suffered mental derangement after having sunstroke—how that fact was relevant to a case of supposed *inherited* insanity appears not to have been asked. One medical authority reported that her face was childlike and asymmetrical with a nose "of striking irregularity" and piercing eyes. She had been "a nervous, irritable child," and in her youth indulged in unladylike activities such as football, climbing trees and roofs, and "silly pranks." She didn't like reading—not even newspapers. Not only that, she was left-handed! All of this was presented by the defense with an attitude that bespoke "Gentlemen of the jury, how much more evidence could you possibly *need?*"

The most electrifying day of the trial was July 27, when the prosecution opened its case. Freda Ward's sister, Mrs. Volkmar, said that Alice seemed to her "wild, wayward and unwomanlike" but not insane. She added that Freda had been so embarrassed after she was caught eloping that family members had a tacit agreement never to bring up the matter. Next witness, Mr. Ashley Rosell, confirmed getting mash notes from both Alice and Freda. The biggest sensation came when Alice took the stand. She recounted the details of her brutal crime without the slightest trace of excitement or remorse—whether she had been coached to answer questions in such a cold, matter-of-fact manner to seem unbalanced is a matter for conjecture. She cried only when she told of walking down the hill with her razor because she "wanted to see [Freda] once more" before the Wards returned to Arkansas. She described what happened next without emotion but with an eye for detail and understatement that prefigures Hemingway:

> When I reached Freda I cut her with the razor. As I cut her throat she tried to say something. I intended to cut Freda's throat and then mine, but her sister Jo made me mad by striking me with an umbrella; so, after slashing at Jo, I followed Freda and cut her again. All I wanted to do was to cut her so as to kill. I loved her better than anyone in the world.

Alice shocked everyone by stating that she had tried to murder Freda on previous occasions. Once, she was prevented from carrying out her intention by her razor getting stuck in her dress pocket; another time, she changed her mind because there were too many witnesses about. She also said that Jo Ward had "told a lot of lies on her" and

Freda Ward. From the *Louisville Courier-Journal*, January 29, 1892. Reprinted by courtesy of the *Louisville Courier-Journal*.

dropped a broad hint that she'd murder Jo too out of revenge if she only could.

Given Alice's bloodthirsty testimony and the reluctance of all-male juries to hang women, the outcome was not surprising: on July 30, the jury decided after twenty minutes' deliberation that she was not mentally competent. She was to be confined for life to the West Tennessee Asylum for the Insane at Bolivar. It was the appropriate place for her if she was actually insane; but if, as seems probable, she escaped justice by pretending to be crazy then she was condemned to live the rest of her life, perfectly sane and cognizant of her plight, in a madhouse. In the latter case, it is difficult to see what she actually gained. It was understood that if Alice regained her sanity she would be tried for murder. If she was shamming, it was in her best interest to keep up the charade indefinitely.

On August 1, Alice was taken by carriage to the asylum. On the way out of Memphis, the carriage passed Elmwood Cemetery, where Freda Ward was buried. Somehow, Alice convinced Deputy Sheriff Perkins to allow her and her parents to visit her victim's grave one last time. She stood silently at the tomb, clearly lost in an emotional reverie. A reporter wrote, "She moved around the little mound and eyed it with eyes wide open, an occasional tear dropping down her cheeks. She stooped over and planted some flowers, which she placed together tastefully and with thoughtful air." Then she announced she was ready to go to her new home. Perkins stated that huge crowds boarded the train to stare at Alice at every stop they made on the way to Bolivar. The last he saw of Alice, he said, she was sitting on the asylum's veranda, playing a French harp for her fellow inmates.

Lillie Johnson remained free on bond. Her attorneys did their best to have her case thrown out, but Judge DuBose insisted she go on trial although an acquittal was practically a certainty. He was adamant that he would hold Lillie until Alice regained her sanity and then he would try both of them. Fortunately for Johnson, when her case was heard at the end of March 1893, it was heard not by DuBose but by his successor, Judge Scruggs. Attorney General Peters, who had prosecuted Alice Mitchell, declared that there was no evidence Lillie was guilty of anything more than having the misfortune to be in Mitchell's presence when she went on her killing jag. Scruggs agreed and charges against Lillie were dropped once and for all. By then, she was much more careful about her choice of companions. Lillie became a recluse, never venturing outside except to go to church. The illness she had suffered during her first courtroom appearance had developed into the dreaded tuberculosis. It is likely she did not live long after her name was officially cleared.

Years passed but not very many. Every once in a while, news crept out about how Alice was faring in the mental hospital. It was reported that she was showing much improvement only a couple of months after she was committed. In March 1893, news came that she was the darling of the asylum. By then, she had been incarcerated for nine months; when the Legislative Visiting Committee toured the place, they found, according to the news item, "[t]he slayer of her girl friend in fine physical condition. She has never been ill a day . . . of her confinement. She has gained twenty pounds in weight and is as handsome a girl as one could wish to see. Mentally, however, she shows no improvement." She seemed only momentarily sad whenever Freda Ward's name was mentioned. All the other patients loved her and she kept them entertained with her harmonica. Her family made frequent visits. November 1893 saw the following report:

> It is said by one of Alice Mitchell's attendants . . . that she is one of the most useful women in the asylum; that she works harder than any attendant in the wards. She scrubs the floors, washes the dishes and assists in every way in keeping things in order; that she shows the greatest interest in the patients, especially the old women, to whom she is tenderly kind.

Whether Alice was authentically insane or faking it to avoid prison or worse, life at the West Tennessee Asylum became onerous to her. In June 1895, she attempted unsuccessfully to drown herself in the reservoir on the building's roof. An inmate found her suicide note and informed a doctor, who rescued her just in time.

Less than a month before the United States declared war on Spain, unexpected news came that Alice had died in the asylum on March 31, 1898. She was about twenty-five years old. No newspaper appears to have related the cause of death, but it may have been something highly contagious since she was buried at Elmwood Cemetery, the same graveyard containing her victim, just a few hours after she died. Let's hope she was not accidentally buried prematurely, as happened so often then. A week later, the *Bolivar Bulletin,* the newspaper in the town where the asylum was located, ran some lines describing her rapid decline. It makes for harrowing reading:

> When first confined, she was the picture of health, participated in the dance, furnished music for the entertainment of visitors and patients, delighted in out-door exercise and on account of her accomplishments and cheerful, happy disposition she was a great favorite. As time wore on the above amusements lost their charms for her. She gradually withdrew from the public gaze and finally sought the solitude of her room. Her once handsome figure wasted away and a month prior to her death she would scarcely have weighed fifty pounds. Several days before her death she became partially paralyzed. She never alluded to her crime.

Alice Mitchell had passed from this vale of tears but her reputation as America's most notorious lesbian lingered until her case was gradually forgotten. For several years, newspaper accounts mentioned her when describing stories of a similar complexion. In February 1894, a mesmerist at New York City's Bellevue Hospital allegedly hypnotized two girls into believing they were a boy and his sweetheart, whereupon they went insane; the *Louisville Courier-Journal* headlined the story "Two Queer Girls . . . Just Like

Alice Mitchell." When Mrs. William Hickman and Mrs. H. A. Hassall of Stockton, California, entered a suicide pact "over a perverted infatuation" in May 1899, news reports commented, "The case is similar to one which occurred at Memphis a few years ago."

But Mitchell's greatest claim to fame—or infamy— came when her story was featured in a later edition of Dr. Krafft-Ebing's *Psychopathia Sexualis* (1886), a legendary Victorian-age book that examines a smorgasbord of deviancies and sexual eccentricities in lavish detail—for readers fluent in Latin, anyway—and which for years was favorite reading for doctors, psychologists, and college boys looking for a cheap thrill. Alice is given semi-anonymity as "Case No. 236" and enshrined alongside other nineteenth-century sexual bogeymen such as Sergeant Bertrand, Jesse Pomeroy, and Jack the Ripper.

The Two Mr. Rathbuns

Frank Ogden, proprietor of the Falls City Hotel in Jeffersonville, Indiana, was worried. The occupant of room number 50 was not up and stirring even though it was noon on this seventh of November 1901, so Ogden thought he had better check on him. The door to number 50 was unlocked, and when Ogden entered, he found the occupant dead in bed, seemingly of natural causes. A statement in the dead man's memorandum book revealed that while he had died in Indiana, he was from the Deep South: "My name is Newell C. Rathbun. In case of accident or death notify my wife, Sue Rathbun, 1204 High Street, Little Rock, Ark." When the authorities rummaged through his personal effects, they found several letters from Sue to Newell, begging him to come home and urging him not to commit suicide. They also found that Rathbun had been a member of the Twenty-Seventh Infantry, Company K, stationed at Plattsburg, New York. Evidently, he had been traveling from Little Rock to Plattsburg and died at Jeffersonville en route.

The mystery of the deceased's identity, it seemed, was solved. Yet there were many nagging details. When Rathbun checked in on November 6, he had been accompanied by a man calling himself William Ten Eyke, who had paid for both men's lodgings. Ten Eyke wrote in the hotel registry that he was from Watertown, New York. Ogden had observed that the duo seemed unlikely traveling companions: Ten Eyke wore a nice suit while Rathbun was dressed like a hobo with a small derby hat, a shabby brown coat and vest, and buttonless pants that were held up with pins. He had neither collar nor tie, which made him stand out like the clichéd sore thumb by the sartorial standards of 1901. But not long after they checked in, Rathbun had turned up in a fine new gray-striped suit, which he said Ten Eyke had given him. The gentlemen had left the hotel after supper; when they returned late that night, Rathbun appeared to be in a state of beastly intoxication.

The next morning, Ten Eyke told Ogden, "Mr. Rathbun got drunk last night and wants to sleep as long as possible. Tell him he can find me where he met me in Louisville if he wants to see me." After which the dapper Mr. Ten Eyke had his breakfast—and then disappeared from the hotel. At noon, Ogden went to room 50 and found his dead guest.

Deputy Coroner Frohman Coots examined Rathbun's corpse and found that his heart was too full of blood; the official was inclined to believe the man had somehow committed suicide, perhaps by ingesting drugs. Coots was eager to ask questions of Mr. Ten Eyke, but that worthy man failed to return to the hotel. Coots became suspicious and felt that Rathbun had been poisoned, although no noxious substances were found in the room. Curiously, however, the coroner did not perform an autopsy to confirm his suspicions. While embalming the body, Coots smelled such a strong odor of laudanum emanating from the stomach that he had to step outside. He later insisted to reporters that he could prove the body had enough laudanum in it to kill two men, but he did not care to "divulge the secret" of his methods. His opinion was supported by a druggist named Doolittle. The record does not state whether this Dr. Doolittle could talk to the animals, but he was present during the embalming and was certain that laudanum was the cause of death. As a precaution, Coots saved a bottle of fluid taken from the stomach for later testing. If Coots was right, the "drunken" Rathbun actually may have been staggering about due to the effects of the poison, and Ten Eyke was Suspect Number One. Ten Eyke would have been lying when he said his companion was only drunk, he appeared to be stalling for time when he told the hotel staff not to wake up Rathbun, and his vanishing act certainly did not redound to his credit.

When filling out the death certificate, Coots declared that the cause of death was "regurgitation." He meant that some substance had caused the victim's blood to flow into the heart more rapidly than the arteries could disperse it. Some would misinterpret the certificate to mean that death was due to "natural causes."

On November 9, the coroner received a letter from Ten Eyke nonchalantly telling the story of Rathbun's demise as it already had been reported in the papers. The letter bore no return address. At the same time, information from Little Rock deepened the mystery: Rathbun's corpse had been shipped there for burial in Oakland Cemetery (the local Citizens' National Bank generously paid for the expenses)—but no one recognized the body. Newell Rathbun had been an army lieutenant and a recruiter, a job at which he excelled—in fact, upon his return to Plattsburg, he was to be placed in charge of a recruiting station. Rathbun was of respectable appearance and gainfully employed, but the poisoning victim in Jeffersonville had been nothing of the sort. He had worn tatty cast-off clothing and died penniless.

On the other hand, William Ten Eyke had been well-dressed and had plenty of money. The police came to the conclusion that the reader has probably reached: Ten Eyke actually *was* Newell Rathbun using a pseudonym. But if Rathbun was alive, who was the dead man? And if it was a poisoning, what was the motive? The former question could only be answered by Rathbun, but the latter question was answered by Samuel Powell, Arkansas state manager of the Metropolitan Life Insurance Company, whose firm definitively proved that the corpse was not Rathbun. The "late" Mr. Rathbun recently had purchased two policies on himself totaling $4,000 (modern equivalent would be more than $100,000). Mr. Powell had been astonished when he read of the death in the papers; he had sold Rathbun one of his two policies, and he remembered his client as being the picture of good health. When the body arrived in Little Rock, Powell and the company physician, Dr. Jennings, examined it and knew immediately that it was not the same man who had bought the policies. They called in a parade of people who had been well acquainted with Rathbun to view the body. Rathbun's former landlady agreed that whoever the corpse was, it wasn't he. William O'Connor, who had previously boarded with Rathbun, concurred, as did Durand Whipple and Emil Gloeckler, close friends of the "deceased." Most damaging of all, Ms. Corinne Pryor told the authorities that Rathbun had proposed marriage to her last spring and told her that he had a cunning plan, which would provide a life of ease for them: he would insure himself to the hilt, buy a house, kill someone in his place, and burn the house down! She would only have to identify the body as being his and collect the loot. Ms. Pryor was not charmed by her suitor's criminal ambitions, and a few months later, Rathbun married the apparently less choosy Sue Lundy. When Rathbun's family in Little Rock saw the well-preserved remains, they unanimously declared that it was not Newell. Interestingly, one person who did not look at the body was the alleged widow, who claimed to be too prostrate with grief to come take a peek. When finally inveigled to do so, she said it was not her husband.

Before proceeding with the story, I would like to provide helpful hints, all well illustrated by Rathbun's stupidity, for would-be life insurance cheats:

1. Have the decency to wait a few years after taking out your policy before engaging in murder and other skulduggery. Rathbun bought his policies in summer 1901 and pulled off his none-too-clever fraud in November, which means he had barely even paid any premiums. Such suspicious circumstances will make insurance companies and the police take notice. Patience!

2. Don't let greed inspire you to overinsure yourself to the point of absurdity, as Rathbun did. You will make yourself memorable to the friendly folks who sold you the policy.

3. If you must murder someone in your place so that you can start a new life under a false identity, at least have the sense to kill a person who resembles you. Rathbun's choice of a substitute not only bore merely a superficial facial resemblance to him, but he was shorter, had a tattoo on his forearm, and differently colored hair. It was hard enough to get away with this sort of thing in 1901; now, with the advent of DNA testing, it is nearly impossible.

4. Don't try it in the first place. It requires a criminal genius on the order of Professor Moriarty to succeed at a life insurance fraud that involves getting a corpse to take the place of the policyholder; the annals of crime are choked with the bodies of persons who tried it and got hanged for their pains. Too many things can, and likely will, go wrong. A trivial detail will trip you up, and then someone somewhere will write a true crime book commemorating your blunders for the entertainment of posterity.

On November 11, Louisville police received a call about a peculiar fellow trying to enlist at an army recruiting station. It had been observed that said peculiar fellow bought every Louisville paper he could find and leafed nervously through them. He claimed to have never served in the military before, but the doctor who gave him a physical examination noticed that he was wearing government-issued underwear. He called himself Lou Root of Detroit, but manifestly he was Newell Rathbun; in short order, he was in police custody.

He made two contradictory confessions. First, he admitted that he was indeed Newell Rathbun and that he had deserted the army; he was trying to hide from the authorities by reenlisting under an alias. He claimed that the dead man was really William Ten Eyke. The two had plotted to "procure a stiff" and pull off an insurance swindle—which, incidentally, would require burning down the hotel where the false Rathbun was stashed—but to Rathbun's good fortune, Ten Eyke coincidentally happened to die himself. Not one to overlook a favor from the gods, Rathbun followed through with his plan using Ten Eyke's body. In other words, Rathbun confessed that there had been an insurance swindle, but he claimed murder was not involved. Quick detective work revealed that no such person as Ten Eyke existed, so Rathbun had to cook up another story. This he did with aplomb, stating that he had had a partner in crime named Corporal Blanchard. "[W]e fixed it up to slip a stiff into some hotel, then set fire to the building after having left letters and papers of mine in the pockets of the stiff's clothes. Of course, when the hotel burned, we expected the stiff to be burned up too, or at least so scorched that no one could recognize him." (Rathbun did not explain how the evil geniuses planned to arrange it so that the fire would destroy the hotel and the "stiff," yet leave the papers intact, since if the papers were unreadable the crime would not have succeeded.) As for murder—why, mercy, Rathbun never killed anybody! Blanchard must have done the murdering, he said, or else the bum they intended to kill providentially drunk himself to death. "I was only to furnish the evidence. Blanchard was to get the stiff." He had no idea concerning Blanchard's whereabouts.

"But suppose, Rathbun," said a detective interrogating him, "that you had burned the hotel, don't you think that some persons might have been burned to death?"

"Yes, that might have happened," he agreed. It was fortunate for many that he had developed cold feet when it came to this phase of the plan.

The accomplice Blanchard was fictional; Rathbun had planned and perpetrated the entire crime himself. His pretty story still did not reveal the identity of the corpse. However, that solution too was forthcoming. The staff at the Louisville Salvation Army Hotel noticed that a youthful, good-natured hobo who hailed from Evansville, Indiana, had checked out on November 6—and had not been seen since. This particular hobo had been dressed in the same garb worn by the pauper who had checked into the Falls City Hotel with Rathbun. His name was Charles Goodman, and

Rathbun—whose favorite short story was Conan Doyle's "My Friend the Murderer"—confirmed not only that Goodman was the dead man, but also that he had befriended the vagrant because he seemed like a perfect victim. One fact that came out during the investigation was that Rathbun had considered two other men as potential victims before settling on Goodman.

In the meanwhile, Rathbun's Arkansas wife and relatives made a surprising turnaround. Days earlier they had declared with one voice that the corpse in their midst was that of a stranger; on November 12, they decided that the departed was good old Newell after all. I'm sure the $4,000 they stood to gain from his insurance policy had nothing to do with their reversal. They demanded that the man under arrest in Louisville be brought to Little Rock so they could see for themselves, despite the fact that five thousand curious souls had seen the body and none identified it as Rathbun. A coroner's jury scrutinized the remains, and many of Rathbun's friends and acquaintances swore that it was not him, no way, no how. It appears that the only people in Little Rock who claimed that the body was Rathbun were his wife and his brother-in-law—though Mrs. Rathbun did not come to court when summoned by the coroner on the grounds that she was still "prostrate with excitement."

On November 13, Rathbun was moved from Louisville to Jeffersonville to face a charge of murder. Instead of sending Rathbun to Arkansas, authorities decided that Deputy Sheriff Al Chichester of Little Rock would interview the prisoner in Indiana. The sheriff was accompanied by Rathbun's friend and bartender Emil Gloeckler; when the prisoner saw them he dropped all pretenses. Weeping, he called them by name and admitted again that he was the one and only Newell C. Rathbun. He wrote a document confirming the fact and signed a photograph of himself as well. He hinted that his wife was in on the wicked plot—an assertion easy to believe since she was the chief beneficiary of his insurance policies and had affirmed against all evidence and common sense that the stranger's corpse was her husband, but since the gentlemanly authorities pursued the matter no further, neither shall we.

Then there was the contretemps involving the corpse. It remained in Arkansas despite Coroner Coots's repeated requests to have it sent to Indiana; the Little Rock authorities agreed to release the body after the prisoner's identity was firmly established. Since Coots had embalmed the body but not autopsied it, it would be difficult to find any traces of poison. Repeatedly, Rathbun confidently proclaimed that no laudanum would be found in the stomach. While in the Louisville lock-up, Rathbun, too talkative for his own good, suggested the true nature of his plot several times. He sneered that he never would have been so gauche as to use laudanum:

> I should have used chloroform, then set fire to the bed, turned in the alarm myself and helped fight the flames. . . . That bum's quick shuffling off busted it. He must have died of alcoholism. I was greatly surprised to find Goodman dead [in the hotel bed]. I fully intended to make a stiff out of him but, finding him lifeless, I hastily decided to plant the letters in his pocket. . . . Wasn't it funny that after I planned to make a stiff out of Goodman, he laid down and died himself? No one could have been more surprised than I when I found him dead. I had not expected it so soon.

On one occasion, Rathbun said he had been getting Goodman "in condition for murder." Detectives took this to mean he had been trying to weaken Goodman through drink and/or drugs, so that when he murdered Goodman in the hotel it would look like natural causes or alcohol poisoning.

In other words, Rathbun kept hinting that he had *planned* to murder the hobo, but the intended victim died of some other cause just before he was to be killed. To hear Rathbun tell it, he was guilty of manslaughter but not murder. It was wise policy to keep the authorities guessing. Rathbun went to ridiculous lengths to confuse the coppers and the press; at one point, he said that the victim was his identical twin brother, which came as a surprise to his friends and relatives, who didn't know he had one.

The peculiar twists and turns in the Rathbun saga seemed to be never-ending. Although the authorities in Arkansas had promised to ship Goodman's body to Indiana once it was proved that Rathbun was alive, Little Rock mayor W. R. Duley changed his mind. It seems he was not convinced by Rathbun's confession or by the word of his own Deputy Sheriff Chichester. On November 18, his honor gave the corpse back to Mrs. Rathbun, who likely did not want it even though she still claimed that it was her darling Newell. Much to the disgust of the Jeffersonville police, Indiana would obtain the body only if the "widow" gave permission. Little Rock's coroner Young overruled the mayor and ordered that Goodman's body be removed from the vault at Oakland Cemetery and shipped with due haste.

The body arrived in Jeffersonville on November 22. The Arkansas authorities reluctantly sent Goodman's corpse, but for some unfathomable reason, they failed to send his tattered clothes, the nicer clothes given him by Rathbun, or the letters from Mrs. Rathbun that were in his pocket—all important evidence in proving the suspect's guilt. It was as though someone in Arkansas was determined to obstruct justice. Also on November 22, Rathbun was indicted by the Clark County Circuit Court on six counts of having been responsible for the death of Charles Goodman. Prosecutor Frank Mayfield's document covered all legal bases: it charged Rathbun with killing Charles Goodman, or some unknown male, with murder by poisoning with laudanum, some other yet-undiscovered substance, or by use of an anesthetic such as chloroform. The prisoner pled not guilty.

The long-delayed autopsy on Goodman was finally performed on November 23. Fortunately, the body was in an excellent state of preservation. The postmortem was conducted by Deputy Coroner Coots, his quaintly named brother Glover Coots, and Dr. L. B. Kastenbine of Louisville, who was to analyze the contents of Goodman's stomach.

One thing was immediately apparent: Goodman had been in excellent health, so no one could claim that he had been terminally ill. Afterward, the body was sent to the vault at Jeffersonville's Eastern Cemetery where it lay unclaimed until it was buried in a potter's field. Several suspenseful days passed before the autopsy results were released.

As with most high-profile cases in which the identity of a murder or a victim is in question, the Rathbun-Goodman case inspired in newspaper readers a variety of reactions that ran the gamut, from comical to pathetic. The police were inundated with requests from people who thought Goodman might be a missing relative or friend; they wished to be furnished with a description of the corpse. On the other hand, some readers thought they knew Rathbun's "true identity" and asked for photographs of him. An anonymous crank in Indianapolis, who would have fit comfortably in the modern world, wrote a letter praising Rathbun for his attempt to defraud a heartless insurance company and suggested that the police should just let him go free. In addition, several clearly desperate women claimed to be married to the prisoner. The strangest of these birds was Mrs. Lillie Wilhelmina Stanley Muir Talbert, who claimed that Rathbun had married her on September 8, 1900, and therefore was her estranged husband. Why any woman would want to claim the likes of Rathbun is a mystery within the mystery, but Mrs. Talbert emphatically told a reporter, "That murderer up there is my husband." She was mistaken. Only Sue Lundy of Little Rock was lucky enough to be the official Mrs. Rathbun. I hesitate to say that Mrs. Talbert had problems facing reality, but after this disappointment, she became convinced that her missing husband was not "that murderer" Rathbun but rather his victim Goodman. Somehow, the persuasive lady convinced the cemetery sexton to open his coffin. That must have satisfied her because in June 1903, Mrs. Lillie Wilhelmina Stanley Muir Talbert married a butcher in Memphis, thereby becoming Mrs. Lillie Wilhelmina Stanley Muir Talbert Gardner.

On December 10, Dr. Kastenbine gave his autopsy report to Prosecutor Mayfield. It was supposed to be kept secret, but word leaked out. To nearly everyone's surprise, no trace of laudanum or any other poison was found, just as Rathbun had predicted all along. Mayfield bravely insisted that Rathbun would be convicted anyway, but there was a serious flaw in the prosecution's case: it seemed certain that Rathbun had done something to Goodman, but what? There was no physical proof Goodman had been poisoned, and detectives couldn't find evidence that Rathbun had purchased poison anywhere in Louisville or Jeffersonville. In an editorial, the *Louisville Courier-Journal* pointed out the weaknesses in the state's argument:

> Can it be true, as intimated, that the chemical analysis discloses no poison in Goodman's stomach? But have not sleuths by the dozen flatly told us that Goodman was poisoned, a fact so clear to them that their efforts were directed to scouring the country to find where the poison was obtained? And did not the scientist who sat on the body [Coroner Coots] tell us that though he made no examination of the stomach he not only knew through a secret source of his own that there was poison in it, but he knew what poison it was?

Rathbun's trial began on December 16. The prisoner was said to be more worried about being court-martialed for deserting the army than about the possibility of being convicted and hanged for murdering Goodman. Prosecutor Mayfield traced the movements of Rathbun on the night of November 6; pointed out that the prisoner had confessed several times to plotting insurance fraud, murder, and arson; and asserted that Rathbun had employed "a deadly poison," but Mayfield stopped short of saying what kind. Frank Ogden described the arrival of the well-dressed "Ten Eyke" (Rathbun) and his poorly dressed friend "Rathbun" (Goodman) at the Falls City Hotel. Deputy Coroner Coots told of smelling laudanum as he embalmed Goodman and admitted that he had used formaldehyde, a colorless, pungent gas loaded with chemicals, which meant that even if Dr. Kastenbine had found poison in the stomach, any defense attorney worth his briefcase could have argued that they got there through the embalming process. (I do not know what became of the vial of Goodman's stomach fluid that Coots claimed to have saved before the embalming.) The defense scored several points but lost ground when attorney Harry Phipps made the absurd declaration that his client was not actually Newell Rathbun despite Himalayas of evidence to the contrary, including the prisoner's voluntary admission.

The Neoclassical poet Alexander Pope wrote, "Who shall decide when doctors disagree?" His epigram was vigorously illustrated during the trial by a breathtaking number of professional dissectors of the human body who contradicted themselves and each other. When Dr. Kastenbine took the stand, the defense got him to admit that he could think of at least three possible nonsinister causes of Goodman's demise: the kidney disease nephritis; syncope caused by stoppage of the heart; or a blood clot. In other words, Goodman might have died from natural causes or from alcoholism. The physician also testified that chloroform causes the pupils of the eyes to dilate, but Goodman's were contracted; yet, he said, chloroform might have been the cause since Goodman's brain was blanched, a symptom that could not have been caused by the embalming fluid. In the final analysis, he could not say for sure one way or the other. Dr. Carl Weidner testified that in a case of chloroforming, the brain would be bloodless and the heart relaxed and full of blood. In his opinion, "Death might have resulted from ether or chloroform or an anesthetic," but under cross-examination he agreed that cause of death could just as easily have been an obstructed aorta. Dr. D. C. Peyton opined that Goodman had died quickly of "some deadly poison, probably chloroform," but added that "if all organs were free from disease, no man could explain the cause of death." Dr. E. N. Flynn, a defense witness, believed Rathbun had died from overindulgence in whisky. Dr. G. F. C. Hancock said cause of death was probably alcoholism, but then again it could have been chloroform. Two other physicians, Ruddell and Graham, offered testimony as ambiguous as Dr. Hancock's and another, Dr. Field, called the cause of Goodman's death a complete mystery.

On December 21, the case went to the jury, the members of which were probably reeling in confusion from the wildly contradictory and inconclusive expert medical testimony. The defense expected Goodman to go free; the prosecution was equally certain he would be convicted. In the end, neither side was happy with the verdict. Rathbun's bizarre, ridiculous, and deeply improbable defense—that he had intended to commit murder, but fate had stepped in and did the job for him—actually worked. The state was unable to prove otherwise, and a man can't be executed merely for having bad intentions. Therefore, the jury decided on December 23 that he was guilty of third-degree manslaughter rather than murder. Rathbun did not get off scot-free as the defense hoped, but to the prosecution's disgust, he got a relatively easy sentence since he was found guilty of a lesser charge.

Rathbun called the sentence "a fine Christmas gift." He had no idea how close the jurors came to giving him the death penalty. He was sentenced to not less than two and no more than twenty-one years. Several jurors visited Prosecutor Mayfield's office the day after sentencing and apologized for their wimpy compromise. They all told Mayfield that they believed Rathbun was guilty and some agreed that the punishment they chose did not fit the crime.

Because he was twenty-eight years old, Rathbun was sent to the Jeffersonville Reformatory rather than a penitentiary for more hardened criminals. He received the maximum sentence of twenty-one years; a jail official curtly stated, "One of the purposes of the Board of Managers of the Reformatory is to do what juries fail to do." Superintendent Hart added, "It is the aim of the board to protect society from those whose liberty would be a menace to it." Rathbun expressed his own self-serving view of matters in a letter to his parents in Petoskey, Michigan:

> It's all over. By my sentence you will see that I was not guilty of the crime with which I was charged. I was a victim of circumstances. I sorrow deeply on account of the sorrow I have brought to you. There was no one that testified against me except the police, and they were paid to do so. I hope to be with you Xmas, 1903.

Rathbun went to work in the prison foundry and soon after his incarceration made a name for himself as a model inmate. Remarkably, he never violated a single rule during his stay. He was called "the most expert molder in the shop" and earned spending money by working overtime; he continued his backbreaking labors and refrained from complaining even when he contracted a nearly fatal case of diphtheria. He professedly hoped that his good behavior would result in a parole in 1903, even though the parole board vowed when he entered prison that he would serve his full sentence. He nearly got his wish in December 1903; the army promised to arrest and try him for desertion if he got paroled, but in the end, the board rejected his application after "the enormity of his crime was taken into consideration."

At some point, Rathbun confessed to reformatory superintendent W. H. Whittaker and his assistant Morris Barnard that he had in fact murdered Charles Goodman—and, contrary to all the expert testimony put on by his defense, he did it with laudanum. The much-maligned Deputy Coroner Coots had been correct all along! For some reason, Whittaker and Barnard chose to keep Rathbun's confession a secret. In a way it didn't matter since under the double jeopardy clause in the Constitution, Rathbun could not have been tried again for the murder even if he admitted his guilt to President Roosevelt in person.

After serving less than eight years for the lesser charge of manslaughter, Rathbun was quietly paroled on April 5,

1909, and walked out of jail fresh as a daisy and twice as free. Let us hope he never again was possessed by the urge to insure his own life, kill a hobo in his stead, and burn a hotel down around the cadaver.

Two Shopworn Legal Defenses
for the Price of One

Fathers used to take their daughters' "purity" a lot more seriously than they do now, if we are to judge by the innumerable old news accounts of angry men forcing seducers into marriage with a little double-barreled persuasion. If the cad were so stubborn as to refuse, often the fathers of the "ruined" girls took even more drastic action: they followed the unwritten law.

The unwritten law was invoked throughout the country, but nowhere with more gusto than in the South, where personal honor was traditionally taken very earnestly. Simply put, the unwritten law held that anyone was permitted to uphold the sanctity of home and family by any means necessary, including mayhem, maiming, and murder. So, for example, if Daddy discovered that a moustache-tweaking masher had seduced his daughter, he was entitled to hunt down said masher and slaughter him where he stood. No jury would convict him—he was only following the noble unwritten law. If Daddy had forbearance and a sense of fair play and demanded a shotgun wedding, the wise desecrator of a girl's honor would agree, knowing that if he declined he might be parted from company with his own head and his murderer would pay a minor penalty at worst.

Or suppose Mr. Blank came home unexpectedly after a long day of toil at the buggy whip factory and found a man who happened not to be himself entertaining his wife. According to the magnificent unwritten law, Mr. Blank was perfectly within his rights to beat the other man within a millimeter of his life—or even kill him on the spot—and then thrash or kill his strumpet of a wife. Many a man has walked free after the jury agreed that he was correct to

chastise the adulterous couple. They broke the stately unwritten law!

But lest anyone think the unwritten law was merely a
legal ruse for men to keep women under control, note that
women also took full advantage of it—maybe even more
than men did. My file cabinets groan piteously under the
weight of articles about women who killed unfaithful spous-
es, and/or the homewreckers who led their men astray,
and who afterward faced only the most perfunctory of trials with a foregone conclusion: she had the right to do it.
Sometimes there wasn't even a trial. Girls slaughtered seducers, rapists, and men who merely "insulted" them; the
glorious unwritten law amply covered all of these circumstances. If I have seen one account of a furious woman who
publicly horsewhipped a man (or woman) for spreading rumors about her, I have seen a hundred thousand.

Many recipients of this vintage violence were guilty, and
it could be argued that they got their just desserts; but others were blameless victims of rumor and, often, their innocence was not established until the splendid unwritten law
had already taken its toll. Unquestionably, hundreds of people got away with murder simply by invoking the majestic
unwritten law. If Mr. A wanted rid of his neighbor Mr. B, all
he had to do was kill Mr. B and tell the jury with a straight
face, "He tried to rape my daughter." For many juries that
was good enough, and while invoking the exalted unwritten
law was not foolproof, the canny murderer knew the odds
were in his or her favor.

This preamble leads us to a certain time and place—
Lynchburg, Virginia, on April 22, 1907. Judge William G.
Loving's nineteen-year-old daughter Elizabeth told him that
on the night before, storekeeper Theodore Estes drugged
her and raped her while she was unconscious. (A common
theme in the seduction stories told by tearful women of
bygone eras is that someone drugged them. Somehow, they
never seem to have had sex on their volition; they always
had to be knocked unconscious first, to minimize their

own role in what happened next. Plenty of people believed these unlikely yarns. For generations, mothers warned their daughters *never* to accept a drink—especially a Coca-Cola—from a strange man because he may have slipped a Mickey into it for nefarious purposes.)

Judge Loving—actually a former judge—believed his daughter. After she told the story, he hopped in his buggy and rode ten miles to Thomas Ryan's country estate at Oak Ridge, where he found young Mr. Estes. The infuriated father shot Estes to death without asking him whether the story was even true. According to the judge, "When I heard the awful story from the lips of my dear one I was insane. I wanted to learn all the facts, and then nothing in God's or man's power could have stopped me from taking his life. I did it after careful consideration." Except, of course, he did not trouble to "learn all the facts" and did not act "after careful consideration."

The dead man's friends, on the other hand, said Estes was guilty of nothing worse than giving Elizabeth Loving a shot of whisky when she complained of feeling ill during a buggy ride. The inference was that she got drunk and invented the story of Theodore's wicked intentions to explain her condition when she got home.

When Loving went on trial in June, his attorneys took the obvious route: invoke the awe-inspiring unwritten law! Whether or not Elizabeth's story was true, her father reacted the way any respectable, red-blooded father would. But Loving and his attorneys had reason to be concerned. After all, it was the year 1907, and juries did not let those who murdered due to matters of honor off the hook as consistently as they had in the past. A supporting argument was needed in case the jury did not think the never-to-be-sufficiently praised unwritten law was a good enough reason to shoot a man in cold blood without asking his side of the story. Fortunately, Loving's attorneys had a model to follow—the newspapers were full of one of the most notorious invocations of the unwritten law in the history of American jurisprudence.

In 1904, Harry K. Thaw, disturbed son of Pittsburgh millionaires, married infamously promiscuous Broadway chorus girl Evelyn Nesbit. Before their nuptials, she confided to Thaw that when very young, she had been drugged and raped by noted architect Stanford White. Thaw stewed over the information for a couple of years and then shot White in the face before a horrified crowd at New York City's Madison Square Garden on June 25, 1906. The Thaws used their vast wealth to keep their son out of the electric chair in an excruciatingly protracted legal drama that went on for years, the details of which could fill a book five times the length of this one. Thaw's lawyers pled the agreeable unwritten law—even though White's alleged seduction of Evelyn Nesbit took place *before* she married Harry—and for good measure, they brought in a battery of psychiatrists who declared that Thaw was stark raving crackers. The expert witnesses, who appeared willing to say anything under oath as long as they received payment from the Thaws, even invented a brand new medical term—*Dementia Americana*—to describe the particular kind of insanity a man feels when he craves recourse to the wonderful unwritten law.

Well, Judge Loving's lawyers must have reasoned that if the double whammy of the unwritten law and insanity defense was working so well for Harry Thaw, it could work for their client—even though both defenses were legal clichés that already had been used too many times to free manifestly guilty and sane killers. They were viewed with wide suspicion—if not outright contempt—by the press and laymen alike. But would these shopworn defenses succeed one more time?

Loving's daughter took the witness stand on June 25. Between sobs, she told the same story she told the judge on the fatal morning. She explained how Estes took her for a buggy ride; how he wickedly gave her a sip from a flask; how she felt faint afterward; and how Estes drove to an unfrequented road and there "despite her screams outraged her." She spent the night at the home of her friend, Annie Kidd. The next morning, her father asked how she came to be arriving home so late and in such a stupefied condition. She told all, and off he went with a loaded shotgun and murder in his eye. Gentlemen of the jury, you'd have done the same—you too would have relied on the hallowed unwritten law to annihilate the despoiler of your daughter!

The prosecution—whose own courtroom theatrics included bringing in Theodore Estes's bloody clothes for everyone to behold—countered that it was mighty convenient to blame a man who could not defend himself against the charges. Elizabeth Loving admitted she had taken two drinks that night—one at Estes's store, the other in his buggy. The hint was that she might be wilder than her father suspected.

The defense decided they had better play their other card—the insanity card! Dr. William Tunstall testified that he thought Loving was insane while committing the crime. The doctor's evidence for his belief seems ridiculously thin. Loving failed to speak to Dr. Tunstall before the killing and afterward; in addition, Loving's head "hung low and he was pale." Tunstall testified also that the judge frequently got drunk, sometimes to the point of undergoing delirium tremens. (It sounds as though the good doctor confused the concepts of "drunkenness" and "insanity.") Not only that, the judge was noted for "his temper, his unreasonable acts, his passion and his harshness." Dr. Tunstall admitted that when Loving applied for bail ninety minutes after the murder, he seemed perfectly rational.

The defense picked up the ball and ran with it, claiming Loving was insane due to long years of abusing alcohol. Therefore, he was not responsible for his actions when he shot Estes in a fit of anger. The defense called this "emotional insanity," as opposed to ordinary, mundane insanity.

The prosecution produced Ms. Annie Kidd, at whose home Ms. Loving spent the night after her alleged drugging. Before Kidd could say anything, the defense raised an objection based on a precedent in the Thaw-White murder trial—which proves they, like everyone else in America in 1907, had been closely following the proceedings in that celebrated case. Prosecutor Daniel Harmon argued that Judge Loving could have found out all the facts had he walked a block to the Kidd residence instead of immediately tracking down Theodore Estes. Harmon added that Loving could have taken his daughter to a physician to ascertain whether she had been doped and assaulted, but he did not. Furthermore, the "abandoned road" where she claimed the crime took place was within sight of the town of Lovingston. A Lovingston man of experimental outlook drank the remaining contents of the supposed "drugged flask of whisky" and suffered no unusual effects.

(Let us pause a moment to ponder poor Elizabeth Loving's intolerable situation. If her story was true, by telling it she inadvertently caused the killing of a guilty man. If her story was a lie, she caused the murder of an innocent man. Whether the story was true or false, she risked condemning her father to death or jail. And whether her father was acquitted, imprisoned, or given the death penalty, she was guaranteed to be the object of small-town gossip for the rest of her life.)

On June 27, the judge—the one trying the case, not the one in handcuffs—made a dramatic ruling. He declared inadmissible certain evidence favorable to the state, in particular the statements Ms. Kidd intended to make, which the state claimed would have shown incontrovertibly that Elizabeth Loving fabricated the story about the drugged whisky. As the *Louisville Courier-Journal* neatly summarized it, the court gallantly refused to allow Ms. Loving to be contradicted. The defense, by contrast, was allowed to introduce any testimony they pleased. A victory for Loving was all but assured. Judge Barksdale cited events in the still-unfolding Thaw-White case as precedent.

The prosecution tried to knock the props out from under the insanity plea by bringing in seven witnesses who had known Loving for years. They agreed that he never had been deemed insane. On the contrary, he "had served with honor as a judge and had charge of large estates." The only mental flaws the state conceded were that the judge had a bad temper and got drunk a lot.

The case went to the jury on June 29. Both sides wrangled over the instructions for the jury. The prosecution argued that jurors should not consider the unwritten law as justification for the murder. Judge Barksdale struck out those instructions. It came as no surprise, then, when the announcement came, after only thirty-five minutes of consideration, that Judge Loving was acquitted. The insanity plea and the unwritten law had won the day again! Few people—certainly not members of the jury—stopped to consider that in the Loving case, even the enchanting unwritten law offered no excusable grounds for murder since it was never established that Estes had, in fact, drugged and molested Ms. Loving. Incidentally, the same combination got Harry Thaw off, too. He was sent to an asylum as opposed to a prison; a few years later, his parents got him relieved of that punishment as well. Thaw spent the rest of his long life a free man.

The historical record indicates that the supposedly crazy Judge Loving never performed another insane deed for the remainder of his life. I would guess that Elizabeth Loving took a chaperone on her next date—and that her beau was only too glad to have one along.

Rube Burrows Has His Portrait Taken

In the movies, outlaws—especially bank robbers and train robbers—are usually well groomed, courtly, and possessed of a dash that is the envy of adolescents of all ages. They are generally played by actors such as Tyrone Power, Warren Beatty, Johnny Depp, and Brad Pitt. A common theme in movies and folklore is that these thieves were American versions of Robin Hood: they robbed big institutions, such as banks and train companies, but shared their loot with the deserving poor.

That is the fantasy. The real-life exploits and death of Rube Burrows were the reality.

He was born in Lamar County, Alabama, on December 11, 1854; his surname is given interchangeably throughout his life as Burrow or Burrows. He was the Deep South's equivalent of Missouri's Jesse James. Apologists for James often claim that he was forced into his life of crime by circumstances, particularly the hard times and persecution Southerners faced during the Reconstruction. The same could be said for Burrows, who lived an honest life at first. He worked on the family's farm until he turned eighteen. Then he moved to Stephenville, Texas, where he worked on his uncle's ranch. Burrows had dreams of saving his money and buying his own land. He married and had two children, but tragedy struck in 1880 when his wife died of malaria. He married again in 1884 and moved to Alexander, Texas, still working hard and saving his money.

In 1886, Burrows's crops failed and he faced financial ruin. He chose the path that he could never escape afterward. Train robberies were very much in vogue; the greatest thief of them all, Jesse James, had been dead only four years but had already achieved the status of American legend. Why sweat like a peon on a farm, dependent on the vagaries of the weather for success and the recipient of paltry rewards even when everything went favorably, when all one needed to live in luxury were a handkerchief, a six-shooter, a fast horse, and the element of surprise? Burrows and his brother Jim decided they, too, would rob a train just like everyone else seemed to be doing.

In December 1886, the Burrows brothers and four other men conspired to rob the Denver and Fort Worth Express on its return trip from Indian Territory (Oklahoma). When the train made a scheduled stop in Bellevue, Texas, the bandits climbed aboard with pistols drawn. They were not entirely competent during their first attempt at wholesale robbery. Most of the passengers saw them coming and successfully hid their valuables, so the Burrows gang had only $300 to split amongst themselves for their pains. Even worse, three army soldiers happened to be aboard. The sergeant expressed a desire to ventilate the bodies of the fleeing outlaws; things would have gone badly for Burrows and his men had the other passengers not talked the sergeant out of it.

Despite this inauspicious beginning, however, Rube Burrows was bitten hard by the robbery bug. Easy money, hairbreadth escapes, excitement—it sure beat farming. Maybe someone would even write a dime novel about him someday!

In June 1887, the gang stopped the Texas and Pacific Express heading east from Ben Brook, Texas. The second robbery went much more smoothly than the first. Burrows thought of a clever touch that had not occurred to the late, celebrated Mr. James: he forced the engineer to halt the train on a high trestle over a gorge, which effectively discouraged passengers from running away. (It was the tendency of journalists and dime novelists—and some modern writers who surely know better—to claim that outlaws held up trains in order to strike back at robber barons and greedy capitalists. The reader will observe that Burrows, and Mr. James of sainted memory, picked the pockets of poor travelers when the opportunity arose.) This holdup went so well that Burrows duplicated it in the same spot on September 20. On this third robbery, his gang got away with an amount estimated between $12,000 and $30,000. The equivalent in modern currency would be between $280,000 and $660,000. That would have been enough to keep the criminals well-to-do for quite some time, but greed inspired them to push their luck again less than three months later.

On December 9, Burrows and company held up the St. Louis, Arkansas, and Texas Express at Genoa, Arkansas, and got away with the proceeds of the Louisiana lottery. It was a risky move since the train was guarded by the Southern Express Company. The SEC failed to stop the robbery, but it was in league with the world-famous Pinkerton detective agency. Had Burrows stuck to relatively small fry he might have retired early as a gentleman rancher with a mysterious source of income that neighbors gossiped about. Now he had the Pinkertons after him. Within five days of the robbery, detectives had traced a raincoat left behind by one of the robbers to a store in Dublin, Texas. The clerk identified the purchaser as gang member Jim Brock.

Rube Burrows in life . . . From the *Louisville Courier-Journal,* October 26, 1890. Reprinted by courtesy of the *Louisville Courier-Journal.*

Brock was captured in due haste and confessed. Afterward, he received a letter from an unwitting Rube, mailed from Lamar County, Alabama; he had gone back home to hide until the heat blew over. The Pinkertons invaded the outlaw leader's house on January 8, 1888, but Burrows's luck held. His brother Jim had tipped him off that detectives were on the way and he was long gone when they arrived.

One might think that a sensible outlaw would lay low for a while after such a close escape, but it is the nature of the career criminal to develop a sense of invincibility and correspondingly take greater and greater risks. Only two weeks after the Pinkertons came within a gnat's eyelash of catching Rube, he and brother Jim let their guard down and took a public ride on a Louisville and Nashville train in southern Alabama. An alert conductor saw them and police surrounded the train when it reached Montgomery. The brothers were marched to the police station, but at the foot of the stairs, they made a break for it. Rube got away after shooting—nonfatally, it appears—a printer named Bray who got in the way, but Jim was captured and sent to jail at Texarkana. He died on October 5, 1888, of typhoid and malaria, an all too common fate among the era's jailbirds.

The capture of his brother inspired Rube to hide in the swamps and restrain himself until December 15, when he and S. C. Brock robbed the Illinois Central at Duck Hill, Mississippi. This time, things went badly awry. The conductor panicked and shouted that outlaws were aboard. Two armed passengers—Chester Hughes and John Wilkenson—jumped Burrows. He fired first, killing Hughes instantly. The falling corpse hit Wilkenson, forcing him to drop his pistol. Burrows got away, but he had killed his first man, making the Pinkertons more eager than ever to catch him.

One of the more unintelligent manifestations of human nature is the tendency to root for plunderers of trains and banks, and in later years after train robbing became obsolete, for those who specialized only in bank robbery—as was well documented by the newspapers during Depression-era pillaging by Bonnie and Clyde, John Dillinger, and Pretty Boy Floyd. (Those who cheer when a modern "Robin Hood" steals money from an oppressive institution such as a bank seem not to realize that the money originally came from depositors—the so-called "little guy." Applauding a bank robber is like applauding a man who picks your pocket, directly or indirectly.) Folks admired the wily bandit Rube Burrows, who lived the adventurous life they all secretly envied while dodging the Pinkertons. The great common people bestowed upon Burrows a Robin Hood persona, in the belief that he, like Jesse James, robbed from the rich and gave to the poor—though there is precious little evidence outside of folk legend that either Burrows or the lamented Mr. James ever did anything with their ill-gotten gains other than keep it for themselves.

This ill-considered folk idolization of Burrows came to an abrupt end on July 16, 1889, when he committed his second murder. Evidently, people enjoy it when a robber steals their money from banks and trains, but they draw the line when that robber takes a life. Unlike Burrows's first killing, which could arguably be considered a case of self-defense, the second was cowardly and uncalled for. Having somewhat foolhardily returned to Lamar County, Burrows entered the post office to pick up a package addressed to "Cain." (Perhaps Rube was enjoying a joke with a Biblical flavor.) It contained a white mask he intended to wear during his next robbery. The postmaster, Mose Graves, told him that the package had arrived, but since no one named Cain lived in the vicinity he had sent it back. A heated argument ensued. It ended with Graves mortally wounded on the floor and Burrows holding a smoking pistol.

Graves was a popular man, but Burrows, the former darling of newspaper readers, did not abandon Lamar County. He and his gang hid in a section of rough terrain seven miles from Vernon, described as a "natural fortress" where "ten men can defend it against the approach of a thousand men." Lawmen arrested Rube's father Allen, his brother John, and his brother-in-law James Cash on suspicion of harboring a fugitive. Rube sent word that if his kin were not released he would "make the sheriff suffer." In response, Governor Seay sent a detachment of the Birmingham Rifles and their forty guns after Rube, accompanied by no fewer than seventy detectives. In the meantime, a mob threatened to drag the Burrows men out of the jailhouse at Vernon and lynch them on the spot. Things looked exciting for a day or two but ended in a stalemate: the Birmingham Rifles were unable to penetrate Rube's fortress and were sent home. The three incarcerated Burrows relatives were neither sprung from jail nor lynched, but they were tried on July 31 on charges of being accessories to the murder of Postmaster Graves. Rube's father and brother were freed and Cash was released on a $1,000 bond. This satisfied Rube and he stayed put.

Somehow, Rube and his gang escaped from his stronghold without being spotted. He continued to support himself by his usual means. On September 25, 1889, he and two henchmen held up the Mobile and Ohio Express at Buckatunna, Mississippi, again pulling his favorite trick of forcing the engineer to stop on a high bridge. They got away with $223 and some packages but failed to notice an additional $70,000 in government money, so the joke was on them. During the robbery, Rube remarked, "The Mobile and Ohio dared me to hold up a train, and I wanted to show them I could do it." After the holdup, the men fled back to their natural fortress.

On October 24, Sheriff Morris of Blount County, Alabama, learned that Rube was hiding at the home of Bud Ashworth. The reward on Rube's head was up to $5,000. The sheriff's brother and four deputies could not pass up such an opportunity and pounded on the cabin in the dead of night, guns drawn and probably thinking about all the diamond-studded watch fobs they could purchase with $5,000. Using a woman as a human shield—so much for the fabled gallantry of the old-time bandit—Rube made his way to a clump of trees where he had loaded Winchesters salted away. Burrows got away, but the woman he had used to achieve his escape was so hysterical that relatives feared for her health.

Blount County lawmen had but one collective thought: Rube Burrows is somewhere in the area! A posse of forty gathered at Oneonta and combed the hills looking for the much-wanted "Bandit King of the South." On October 25, they found him—or rather, he found them and they abandoned the chase after he killed two of their number and wounded ten others. When word got back to Oneonta, five hundred armed men indulged in the rare sport of Rube hunting, but Burrows and his men had long since disappeared across the Warrior River and were hiding on Sand Mountain. In the past, Burrows could always count on getting help from farmers and others who found it glamorous to pal around with a notorious criminal. Those days were gone, as noted in a news report about the pursuit: "Burrows has the citizens so scared that they can help but little."

A couple of weeks' worth of wild news reports ensued, contradictorily alleging that Burrows had been caught—no, had been killed—had captured some detectives—better yet, had killed two detectives in a cave—best of all, had abducted and murdered a reporter for the *Atlanta Constitution*. However, none of the stories were true. The truth was that he and his men had left Blount County and nobody knew where they were.

Late at night, November 12, two men went to the residence of Mr. Summers in Vernon, Lamar County, to ask if he would open his general store so they could buy burial material "for a person who had just died out in the country." Summers obliged, but after he opened the store, he found himself looking down a revolver barrel. The men took $400 and left. It was supposed that Rube had returned to his old home.

The rewards offered for Burrows and his gang amounted to $7,500 by this time. Correspondingly, the net began to close. Two of his esteemed associates (and also his cousins), Rube Smith and Jim W. McClung, were captured at Amory, Mississippi, on December 14. By seizing them, detectives thwarted the planned robbery of a Kansas City, Birmingham, and Memphis train.

On Christmas Day came a report that Rube had been killed at McKenzie Lake, Texas. It wasn't him, but by then the genuine article had less than a year to live. He slipped away to Milton, Florida, where he took a job hauling wood. Only a sick ox saved him from capture on February 6, 1890. Burrows wanted to take a team of oxen across a river on a ferry, but at the last moment, one took ill. Upon being informed that the ferry operator was down at the river with a number of hunters, Rube got suspicious and escaped again.

His antisocial adventures continued. In March, Burrows's men allegedly murdered T. V. Jackson, the Southern Express Company detective who had captured gang members Smith and McClung. In April, the gang liberated two men named Warren Lowery and Copps from the Winston County, Alabama, jail—or so it was said. Like all outlaws, Burrows was blamed for every crime committed within the area of several hundred miles; it is often difficult to separate his genuine misdeeds from those of others who found the notorious man a convenient scapegoat. On May 30, some burglars blew open a safe belonging to merchants Crew and Sons in Vernon, Lamar County, taking $100 and then defiantly eating canned sardines on the front steps. Because the robbery occurred in Burrows's old stomping grounds, it was pinned on him, but a reporter noted that the caper "was not committed in Rube's characteristic style."

In short order, more of Burrows's men were caught in the law's snares. Det. T. V. Jackson—who we assume had not been murdered by the gang after all—arrested S. C. Brock, billed as "the smartest of all train robbers," at Columbus, Mississippi, on July 16. A week later, Jack Jennings was nabbed in Birmingham, Alabama. Burrows—running out of henchmen and possibly out of cash as well—returned to doing what he did best. In early September, he held up an express train at Flomaton, Alabama, and got away with a measly $200. It was his final robbery.

On October 7, four men in River Ridge, Monroe County, Alabama, accomplished what dozens of Pinkertons and

$25,000 spent by the Southern Express Company had been unable to do. Wealthy farmer John McDuffie (or McDuffee), merchant Jefferson Davis "J. D." Carter, and two black farmhands—one was John Marshall; the name of the other does not appear—spotted the most wanted man in the South ducking into a cabin. They hatched an instant plot. The farmhands entered the cabin and sat at a table on both sides of Burrows as though they were waiting for a meal. At a prearranged signal, they seized Rube's arms as McDuffie and Carter burst in with guns drawn. Burrows surrendered sheepishly. Perhaps he was embarrassed at having been caught by such a simple ruse after his many years of fortresses, gunfights, clever escapes, and providentially sick oxen. McDuffie, Marshall, and Carter hustled Burrows to the jail at Linden. They arrived in the middle of the night, so the sheriff was not in. The men locked Rube in a cell and spent the night keeping a close eye on him. Carter took the bandit's loot and rifle for safekeeping and went to his store.

The next morning, Rube asked McDuffie and Marshall if they would toss him his satchel, which had some crackers in it. They obliged without first looking in the satchel. If they had, they would have seen that it contained a loaded pistol in addition to the savory morsels. Within moments, McDuffie was behind bars like a real-life Barney Fife while a free Rube aimed a gun at John Marshall.

Burrows could have slipped out of town in the confusion, but he was determined to regain his money and rifle and so hurried to J. D. Carter's store. Carter looked up from his work and fixed his gaze upon the man whom he had helped lock up the night before. After a tense moment, the merchant and the desperado exchanged compliments and vowed to treat each other to dinner with all the fixings— just kidding! They immediately fired upon each other. Carter received a nonfatal wound in the shoulder, as inevitably happens to the good guys in Western movies when they indulge in gunfights. One of Carter's bullets passed through Burrows's body via his stomach. He staggered outside, followed by Carter, and sank to the ground dead with a pistol in each hand.

In those wonderful bygone days, it was the custom whenever an outlaw was killed—especially in the West and South—to put the illustrious corpse on public display, preferably with his weapons. Sometimes, a placard with a pointed message was added to the tableau. Burrows was clapped in a cheap pine casket, and thousands of people came to look at him. Some stole his shirt buttons; some snipped locks of hair; one plucky individual made off with the bad man's shoes.

Once everyone feasted their eyes, the remains were shipped to Birmingham—by train, ironically. In Burrows's time, whenever a famous villain was killed and tastefully mounted, the local photographer would take a picture and sell copies. These treasured mementos would be handed down like heirlooms. Many still exist.

(The tradition continued well into the 1930s. Photos of the bullet-riddled corpses of Bonnie and Clyde and the Ma Barker gang were collector's items and the body of John Dillinger was famously displayed in a Chicago funeral home before throngs of gawkers despite the blistering summer weather. An especially ghoulish photo taken during Dillinger's exhibition depicts a laughing young woman posing by his body while holding her nose. Before we deride our barbaric ancestors, however, it is well to remember that in our own era innumerable Web sites allow browsers to view the goriest accident photos and crime-scene pictures imaginable free of charge and in the privacy of their own homes. Compared to this high-tech voyeurism, those old pictures of dead outlaws are the height of good taste and refinement. Some aspects of human nature never change.)

One of the most famous works from the Dead Outlaw Tintype School of Art—it can almost be called iconic—is a portrait of Mr. Burrows, showing him in a casket eerily standing on end. The photo was taken in Birmingham at the request of the officials of the Southern Express Company and can be seen in sundry books on outlawry and on a number of Web sites. After this great moment in the history of photography, the remains were sent to Burrows's relatives in Lamar County. It is interesting to read a reporter's description of the photo, written only minutes after it was taken:

> The unvarnished coffin was taken into the Southern Express Company's office. The top was removed and the coffin was placed upright in a corner. The dead robber appeared in a standing position. His sombrero hat was then placed upon his head, a pistol was put in each of his hands and his favorite rifle was leaned against him. He appeared just as during life. An excellent photograph was taken by an enterprising photographer. The coffin was then lowered and the crowd was allowed to pass through and gaze at Burrows. He looked every inch the outlaw he was. . . . [H]is general appearance inspired terror. He wore the rough jeans suit in which he was killed and a dirty calico shirt. There was only one wound on his person, the one which killed him.

Perhaps two photos were taken, since the often-reproduced picture shows the coffin leaning against a boxcar rather than standing vertically in the SEC's office. Another description of Rube's famous carcass comes to us from Charles Kensler, detective for the Louisville and Nashville railroad, who was interviewed by the *Louisville Courier-Journal* three weeks after Burrows's death. It takes considerable shine out of movies that depict dandified, well-mannered, and elegant outlaws:

> The corpse was filthy beyond all imagination, and possibly he had not washed himself in years. Dirt was a disguise to him, and even on his face and neck the dirt was so thick that his collar could not have been distinguished fifty feet away. His clothes were old and worn, and the cheap cotton shirt he had worn for months was stiff with dirt.

Similar sentiments were expressed by Lucien Minor, a route agent for the SEC, in a November 1890 interview:

. . . and in death. From the Keven McQueen Accumulation.

He was as low a specimen of humanity as I ever looked upon. When killed he was dirty and filthy in the extreme. The cheap cotton shirt he wore was shiny with accumulated dirt and grease, and his torn and badly-worn coat was in the same plight. The dirt on his bearded face was so thick that it could be scraped off, and he certainly looked as though soap and water were, to him, unknown quantities.

As long as we are stripping away the romance from Rube's life, it should be noted that robbing trains was an occupation that seldom paid well. The Burrows gang rarely got away with more than a few hundred dollars and, because it had to be split among all members, no man walked away with much pecuniary reward for all his risk-taking. Rube spent most of his loot financing his getaways; as a result, he was perpetually broke and might as well have stuck to farming.

Rube Burrows had been the last member of his gang to be captured. All the others wound up in prison. On November 10, 1890, S. C. Brock, aliases Joe Johnson and Joe Jackson—obviously, creativity wasn't one of his strong points—made a spectacle of himself by leaping from a fourth story balcony in the penitentiary at Jackson, Mississippi, and landing on his head at the ground floor. That was the end of the so-called "smartest of all train robbers." Rube Smith went on trial in April 1890 for robbing the train at Buckatunna and was summarily found guilty. In November 1890, Smith was tried a second time for robbing the U.S. mail. The mildest possible sentence was life imprisonment—and that's exactly what he got. On December 8, he boarded a train to the Ohio State Penitentiary in Columbus.

Three of the four men who captured Burrows were rewarded. McDuffie did not claim any money since he was already wealthy. The two farmhands got $100 apiece; Carter received $1,000 since he was seriously injured in the shootout. But, I am pleased to note, they weren't the only ones in the Rube Burrows story who found a measure of financial security. The outlaw's parents sold his coffin and the clothes he was wearing when killed to the proprietor of a traveling museum. The asking price was twenty dollars. To fulfill the financial transaction, the museum owner had Burrows's body exhumed. While the entrepreneur was at it, he had a plaster cast made of the entire corpse. When he took his show on the road, he displayed a life-sized figure of Rube wearing his original grave clothes. The coffin sat nearby as a grim *memento mori* for all introspective persons who had a nickel to spare.

A Farce in More Ways Than One

In the days before convenient home entertainment, our ancestors went to see plays, the vast majority of which have not stood the test of time. Hence the diversion-hungry crowd that assembled at the City Opera House in Chattanooga, Tennessee, on September 22, 1899, to see a new play's opening night. It was a farce comedy by E. A. McCoy called *Mr. Plaster of Paris,* which had been playing successfully on the road for three weeks. The featured actress was twenty-one-year-old Julia Morrison of New Orleans, described as blonde and "exceedingly handsome." Her role was listed on the playbill as "Irene, a Victim of Circumstances."

The play was to begin at 8:00 P.M. Just after the orchestra finished a sprightly overture, three pistol shots rang out as the audience sat looking at an unraised curtain. Seconds later, the acrid odor of gunpowder wafted through the room. The audience thought it was part of the play. A solemn man stepped out of the wings (I fancy that he wore a swallowtail coat and a bat-wing collar) and informed the assembly that there would be no show tonight, many regrets, and would everyone please form an orderly line to the box office to get their money back.

The real theater took place behind the curtain that night. Morrison had shot Frank Leiden (real name, Leidenheimer), the theatrical company's stage manager and leading man. She was arrested, as was her husband Frederick Henry James, who traveled with the troupe although he was neither an actor nor a stagehand. He appeared to be the quintessential hanger-on, turning up everywhere he was not wanted, sticking his nose in other people's business, and enjoying luxuries provided by his wife's income. The other actors said Mr. James instigated the trouble by encouraging Julia to disobey the more experienced Leiden's advice on acting. Mr. James made his own living, incidentally, as a seller of novelty rubber neckties (really).

Morrison granted an interview to a *Chattanooga Times* reporter, during which she behaved like an *actress*. Her greatest strength was definitely not subtlety. She started by moaning, "Ooooh! I don't know what to say. It's all—oh, it's so awful; and I can't bear to talk about it." Then she proceeded to "talk about it" in lurid detail while staggering about in her cell. Perhaps attempting to turn public opinion in her favor, she told about the insults and salacious propositions heaped upon her by that horrid beast Leiden. (For example, he supposedly told her, "If you kiss me I will give you no more trouble.") The entire theatrical company had conspired to keep her husband away from her so that she would have to be alone with Leiden. He had even threatened to take her life! She screamed before the reporter and assumed a crazed look. She struck a pose by clasping her hands tightly in the finest "but I cannot pay the rent" fashion and claimed she could see the spirit of Leiden coming to get her! "Oh, help me, help me!" she cried to the journalist. "There he is! Look! Look! He is coming towards me! Oh, what shall I do?"

Could anybody possibly have been fooled by such stark nonsense? Unfolding events suggested that plenty of people were.

No one disputed that there was bad blood between Morrison and Leiden—and the coroner's inquest uncovered plenty of proof. He called her a lousy actress and a rank amateur. A few hours before shooting the man, she slapped him. (It is darkly amusing that these two performers who loathed each other in real life had to pretend to be in love onstage every night.) Julia set to work blackening Leiden's character, telling the coroner that despite his slighting remarks about her acting skills, he was infatuated with her and had "insulted her." In other words, he sexually propositioned her. She shot the masher in self-defense. The other members of the troupe sided with Leiden. They universally detested Morrison, whom they called stubborn and contentious. They confirmed that she was a bad actress who had gotten her role through misrepresentation; she claimed more onstage experience than she actually had. More to the point—since bad acting is regrettably not a punishable crime—they said the shooting was unjustifiable and premeditated. The coroner's jury agreed and Julia was taken to jail to stand trial. Charges against her husband, Mr. James, were dropped and he was free to go on peddling rubber neckties.

Julia Morrison was an actress in an era when actresses were considered little better than prostitutes, but she was not friendless. "While the terrible crime is not condoned," wrote a reporter, "there is deep grounded belief that there are mitigating circumstances which have not come to light." The socially prominent women of Chattanooga took up her cause and brought her bouquets, fruit baskets, and the latest works of popular literature—in which, no doubt, every other line of dialogue spoken by the heroines started with the exclamation "Oh!"

(Women were not the only ones who hoisted the banner in defense of Morrison. A furniture dealer sent some of his wares to make her cell cushier and a letter signed "A Southern Man," which appeared in the *Chattanooga Times* on September 26, included these sentiments: "I do know that a woman is in trouble and as a southern man, born with the chivalric ideas of that class, I deeply sympathize with her." The mayor of the city was reportedly among the bringers of flowers and fruits.)

On September 25, Joseph Harris, manager of the acting company, visited Julia in prison. Previously, he had been heard to denounce her as a cold-blooded murderess, but after speaking with her for a half-hour, he left convinced the killing was justified.

The prosecution faced an uphill battle from the beginning. The entire *Mr. Plaster of Paris* company was to be subpoenaed, but they left for New York City before the papers could be served. The show must go on, with or without a leading man and a mediocre lead actress! The fleeing troupe included manager Harris, who had declared he would do anything in his power to help Julia; perhaps he thought he could help her best by getting out of town and taking all his potential hostile witnesses with him. The state certainly could have used the testimony of actor Joseph Kearney, who undertook the role of "John Plaster of Paris, Kentucky." He told the newspapers that he heard an argument between the accused and the victim after rehearsal on the fatal day, during which Julia threatened to "put a ball [bullet] through" Leiden—a moment also witnessed by the company's assistant manager Roger Ryerly.

Julia Morrison strikes a pose. From the *Chattanooga Times,* September 24, 1899. Reprinted by courtesy of the *Chattanooga Times Free Press.*

A second problem facing the state was that the prosecutor, George Antz of New Orleans, happened to be the victim's brother-in-law. It was a conflict of interest that seemed to raise no eyebrows, but it gave the defense ample grounds for a retrial in the event Morrison was found guilty.

A third problem was the court's prejudice in favor of the defendant. After the trial, Antz complained that the defense was allowed to introduce depositions instead of witnesses while the state was forbidden to introduce documents attesting to Leiden's sterling character, such as letters from former employers. Even more startling, on September 28, the grand jury indicted the actress for murder—much to her surprise, as she expected to be set free with no further ado—but afterward jurors visited the prisoner's cell and reassured her that she would be acquitted! The record does not state whether they comforted her with friendly winks.

At an October 3 hearing, Judge Floyd Estill was to decide whether the prisoner could be set free on bond. The defense provided witnesses from the opera house staff, since the entire acting troupe had fled to New York. Joseph Breeding swore Leiden threatened Morrison with a cane; that he "applied opprobrious epithets" to her at the show's rehearsal and often had used obscene language before her; that he struck Morrison several times and kicked her downstairs. Where her husband had been during this mayhem, no one explained, and of course no one was about to be so ungentlemanly as to ask Morrison to display her bruises. Frank Shipp said Leiden had been about to strike Morrison with a cane when she shot him. In addition, physicians testified that the prisoner was pregnant and prolonged confinement in the jail cell would be bad for her health. They opined that the stress of pregnancy might have been the reason the delicate little dove's mind snapped!

Despite the testimony, Judge Estill refused Morrison bail. He explained, "It was shown to the court that they had a quarrel on the day of the murder but that the defendant was the aggressor, calling Leidenheimer a liar and slapping his face. The proof as to the deceased ever having attempted to assault her is conflicting." Judge Estill added that if it appeared at any time that her health was in danger, he would immediately allow bond. The *Louisville Courier-Journal* applauded the justice's ruling:

> The attempt to make a heroine of a commonplace murderess at Chattanooga has not impressed Judge Estill. The Judge refuses her bail upon the ground that her crime was a premeditated and heartless one, and that there is nothing in her condition which makes it necessary that she should be released. Judge Estill has not forgotten that a Judge must be just before he is merciful, and certainly before he is mawkish.

As time passed, it became obvious that Morrison was not actually pregnant. Let us be charitable and assume the doctors were mistaken, or perhaps they just took her word for it that she was expecting.

When Morrison went to trial on January 4, 1900, both sides had their strategies planned. As summarized in a carefully worded news account, "the defense will seek to establish a spotless moral character and will introduce a large number of dispositions to show that Miss Morrison had been persecuted by Leiden because she refused to maintain undesirable relations with him." The prosecution, by contrast, would attempt to show that the murder was carefully planned and not committed in self-defense.

When the prisoner entered the courtroom, the first thing everyone noticed was that confinement had not harmed her health in the least. She weighed 180 pounds when first sent to her cell and now she weighed at least twenty more. She was dressed in black and wore—nice touch!—a prominent crucifix. She laughed and chatted with her husband and her friend Mrs. E. E. Geese and did not seem worried about the proceedings. After all, had not the grand jurors told her months before that she was certain to be acquitted?

The first witness was W. J. Patterson, stage manager of the opera house. He said that although Morrison arrived an hour before the show was to begin, she had neither unlocked her stage trunk nor prepared for the performance. It seemed she had no intention of going onstage that night. (Her lack-adaisical attitude neatly fits a theory proposed by some that she knew she was about to be fired.) When Patterson told her that the audience was waiting, she said, "All right, I'll go." She left for the stage in her street clothes rather than her costume. But as she ascended the stairs leading to the stage, she encountered Frank Leiden in costume as the character "Dr. Abindad Binns," superintending the lights and the curtain. Seemingly without provocation, she "drew from her bosom" a .38-caliber revolver and fired three times at Leiden's head from a distance of three feet. He died five minutes later, still wearing a grotesque comic wig. Under questioning, Patterson said he had not witnessed any arguments between Leiden and Morrison, but Leiden told him confidentially of their animosity. Patterson's version of events was corroborated by other opera house employees, including W. H. Womble and electrician Leon Joseph.

Julia Morrison took the stand and revealed that, contrary to previous reports, she was not from New Orleans. "I was born, to the best of my knowledge, in Kansas. My parents died when I was an infant and I have known only foster parents, whose name was Dale." She told a story of constant persecution at the hands of Leiden. She claimed that he had used such obscene, belittling language in her presence that she requested to write his words rather than sully her tongue by saying them aloud. He had been friendly, she said, until he discovered that she was married and that her husband intended to accompany her on the road. Then he started making "improper proposals," became verbally and physically abusive, and, perhaps worst of all, insulted her acting abilities. (Her story would make more sense if she had been a single, unescorted woman rather than married, but men will do strange things.)

At last the day came when she could take it no more! On the night of the murder, she had been feeling ill, and when she was in an opera house toilet room, Leiden came along and "offered an indignity which she told to the court," according to a reporter—note that the journalist dared not give details for fear of offending readers. That was the last straw. As she hurried to the stage so as not to miss her cue, there stood her tormentor at the top of the stairs. (Witness Patterson placed Leiden behind the stage tending to the lights, so either Patterson or Morrison was mistaken or lying.) He raised his cane and called her a "foul name." At this point, her memory conveniently went blank. She did not remember what happened next, but as she wound up at the station house and Leiden had three bullets in his head, she assumed she must have killed him. And why was she walking around with a loaded gun—on the way to the stage, yet? She explained that she "always carried a pistol in her bosom" (even when she was acting?), although other members of the acting troupe had stated that she bought the gun the day before the shooting. On cross-examination, she admitted that she had been especially on edge before the murder because she had heard rumors that she was to be replaced with another actress when the company reached Atlanta. Some cynics thought that was her *real* motive for shooting Leiden.

The next day, the formerly happy-go-lucky Julia, realizing things weren't going so well for her, came tottering into court, dramatically supported by her husband and officers. She seemed weak, nervous, and "suffering great mental anguish," all of which suggests that she may have been a much better actress than her victim Leiden thought. Her attorneys said they would enter an insanity plea if it looked like the self-defense plea was not going to work. Allegedly, they had twenty-five physicians on call to confirm Julia's insanity.

The defense scored some points with a series of depositions taken among stage managers and playhouse employees on the route the *Mr. Plaster of Paris* company had taken before reaching Chattanooga. They agreed unanimously that Leiden "abused and continually insulted Miss Morrison in their presence and on many occasions." But prosecutor

Antz went to Knoxville and secured sworn statements that the would-be fragile flower Morrison hurled unladylike insults right back at Leiden and that her language was more violent and threatening than his. Obviously, the reporters who praised the dainty Julia's "refinement," "gentleness," and excellent manners never had the privilege of seeing her in unguarded moments.

Julia's lawyers had her examined by three leading Chattanooga physicians in hopes of proving she was "emotionally insane" as a result of "nervous weakness," terms so vague as to be meaningless. These doctors made their court appearance on January 8. They revealed that Julia had been kicked in the head by a horse fourteen years before and they thought this injury could later result in "emotional insanity" if she were under pressure. The prosecution cuttingly pointed out that some of the same doctors had also sworn under oath at her application for bail months before that Julia was pregnant, which turned out not to be true.

The defense continued to display witnesses who had heard arguments between Morrison and Leiden. Boyd Browder of Knoxville testified that Leiden said he would replace his starring actress with any woman within a fifty-mile radius if he could. Joseph Breeding, who had testified at an earlier hearing, recalled vociferous altercations between artiste and manager, including one in which they took punches at each other. The defense seemed unaware that this testimony was a sword that cut two ways. While it proved there were bad feelings between Morrison and Leiden, it also made Morrison look as bellicose as Leiden and suggested that she had a motive to kill him since he wanted to fire her at the first opportunity. The defense's most valuable testimony came from Frank Shipp, an opera house worker who said that Leiden had raised a cane as though to strike Morrison before she shot him.

For rebuttal, the state tried to show that the defense's witnesses could not have seen the shooting from the sections of the theater where they claimed to have been standing because curtains would have obstructed their view. A witness for the prosecution stated that Leiden was merely holding his cane (and his hat) before Morrison shot him and had made no threatening gesture with it. Morrison had stated under oath that Leiden made an indecent proposal to her in a bathroom just before the show began, but stage manager Patterson swore that Leiden had been onstage constantly for twenty minutes before the shooting, arranging the stage and getting all the props ready—which was his job, after all. Defense witnesses had said that Leiden struck Morrison in their presence before noon on the day of the murder; contrarily, state witnesses said Morrison had hit Leiden, and that he only raised his arm to ward off the blow.

Both sides finished their cases on January 10, and the jury's verdict came in the afternoon. The gentle flower of womanhood, who packed a good wallop and said she carried a pistol in her bosom at all times, was acquitted to wild cheers in the courtroom. (She had also received a round of applause—nectar to an actress!—when she entered the courtroom that day, which prefigured the verdict. It helps to be young and pretty if you are charged with murder.) The foreman later said that they acquitted her on grounds of self-defense and "emotional insanity." Some critics pointed out that the two defenses were not necessarily logically compatible: could a crazy person be cognizant of personal danger to the point of using self-defense?

As in a scene from a stage melodrama, Morrison was permitted to make a speech before the court "in a strictly Shakespearean style," according to a reporter. Predictably, she thanked her attorneys and the jury. Then she turned toward Mrs. Eva Antz, sister of the murdered Leiden, who had attended every court hearing and burst into tears when the jury decided that her brother's killer would pay no penalty. With unbecoming vindictiveness, Morrison said, "As to my persecutors, I leave them to their consciences and their

Frank Leiden. From the *Chattanooga Times,*
September 24, 1899. Reprinted by courtesy of the
Chattanooga Times Free Press.

God." She added, "I forgive you." Mrs. Antz was heard to
remark, "She killed our brother and now forgives us for it."

After leaving the courtroom, Morrison announced plans
to go on a lecture tour, an action taken by every woman acquitted on a charge of murder in those days, or so it seems.
She would begin her tour in Chattanooga; somebody had
the bad taste to suggest that perhaps she could first appear
in the opera house where she had murdered Leiden. Her
speech was to be called "The Other Side of the Stage," and
its lofty theme was "the dangers that confront the virtuous
girls who are lured from happy homes to follow the stage

as an occupation." A speech on the dangers that confront stage managers might have been good, too.

And then something strange happened—or maybe not so strange. The public, which cheered and hurrahed Julia Morrison as Woman Triumphant when she was acquitted, had second thoughts after their emotions cooled. A day after the verdict, the *Times* polled 215 men; a whopping 70 percent thought Morrison should have received punishment of some sort—and men of the era were notorious for their reluctance to punish women who committed murder. A couple of weeks after Morrison's acquittal, it was reported that her proposed lecture tour was cancelled because public sentiment was against it.

Christmas for the Sims Gang

Bob Sims and his gang of brigands, composed largely of family members, lived near Womack Hill in Choctaw County, Alabama, at the end of the same century that gave the world Abraham Lincoln. Sims differed from the myriad thugs, cutthroats, and gang leaders of his age in that he invented his own religion, the main tenant of which was that everyone—especially its founder—should do exactly what they pleased, regardless of the law. Sims and his followers broke the law in every possible way and used his trumped-up "religion" to justify everything they did.

On or around August 20, 1891, Sims was arrested for running an illegal distillery. His novel argument that God gave him special permission to make moonshine was not generally believed, and he was carted off to jail. Two of his brothers and a son rescued him, shooting a bystander and wounding the sheriff in the process. One Sims brother was killed outright and the son was hurt. A mob relieved the officers of the injured Sims and lynched him. Bob and his brother Neal escaped and terrorized the region. There was no crime on the calendar that the abused citizens would "put past them."

A vigilance committee headed by John McMillan, a Choctaw County merchant, forced Sims and thirty of his admirers to vamoose to Mississippi. While there, according to one account, the holy terror issued "appeals to the Governor of Alabama and the President of the United States, setting forth what a peaceable and law-abiding person he was and what an outrage had been committed upon him." After a few weeks in Mississippi, Sims decided to follow his own creed and move back to Choctaw County no matter what anyone else thought about it.

A couple of days before Christmas 1891, John McMillan was taking stock of a wagonload of merchandise. The desperado Sims rode up, aimed a shotgun at the wagon driver, and forced him to deliver all the goods to the Sims household. As a parting (verbal) shot, Sims told McMillan that he could expect to be murdered and have his house burned—*soon!*

The outlaw was "as good as his word," as Dickens wrote in another, very different sort of Christmas story. On the night of December 23, seven members of Sims's gang set the merchant's house on fire and shot every person who ran out. John McMillan was fatally wounded by three shots; his father-in-law, John Kennedy, was killed, as were a twelve-year-old niece and a ten-year-old nephew. The boy was shot and left to burn in the house. Belle McKenzie, a schoolteacher who boarded with the family, was critically wounded by two bullets through the neck.

After thus putting themselves on Santa's naughty list, the gang gave themselves holiday treats by breaking into McMillan's store and setting it on fire, but not before pilfering every item they wanted. They fled into the night, leaving a trail of abandoned shoes from the store and vowing as they departed that they would return and kill citizens named Dr. Brown and Frank Tate on Christmas Eve. Remarkably, two of the assassins were Sims's daughters, dressed as men and brandishing Winchester rifles.

The gang didn't have a chance to share their peculiar idea of Christmas cheer with Brown and Tate. Sheriff D. C. Gavin (whose name is also given as Calvin and Garvin) and a posse trailed them to their house, located six miles from the scene of the massacre. On Christmas Eve, as children everywhere had visions of sugarplums dancing in their heads, sixty angry men surrounded the Sims house. Shots were exchanged to no effect, except for the capture of gang member John Savage—who was promptly lynched—since the Sims had fortified their cabin in the event of such an onslaught. The sixty men soon swelled to more than seven hundred. The sheriff telegraphed for help, and Governor Jones ordered the First Regiment of state troops to go to Womack Hill. These military men were requested to bring candy canes and gingerbread men for negotiation purposes—pardon, my mistake, they were to bring a six-pounder field piece to blow the cabin into Yule logs if the outlaws did not surrender.

But the military arrived too late to be useful. Hearing that a cannon was on the way, realizing the gang was greatly outnumbered and would run out of stolen provisions eventually, and mindful of what had just happened to John Savage, Bob Sims surrendered. The posse was at first in no mood to

Bob Sims, leader of the gang. From the *Louisville Courier-Journal*, December 29, 1891. Reprinted by courtesy of the *Louisville Courier-Journal*.

bargain with Sims, but since there were womenfolk in the cabin, they agreed to be merciful. At 4:30 A.M., the door opened and the outlaws stepped outside. The posse expected a couple dozen rawboned bruisers; instead, the occupants consisted of Sims, Tom Savage, an unnamed Savage boy, and four women—Mrs. Sims and their daughters. The male and female gang members were taken away in separate wagons. Before they left, Bob Sims begged Sheriff Gavin to protect him from lynch mobs. The lawman said he would do his best and surrounded the wagon with fifty men.

The posse was en route to Butler with their prisoners when they were intercepted by a mob that must have numbered far more than fifty. They hanged Bob Sims and the Savages from an oak tree like stockings hung from the chimney with care.

The Sims women were detained for a day, then released. They unwisely returned to their cabin. The lynching had done nothing to cool the mob's ardor to get the rest of the despised gang. On the night of December 26, Bob's brother John Sims and nephew Mosely Sims were seized and hanged without a trial. For good measure, the mob torched Bob's house to retaliate for the gang's burning of McMillan's house and store. At least they spared Sims's grieving wife and daughters, who hid at a neighbor's house and vowed to reform and leave the state.

As of December 28, John Savage's body still swung from a tree limb, not unlike a gibbeted pirate in days of yore. The bodies of Bob Sims, Tom Savage, and young master Savage were cut down and flung over a graveyard wall, though not buried. Citizens were not yet satisfied. Rumor held that Bob's brother Neal had organized a band of forty desperados who intended to burn every house in Womack Hill. Hence the mob set out to find Neal before he could put his dastardly scheme in place. Reportedly, they found him on January 6, 1892, and celebrated the New Year by hanging him, two gang members who happened to be present, and Bob's daughters Laura and Beatrice. The story was false, but the truth wasn't much better. At the time he was supposed to have been lynched, Neal Sims was in a swamp hiding from people who intended to stretch his neck if they got their hands on him.

A posse tracked down and wounded another gang member, Harry Hinton, in a Marengo County swamp. The authorities were determined that Hinton, at least, would receive a fair trial in a courthouse and did all they could to spare him from the mobs. He was taken to the jail at Butler and guarded like a Fabergé egg. But on January 16, a bloodthirsty throng knocked on Sheriff Gavin's door and requested that he hand over Hinton.

"Hinton has died of his injuries," fibbed the sheriff.

The mob left and mulled that one over for a while. They came back the next day with a simple demand: "Show us the corpse." When none was forthcoming, they broke in, seized Hinton, and manufactured one by hanging him from the same oak that had been adorned with Bob Sims and the Savages. They had to carry him twenty-three miles to Womack Hill to accomplish this, but they must have thought the symbolic value was worth all the trouble.

After Hinton's lynching, tempers finally cooled and the war in Choctaw County came to an end. Belle McKenzie, the schoolteacher, who had been shot by the Sims gang during the raid on the McMillan house, languished until she died in mid-January 1892. Neal Sims escaped before the mob chastised him in its unique way. Allegedly, he took up residence in a swamp in Leake County, Mississippi. Laura and Beatrice, daughters of the infamous Bob, lived at their uncle's house. Let us hope that for the rest of their lives the only unruly crowds they faced were at taffy pulls.

The *New York Times* reported these events in the arch, condescending tone the paper usually adopted when editorializing about violence in the South, implying that every person below the Mason-Dixon Line was an unwashed barbarian. The paper failed to see similarly instructive broad social lessons in horrendous crimes committed by Northerners, details of which graced the pages of the *Times* itself.

Crime and Punishment on the Fast Track

L. Britton Lewis and his wife were among the wealthiest citizens of Levy County, Florida, until the hot summer night they lost everything. Mr. Lewis was found dead from two shotgun blasts on August 29, 1902. Evidence indicated that his wife, America, had been shot in the mouth when she investigated. Two more shots ended her life. Her body was found slumped over his. Whoever committed the double atrocity made an unsuccessful attempt to open Lewis's safe. It was just as well that they did not succeed. Disappointment would have been their portion if they had, since instead of the rumored thousands of dollars, the safe contained only $215.54.

The couple's bodies were found by James Lewis, one of their sons. His wife was ill, and the shock of her in-laws' murder was so great that she expired within little more than a fortnight. One of the Lewis's daughters, Mrs. W. A. Jones of Otter Creek, became sick the day after the crime was discovered and a few days later was reported to be "lying at the point of death . . . in an unconscious condition."

Sheriff Sutton and a large posse searched for multiple killers because two different weapons, a shotgun and a rifle, were used. Within days, four suspects were arrested: Tom Faircloth, S. W. Wilkinson, Joe Martin, and Theodore Smith. Of these, twenty-one-year-old Faircloth was considered the most likely culprit. He could not have behaved more suspiciously if he had tried. He borrowed a shotgun the day before the murder, returned it the day after, and had recently purchased shells identical to empty ones found at the crime scene. Faircloth was taken to the jail at Gainesville since the folks back home in Bronson wished him nothing better than a closed-casket funeral.

On September 12, Faircloth confessed to Gainesville's
Sheriff Fennell. He committed the murders with help from
one of the other suspects, twenty-six-year-old Theodore
Smith. They had spent two months planning the home in-
vasion and gathering their courage before committing it.
Their chief motive, it appears, was that they had a distaste
for manual labor. "Last spring Smith and I were employed
cutting cedar logs in the hammock of Lafayette County,"
related Faircloth.

> We were working hard and it was I who suggested the rob-
> bery. I decided that that would be a good way to make mon-
> ey, and that we could kill the old people, make way with
> their money, and never be detected in the crime.
>
> I knew that the money was kept in an old safe, knew the
> surroundings of the house, and felt certain that if we man-
> aged the thing properly we could succeed. The day before
> the killing we met near Bronson and made up our minds
> to do the work that night. I had no shotgun with me and
> borrowed one from a friend. I was careful in what I did. I
> wanted powder, but was afraid to purchase. Luck came my
> way. Father sent me to purchase ten cents' worth of powder.
> I went to the store and bought a quarter's worth. When I got
> to the house my father and brother were away, and I suc-
> ceeded in taking what I thought to be fifteen cents' worth of
> the powder and some buckshot which my father had in the
> house. With this I left and met my friend, after borrowing
> the shotgun and some empty shells.
>
> We then went a short distance from the house. We ar-
> rived at our place of concealment sometime in the after-
> noon. Late in the evening we advanced to an old grapevine
> where we could hide. There we ate a lot of grapes. We had
> been drinking bitters and were pretty near drunk, and the
> grapes served to sober us considerably.
>
> We had made two billies or cudgels of pinewood knots
> and had determined to knock the aged couple in the head
> in the event that we found them asleep. We advanced to
> the house at dark and found that there was no one at the
> house. We went through the house and found the old man's

gun and rifle. We took the rifle and found that it was loaded. Smith went to the safe with the drill which I had stolen from my father and was working to get an opening for the powder with which we were to crack open the safe. I was on the outside and when I saw the aged couple coming I yelled to Smith, "Here they come now." I had the shotgun and Smith the rifle. When the old man approached the door I shot him in the breast with the gun and shot the old lady in the mouth with the other load. Smith had the rifle and when the old lady attempted to run and scream, he shot her twice in the head and she fell dead. Another shot was fired into the body of the old man to insure death.

When the killing had been done I realized the awful crime, and yelled to my partner to come and get away from the place. He came out with the drill and bit. The drill was lost in going to the gate. We threw the pine cudgels under the house, took the rifle and shotgun and made for the woods as fast as we could travel.

We knew that sooner or later there would be bloodhounds on our trail, and we walked down to the creek for over a mile to throw them off the scent. We parted in the morning. I went to the home of my grandmother and changed my clothes.

I determined to make for the Suwannee River. The bit was secreted under the bridge of the public road at Waccasassa Creek and the rifle was thrown into the stream. You know of the story of my arrest and how I came to be here.

Faircloth ended this Dostoevskian story of crime with a request for corresponding punishment. "I deserve to die and am perfectly willing to die provided that I am permitted to die like a man. I want to die in public to have an opportunity to ask the forgiveness of the people of Florida for my awful crime. I wish you would send me a preacher. I want to prepare for death now." The lawmen brought Rev. J. B. Holley to offer spiritual advice to Faircloth, who certainly was in dire need of it.

Sheriff Fennell arranged to take Faircloth to Levy County so he and Sheriff Sutton could check out the details in the confession and determine its truth. But how could Fennell get Faircloth safely out of the jail and into territory where the very sight of the prisoner would provoke a lynching? The sheriff hit upon the novel idea of darkening Faircloth's skin with burnt cork as though he were auditioning for a minstrel show. The absurd disguise succeeded. In Levy County, the authorities found the drill bit right where Faircloth said it would be. They were unable to retrieve the rifle from the creek due to high water.

The other men arrested on suspicion, Wilkinson and Martin, were released. Theodore Smith, seeing that the game was up, wrote a rambling confession. He started with the sentence, "God knows I did not murder anyone," but a few lines later, he added, "Tom shot Mr. Lewis from inside the yard. Tom told me, 'If you don't kill her I'll kill you.' Then I shot Mrs. Lewis with the rifle." He concluded, "I am sorry for what I have done, but will die brave. I would like to see my brother Jim. I have a wife and two children."

Both Faircloth and Smith came from good families but had reputations for being reckless when drinking. Feelings were so bitter against them that Governor Jennings called a special term of court so they could be tried as quickly as possible. Faircloth agreed with the action, stating that he was ready and willing to pay for his crime but was afraid of being mobbed. Some residents of Bronson stated that they were determined to lynch the prisoners even if they had to travel all the way to Gainesville.

Hamlet complained about the "law's delay" in his most famous soliloquy, so he might have been gratified to see how quickly the wheels of justice turned in the Lewis murder case. Faircloth and Smith knew the death sentence was a certainty and told reporters they would plead guilty and not ask for mercy and would bypass the entire process of having a trial if possible. When they had a court hearing in Bronson on September 20, Faircloth did not even trouble to bring an attorney. Smith did have one, J. A. Williams, who faced a Homeric battle to save his client's neck. Judge W. S. Bullock insisted that there must be a trial and would not allow them to plead guilty. Before the day was over, all of the witnesses had been heard, the evidence had been presented—including the cudgels and the rifle, which had been fished out of the creek—and the jury retired for deliberation. At 10:00 P.M., the verdict was delivered for Faircloth: guilty as sin. Three hours later, Smith received the same verdict. The sentence of hanging was passed at 1:00 A.M. Judge Bullock remarked that it was the "saddest duty of his life" and wondered how the young men could have committed such a brutal and cold-blooded crime. The *Florida Times-Union and Citizen,* a Jacksonville paper, commented:

> The sentence of two young white men to the gallows in Levy County has deeply stirred the sympathies of that community, but the jury and court should be commended and the effect of the punishment preserved for the good of others instead of being lost in maudlin sentiment. We can be sorry for the guilty without condoning the guilt.

The prisoners' families were highly upset, but Faircloth and Smith were content with their lot and displayed coolness that impressed everyone who came into contact with them. They requested that they be hanged just as soon as humanly feasible, and the court obliged them by setting Tuesday, September 30, as the date and Gainesville as the place. This was a deviation from the norm, since executions were usually held on Fridays.

When Sheriff Sutton received the death warrant from the governor, it was lined in black crepe because they knew how to do such things with style in those days. The murderers had repeatedly expressed a wish to "die like men" and their nerve never failed them. They slept like babies on paregoric the night before their execution and ate with good appetites on their final morning. They were given an opportunity to critically inspect their coffins, which they declared "all right." The wreaths atop them also met with their approval, and each wished to know which coffin he was to be buried in. Faircloth's coffin was made watertight so Rev. Holley could baptize him in it. Faircloth, who was engaged to be married when he committed his crime, wanted to have the nuptial ceremony performed right before he stretched hemp, but the sheriff believed this was carrying things a little too far and refused.

The condemned men walked to the gallows with a firm step and addressed the crowd in clear, unfaltering voices, cautioning everyone to avoid bad company and whisky and to lead Christian lives. They beseeched listeners not to place any blame on their poor families, declared they were ready to go, and asked God to bless everyone present— which included the sons and daughters of the Lewises, or at least the ones who had survived the shock of their parents' murder. Faircloth and Smith kissed each other goodbye, something that men could do without raising eyebrows in the days before Dr. Freud altered our collective interpretation of virtually everything. The black caps and ropes were appropriately placed and the traps sprung. Both men's necks were instantly broken; Smith had the added advantage of being nearly decapitated.

At the dead men's request, they were buried side by side in the Smith family burying ground. The Lewises were murdered, their killers found, the trial held, guilt established, the sentence passed, and the executions performed—all within one month!

A Murder Ballad

The date was June 6, 1901, and the black community in Louisville, Kentucky, was horrified by the news that sixteen-year-old Artie Smith had been shot in the head at her Green Alley home by her boyfriend, Matthew Kelley, a waiter at Senning's Hotel. The community did not have much use for Kelley, but everyone sympathized with Smith. After Kelley blew out Smith's brains, he shot himself. Even at this early stage in his career, Kelley felt compelled to express his thoughts, leaving his boss an elaborate farewell on hotel stationery:

Mr. Senning, I am sorry to say I have to leave you. I'm in trouble. I owed everybody. I owe $117.50. I am going to the dogs. I am in disgrace; but it will soon all be over.

Now, good-bye, and kiss mother my last time. The insurance is paid up. Good God will forgive me for this rash act. The hard luck has brought me to this. Good-bye, dear parents. Mother, good-bye; it is all over now. Boys, listen to your dear parents and you will always go right. I wouldn't listen; now I go to the dogs. Take this pistol to 1129 Madison Street. Good-bye, Mr. and Mrs. Senning.

According to a newspaper report, "[P]hysicians at the City Hospital say he has not one chance in a thousand to recover." But that one slender chance was sufficient, and Kelley recuperated after losing his hearing in one ear. He was sentenced to life in prison on January 8, 1902. The Board of Prison Commissioners paroled him on August 3, 1909. Kelley was again free to walk the streets of Louisville—or anywhere else he pleased—and got a job at the

Standard Sanitary Manufacturing Company. The parole board no doubt slept securely in the thought that the thirty-six-year-old Kelley had reformed and would cause society no further trouble.

Despite having murdered his former girlfriend, Kelley had no problem attracting a second one: Clara Hamilton, age twenty-four. He ended her life as well but far more brutally. On the morning of May 20, 1911, Kelley went to Hamilton's apartment at 1027 West Walnut Street. Pearl Evans, age thirty-five, was also there. Kelley crushed their skulls with a hatchet, cut their throats, and nearly beheaded them. Overturned furniture proved that they had not gone gently into that good night. The *Louisville Times*'s description of the scene was more colorful than the *Courier-Journal*'s: "The dead bodies were lying on the bed, their clothing and the floor saturated with blood. The room had the appearance of a slaughter pen, so besplattered [sic] was it with blood." The *Times* man added helpfully, "The heads were hacked and crushed and were held to the neck by strings of flesh."

After committing his atrocious crime, Kelley did not behave the way a normal murderer would. Instead of fleeing, he wrote a six-page confession to the police entitled "To the Officer Who May Arrest Me":

> At 1:30 o'clock this morning I killed two women. First Clara, my sweetheart, then Pearl, my sister-in-law. Thursday night my sister-in-law came in and we got to talking very familiar. Both of us were drinking and Friday she spreads to her lady friends that I insulted her, which I didn't.
>
> There are two other women I got that needs killing. Mollie Smith and Bessie Coffin, but I will let them go.
>
> Laura Davis needs killing. She helped Pearl to hide my dark clothes. Their brothers and sisters will have to bear it the best they can. All I can say is that it will be a hard shock to my friends to hear this of me.
>
> I have had lots of trouble with women and money matters and my white friends are sore on me and I am

worried. . . . Turn all my money over to Walter Evans for
my burial expenses. I believe Laura is safe. She has her
arms crossed awfully nice. This is three women I have
killed in ten years. I will take it easy and before leaving
this and before falling into the hands of the law I will try
to meet my mother in heaven.
   But I am almost a maniac and my heart is stone.
   It is 3 o'clock and I am sleepy, so I'll lay down and sleep.
I can now hear the darkies say "this and that."
   Arevior, but not good-bye.

After thusly unburdening himself in prose, he stretched
out on a lounge and spent the rest of the night sleeping with
untroubled dreams a few feet from the gory corpses. He arose
at 6:00 A.M. and strolled to the corner of Tenth and Walnut,
where he confided his peculiar accomplishment to his friend
Henry Smith. The civic-minded Smith immediately told Patrolman J. W. Hunt, who broke down the door at West Walnut
and stood aghast at the enormity—as did a crowd of more
than one thousand of the unhealthily curious, who came to
look after the word got out. The police kept them from entering the house only due to a determined application of might.
   Kelley called the police at 8:00 A.M. and said they could
pick him up at the entrance to Iroquois Park. The authorities found him right where he promised, chewing gum and
sitting on the curb. As they drove him to the station, said
the *Times*, "Kelley appeared to enjoy the excitement he
had caused, and laughed and talked freely about the crime.
He is displaying a spirit of bravado."
   At the station, Kelley confessed again. His motives were
that Clara Hamilton had been "going with other men" and
that she and Pearl Evans had been "talking about him." He
said that he had intended to murder only Hamilton, but
when his sister-in-law awoke during the proceedings, he felt
it wise to kill her as well. He continued to talk himself into
the electric chair by reiterating that he wasn't remorseful
and could think of two or three other women he wished he
had tomahawked while he was at it.

Kelley was untroubled; he thought an acquittal was in the bag, and he felt that even if convicted he would get a pardon or a parole with ease. He can be excused for thinking that, having been released from prison after serving merely seven years of a life sentence for shooting a woman in the head. It was the duty of the legal system—which had given Kelley a break once before with disastrous results—to make sure that he didn't so easily escape his present predicament. On May 23, only three days after his double homicide, a coroner's jury returned a verdict of murder. He was arraigned in criminal court and refused to enter a plea.

Kelley's trial came in June. He wrote a letter to Jailer Pflanz dripping with pathos, twenty-four karat weirdness, and unconscious humor. He requested that a medium visit him in jail so that he might communicate with the spirits of dead relatives and cohorts, including his victims:

> Mr. Pflanz—Kind Sir: Will you please send me a medium by Thursday, if you please. I will be more [than?] thankful to you. I want to have a talk with my dead friends, mother, Artie, Clara and Pearl.
>
> Please do this for me, Mr. Pflanz? I want to have a talk with them before I die. I want to see how many is up and how many is down. Still, I want to go where mother is. I think she is in heaven. I am guessing about Pearl Evans and Artie Smith.
>
> Mother died with grief about me when I was in prison. I have not but a few nickels. Please let me know what she [the medium] will come up for and have them talk to me. You have them come Thursday, as I can get the money some way, please.
>
> Your unfortunate prisoner and woman lover,
>
> MATTHEW KELLEY.

The record does not reveal whether the medium visited Kelley, but soon he was given the chance to speak to his victims without having to resort to a middleman. Perhaps to make up for the embarrassment wrought by turning Kelley loose prematurely, the jury at his trial on June 23 took less than four minutes to find him guilty. The verdict was not unexpected, considering his numerous detailed, downright eager confessions; Kelley's defense attorney had no conflicting testimony to introduce and did not bother to put his indifferent client on the stand. He was sentenced to be executed on September 28 in the state's newfangled electric chair.

In late August, Kelley was sent to Eddyville to await his sentence. Fellow Louisville murderer Oliver Lock, who had ended his domestic unhappiness by decapitating his wife with a butcher knife in July 1910, preceded Kelley to the chair by a month. Lock left behind a lengthy missive in which he forgave everyone and expressed the wish that he might meet his friend Matthew Kelley in heaven. When Lock was strapped into the chair on August 22, 1911, things did not go as well as they might; he was so strong that he broke the straps while the electricity coursed through his body. The second jolt sent him to the Promised Land. The story of the execution could not have come as welcome tidings to Matthew Kelley. Unfortunately for him, the chair was fixed as good as new a few days after Lock broke it.

Perhaps Lock's unpleasant end was a wake-up call for Kelley, who took up religion with admirable sincerity. On September 2, he was baptized in a prison hallway by the chaplain, Rev. J. A. Holton. Kelley took great comfort from repeated readings of the twenty-fifth chapter of the Gospel of John and wrote another extraordinary letter to his jailer in which he claimed that he had repented after having served Satan and his imps for eleven years.

To my kind jailer and jail officials: I thank you all for the kindness and courtesy you have shown to me since I have been here. May God bless each and every one of you. I may write back to you all again before leaving this old sinful world. I knew not that I was going away untill this morning. I was call and notified. I thank God that I was and am ready for his call at any time, as he has promised me after all a home in his peaceable kingdom.

I have not had any peace in this world for eleven years, serving the devil and his angels. I thank God that He has heard my prayers. It seem to me I have wrong my best friends only. I was good and a peacefull boy, but I just could not get along with the women, in misery all the time. I am still praying and trusting God to let me in his peacefull kingdom on the day of resurection. Men repent of your sin and get ready to die. I mean to-day, for we might be called to-night while we are asleeping. I am glad now that I listened to Brother Oliver Lock. He told me to pray. I says: "Brother Oliver, I am so full of sin and have committed so many crimes. I can't pray," and he kept right on after me. I went to pray and said and meant it. I want Jesus to relieve me of this burden.

I had intended to committ suicide, but it seem like my dead mother stood in front of me one night and said, "Meet me in heaven."

I feel now that I will not only meet her, but all who will come to Jesus and do his will.

                                        MATTHEW KELLEY.

One wonders whether Kelley had Clara Hamilton and Pearl Evans in mind when he wrote that "we might be called to-night while we are asleeping" since those were exactly the circumstances under which he had dispatched them.

On September 28, Matthew Kelley entered the execution chamber wearing a spiffy new suit. He remarked, "This is the last time I will dress in this world, but I will next put on a white robe in heaven, which will last forever." These were probably his last words. Unlike Oliver Lock, Kelley was dead only ten seconds after the first current was applied. He was the fourth man to be executed in Kentucky's electric chair.

While Matthew Kelley is forgotten today, his gruesome murders must have been of abiding interest in Louisville. British blues aficionado John Newman has noted that Kelley's murders were the subject of a song, "Clair and Pearly Blues," recorded in Louisville by Cincinnati bluesman Kid Coley on the Victor label in 1931—two long decades after the incident. The song was co-written by Coley and Louisville musician Clifford Hayes; Coley appears to have also been known as Walter Cole, Walter Coleman, Bob Coleman, Kid Cole and (best of all) Sweet Papa Tadpole. The lyrics re-create the details of the crime with a minimum of artistic license, right down to Kelley's last words:

> Now, come listen, people, while I sing one song so lonesome and so blue.
> Now, come listen, people, while I sing one sad song
> 'Bout two girls that I really knows well, and I haven't composed it wrong.

> It was on one Friday, between midnight and day, so lonesome and so blue,
> It was on one Friday, between midnight and day
> That Clara and Pearl, Matthew Kelley laid these two girls away.

> Now, Clara and Pearl lay down to go to sleep in their lonesome bed, I mean;
> Now, Clara and Pearl lay down to go to sleep;
> Matthew Kelley woke up and through their back door did creep.

> First he had a butcher knife, some dirty work to do, so lonesome and so blue;
> First he had a butcher knife, some dirty work to do;
> He suddenly glanced himself a hatchet, said, "I swear I'm gonna fix both of you two."

> Finally, Matthew Kelley approached them, found the girls still asleep in their lonesome bed, I mean;
> Finally, Matthew approached them, found the girls both still asleep;
> Matthew Kelley buried the hatchet in poor Clara's head deep.

> Matthew Kelley walked to the electric chair with his hair combed out in a curl, so lonesome and so blue.
> Matthew walked to the electric chair with his hair all out in a curl;

Tryin' on a brand new suit of clothes, Matthew said, "It'll be the last I try on in this world."

Now, if anybody should happen to ask you who in the world wrote such a song, so lonesome and so blue;
If anybody should happen to ask you who in the world wrote such a sad song,
Tell them it was Kid Coley and he never composed it wrong, and it wasn't no lie.

The Reprehensible Mr. Powers

Mrs. Asta Buick Eicher was delighted in the summer of 1931, for she had received another love letter from Cornelius O. Pierson. He had gotten her address from a matrimonial bureau, the American Friendship Society of Detroit, and had been wooing her via the mail for some time. In his most recent letter, he asked if she would be willing to move from her home in Park Ridge, Illinois, to his home in Quiet Dell, West Virginia, a suburb of Clarksburg. Of course she was welcome to bring her three children: Greta, age fourteen; Harry, age twelve; and Annabel, age nine. It was an offer the fifty-year-old widow could not turn down. Her husband Henri, a silversmith, had left her a home and a modest income when he died in 1927, but it could not hurt to have more money in these bleak early days of the Great Depression. The children were growing up and she needed help raising them. Besides all that, she was lonesome. Though she was of an artistic bent, music and painting had not been enough to assuage her grief.

Mrs. Eicher's friends pointed out that she really did not know much about this Mr. Pierson. His matrimonial ad could not have sounded fishier. It read as follows:

Civil engineer, college education. Worth $150,000 or more, has income from $400 to $3,000 per month. My business enterprises prevent me from making many social contacts. I am unable, therefore, to make the acquaintance of the right kind of women. As my properties are located through the Middle West, I believe I will settle there when married. Am an Elk and a Mason. Own a beautiful ten-room home, completely furnished. My wife would have her own car and plenty of spending money. Cornelius O. Pierson, P.O. Box 277, Clarksburg, W. Va.

In order to believe all of this, Mrs. Eicher had to take Mr. Pierson's word for it. Blinded by infatuation, she never bothered to ascertain whether such a person actually existed in Clarksburg.

The widow was not to be deterred by her friends' warnings. The letters from Pierson kept coming, peppered with romantic phrases he had cribbed from "Advice to the Lovelorn" newspaper columns and bits of sentimental poetry. When her correspondent came calling in person on June 22, 1931, she told neighbors he was "just an old friend of the family." Pierson left for home on June 27, but the next day Mrs. Eicher packed her valuables and drove to West Virginia. A few days later, Mr. Pierson returned in a car bearing West Virginia license plates. He came to retrieve the Eicher children, who had been left in the care of Elizabeth Abernathy, a nurse, and a boarder named Jack Williams. Pierson promised the children a trip to Europe and extravagant gifts. Greta would receive a small toy automobile and a piano; Harry, a pony and a dog; Annabel, a doll and a chance to study the violin in Europe. According to nurse Abernathy, the driver left in such a hurry on July 2 that the children did not even get to change out of their bathing suits.

A month after she arrived in Quiet Dell, Mrs. Eicher met a woman in the very same boat, fifty-year-old Dorothy Pressler Lemke of Worcester, Massachusetts. Mrs. Lemke was under the impression that she was about to marry Mr. Pierson, whom she knew from his correspondence as D. P. Lowther. She also had met the letter writer through the American Friendship Society, and he had brought her to West Virginia on July 28. We can only wonder what the women felt when they realized the same man had promised them both marriage and a good life, but they did not have much longer to be troubled by puzzles and contradictions.

After several days passed without Mrs. Eicher's sending word to friends and relatives back home, Park Ridge chief of police Harold Johnson became suspicious. His doubts were fattened when Mr. Pierson came back to Park Ridge the third week of August and laid legal claim to the Eicher home. Johnson found Pierson stacking the widow's furniture in her garage; the chief of police challenged Pierson to come to the station the next day and prove the house had been sold. Instead, Pierson fled town.

A few days later, Chief Johnson entered the deserted Eicher residence. He found several of Mr. Pierson's love letters to the widow in her house and informed the Clarksburg, West Virginia, police about his misgivings. The authorities quickly traced Pierson's post office box and made discoveries that would have been to Mrs. Eicher's advantage had she done a little amateur detective work. The man claiming to be Cornelius O. Pierson was actually Harry F. Powers; that may not have been his real name, as some contend he was born Herman Drenth. Various sources give his age as ranging from thirty-eight to forty-five. He was not a civil engineer but the owner of a grocery store in the Broad Oaks section of Clarksburg. Powers was neither suave nor rich; he was short, pudgy, adorned with horn-rimmed glasses that covered tiny blue eyes, and ugly enough to breed the bogeyman. He had served time in other states for defrauding widows. In addition to these shortcomings, he already had a wife named Luella, whom he had married in 1927. Worst of all, he considered murder a *career,* not a job.

Powers was arrested despite his protests that Mrs. Eicher was alive and had gone to Colorado to marry another man.

At this stage in the investigation, the police knew the Eichers had disappeared and that their destination had been the farm of the pseudonymous Mr. Powers. Suspicion immediately centered on a garage on Powers's property that he had constructed in June 1931. He never seemed to use the windowless garage for any functional purpose, but locals had seen him going there late at night. Clarksburg chief of police Clarence Duckworth inspected the building and found a trunk containing Mrs. Eicher's clothing, jewelry, and correspondence with "Pierson." Also found were several pairs of children's shoes, clothes belonging to many different women, and a ring engraved "C. O. P. to E. F." Another trunk held fifty photographs of women, a book listing a hundred birthdates, and several guns.

On August 28, officers found the remains of the four Eichers in a shallow grave beneath the floor of the garage. Each body had been buried in an individual burlap sack. Coroner Leroy Goff determined that the women had been strangled, but Harry Eicher had died of blunt force trauma to the head. A ball peen hammer found in Powers's garage matched fractures in the boy's skull. Another sinister discovery was found in the garage: a trapdoor, over which dangled a rope tied to a rafter. It looked like a homemade gallows.

The next day, the body of Mrs. Lemke was found buried in a sewer trench, her hands still bound before her and a piece of webbing around her neck. A Baptist minister, T. E. Gainer, persuaded Powers to confess, which he did verbally and then in writing, "crying like a baby" all the while. He insisted that his wife Luella knew nothing of his murderous proclivities; she seemed unmoved by the charges against her husband and, when she visited the prison, declared that she would "stick by him." (She had met him, as seems only fit, after a "mail courtship.") No doubt he was glad to get the support, for already threats of lynching against "the American Bluebeard" had inspired Sheriff Will Grimm to call out the state police to guard Powers. By September 2, however, Mrs. Powers had changed her tune, declaring that she wouldn't have him out of jail for $100 million.

It took Harry Powers a couple of days to finally confess all the ghastly details of his slayings. He had fancied the place where he committed the killings his "murder farm" and had built the garage to provide an ideal private site for perpetrating his deeds. He told police that he had killed all four Eichers and Mrs. Lemke on the same day, around

August 1—he seemed unsure of the date. (Powers was in error, as a receipt proved that Mrs. Eicher had purchased silverware in Chicago on that date.) He forced each member of the Eicher family into individual soundproof tile chambers he had constructed in the garage's basement. When Mrs. Lemke arrived from Massachusetts later, he imprisoned her there as well. One by one, he brought his prisoners upstairs and hanged them from his gallows and then beat the corpses' heads with a hammer, just to make sure. Sadistically, he made Harry Eicher watch the execution of his family, then he bludgeoned the boy: "I was permitting little Harry Eicher to watch the killing of his mother and the others, but in the middle of it he let out an awful scream. I was afraid the neighbors would hear it so I picked up a hammer and let him have it." It is unclear how much money and property Powers gained from his dastardly scheme, but a relative of Mrs. Lemke's claimed that she left her home in Massachusetts with $4,287 in cash, up to $8,000 worth of bonds, and jewelry valued at $1,500. Ironically, after Mrs. Eicher's death, it was revealed that she was far from being the wealthy widow Powers expected; her home had been heavily mortgaged and she was in considerable debt.

Powers admitted that under pen names he had been writing to lonely women all over the country via matrimonial agencies in hopes of obtaining their property and bank accounts, with intentions to kill them once he lured them to his "murder farm" in Quiet Dell. After his arrest, he continued to receive letters from unwitting correspondents at the rate of about twenty per day. When arrested, he was about to mail five more letters, including one to a woman in Hagerstown, Maryland, whom he had been planning to visit. Had Powers's career not been nipped in the bud, he might have killed many more unsuspecting women. Even so, his final toll may have been more than five victims. Detectives found hundreds of letters from women from all over the country hidden in Powers's house and garage. One woman who may have barely escaped an awful death was Edith

Simpson of Detroit, who had corresponded with "Pierson" and was scheduled to marry him in September 1931. She had already bought her wedding dress. Police in Washington, D.C., suspected that Powers had killed Mary Baker, a navy department stenographer, in 1930. Mrs. J. B. Dawson, a boardinghouse owner in Morris, Illinois, claimed Powers had rented a garage from her two years previously and fled town just before the body of an unidentified woman was found in a ditch on Labor Day 1929. The mysterious stranger had posed as a paint salesman, driven a car with West Virginia license plates, and called himself Powers.

(Powers is sometimes referred to as an early American serial killer, but the label does not fit him well. The typical serial killer murders for the fun of it; despite the depraved cruelty of Powers's murders, his ultimate goal was always financial profit.)

When police asked Powers how many people he had killed, he answered with a shrug: "I don't know." Convicts dug all over Powers's property and a high-tech apparatus was used to drill in his well, but no more bodies were unearthed. Several bones found near the fireplace of an abandoned cottage on his property turned out to be sheep bones. The "murder farm" attracted crowds hoping to find an overlooked corpse or at least see the garage where the atrocities occurred; an enterprising leaseholder put up a wooden fence so the mob would have to pay admittance, but indignant sightseers burned it down. The leaseholder retorted with a sheet iron fence, and tourists again had to pay for their thrills. They didn't find any bodies, either. By December, the milling crowds had destroyed Powers's infamous garage.

Powers claimed that a head injury he had received during military training in World War I caused him to see visions and have "uncontrollable impulses." He intended to plead insanity and claimed, "I never have confessed and I'll tell my story at the trial. I have no interest in religion and only called the minister to get out of the agony which officers were putting me in." But Dr. Edwin Mayer, a psychiatrist from the

University of Pittsburgh, examined Powers and declared him legally sane: "He is perfectly normal as to physical brain diseases. Powers is a psychopathic personality. He is not insane, but has been a borderline case all his life. He is capable of distinguishing between right and wrong."

The police detained Powers's wife Luella Strother Powers and her sister, Eva Belle Strother, because they disbelieved the prisoner's assurance that his wife knew nothing of the murders. Silver belonging to Mrs. Eicher was found in the Powers house, as well as clothing labeled with the names of both Mrs. Eicher and Mrs. Lemke. It appears the women told a convincing story, for neither faced charges. West Virginians proved less inclined to show mercy to Harry Powers; nearly a month after his arrest he still faced the possibility of being lynched. By September 20, the public's indignation manifested in the form of a crowd of 4,000 surrounding the Harrison County jail. The fire department arrived to hose the crowd down if necessary, but the mob cut their hoses. Deputies arrested three ringleaders; city, county, and state officers set off tear gas, which had the desired effect of encouraging the crowd to go elsewhere. The authorities took the further precaution of spiriting the weeping Powers away to the jail at Moundsville. Prophetically, though Powers still had not gone to trial, he was placed in a cell on Death Row for safekeeping.

When Powers's trial began on December 7, 1931, for the murder of Mrs. Lemke, the Clarksburg courthouse was in a state of reconstruction. He was tried instead in Moore's Opera House before a capacity crowd of 1,200. The *New York Times* reported the surreal blend of grotesque reality and airy fantasy that marked the makeshift courtroom; the murderer was flanked by papier-mâché trees and behind Judge John Southern stood a painted backdrop showing a "typical small town street" complete with a church. Reporters filled the orchestra pit and box seats. Sidney Whipple, a United Press reporter, thought Powers seemed, of all the characters onstage, "the coolest, the most self-possessed, the actor with the greatest stage presence." The trial drew a much larger crowd than the film playing at the opera house, *The Guardsman.*

Powers, never the object of much sympathy to begin with, did not improve his image with his incessant gum chewing or by yawning as the prosecution accused him of the murders of two women and three children. He showed little emotion throughout the trial, even when the prosecution urged that he receive the death penalty. Out on the street, a carnival atmosphere reigned; hawkers sold photographs of Powers, his garage, and the victims' bodies, as well as quickly printed books about the local atrocities and copies of a murder ballad called "The Crime at Quiet Dell."

Defense attorney J. Ed Law requested a change of venue on the grounds that a local jury would not give his client a fair trial. Judge Southern denied the motion. Law also expressed the touching belief that despite the evidence against Powers, including his freely given confession, "the State would not be able to prove its case." The prosecution dashed Law's dreams by displaying Mrs. Lemke's clothing, including a bloody dress, all of which had been found in Powers's house; by putting on the stand Mrs. Lemke's sister and brother-in-law, who positively identified Powers as the man who had visited the victim in Massachusetts; and by providing witnesses who saw Powers digging a hole near his "death garage."

When Powers took the stand on December 9, he did plenty of crying and claimed he had been nearly driven crazy by his unhappy marriage. He also claimed that two other men, Cecil Johnson and Charles Rogers, had committed the murders. Johnson, he said, had stolen Mrs. Lemke from him in Uniontown, Pennsylvania, and Rogers had a key to the garage. Maybe it was not just happenstance that "Charles Rogers" was one of the many aliases Powers employed when wooing widows by mail. The jury did not buy his story; they met on December 10 in one of the opera house's basement dressing rooms and pronounced Powers guilty after deliberating less than two hours. The prisoner chewed gum as the dreaded sentence was read. Despite defense attorney Law's pleas for Powers to receive life in prison, the killer's hanging was set for March 18, 1932. In a reversal of traditional roles, Law became so agitated while pleading for his client's life that the dispassionate Powers repeatedly tried to calm him down. "He seemed puzzled by Law's display of emotion," wrote an Associated Press reporter.

Law argued for a new trial on December 12, but the motion was overruled and Judge Southern fixed March 1, 1932, as the limit for appeals. Powers was more concerned with getting a chicken dinner that night at the jail and laughed as he was led back to his cell. Noticing a looped electrical wire hanging near a stage door, he wisecracked, "There's the noose!"

Powers rarely lost his nerve while awaiting his final day in Moundsville State Penitentiary. He told reporters that he had written a song and expressed the wish that the royalties would go to his soon-to-be widow Luella. They must have reconciled, since she sent him a letter just hours before his death:

> I am heartbroken and so distressed I can hardly live. Oh, I think it is terrible to give you up under such circumstances. Oh, Harry, dear, may God have mercy on you and when you are through with the trials and troubles in this life, may you have a home in heaven where there is no sorrow and some sweet day I will come to see you, dear, and live forever with you. . . . If I get your letter in time, I will write again, dear. If not, I shall say goodbye forever.

Powers was on the verge of a nervous breakdown an hour before his death, but he quickly regained his composure and walked to the gallows with a smile on his face. He was hanged at 9:00 P.M. on March 18 and pronounced dead eleven minutes later. He was such a universally reviled human that, so far as I can tell, his death was unlamented even by those tender souls who make it their business to generate petitions in an attempt to spare murderers the death penalty and keep them alive in prison where they can plot further mischief.

Harry Powers claimed innocence several times, but admitted his guilt in a hefty 50,000-word confession written to a Clarksburg physician, H. H. Haynes. Immediately after Powers's execution, Dr. Haynes announced plans to sell the letter to the highest bidder, explaining "that the proceeds would reimburse him for financial aid he gave Powers in his legal fight to evade death on the gallows." The confession was corroborated by prison guards, who stated that the convict privately had admitted to all five murders, plus one hitherto unsuspected. Dudley C. White, a Clarksburg salesman, had disappeared in 1928. He and Powers were coworkers at a carpet factory. Powers, who became head of the agency after White vanished, told police that White had stolen some of the company's sweepers and run away. After Powers's arrest for the Eicher-Lemke slayings, police found the missing sweepers in his garage.

Harry Powers was buried in the Whitegate Penitentiary Cemetery in Moundsville. He unknowingly made a mark in the worlds of literature and cinema. The Southern author Davis Grubb was from Clarksburg, and Powers was the prototype for the deranged preacher/serial killer Harry Powell in Grubb's novel *Night of the Hunter*. The story was made into a classic film in 1955, with Robert Mitchum turning in an unforgettable performance as the psychotic Powell.

Bibliography

The Axman Came from Hell

Douglas, John, and Mark Olshaker. *The Cases That Haunt Us*. New York: Pocket Books, 2001.

Louisville Courier-Journal, "Taylor Had Clipping . . .," February 9, 1922.

Monfre, Joseph. Death certificate. State of California Department of Health Services, state file number 75-015613.

Monfre, Joseph. Louisiana State Penitentiary record number 4724. *Register of Convicts Received 3801 to 6800, Sept. 17, 1907 to Dec. 5, 1911*. Courtesy of the Louisiana Secretary of State: Archives Division.

New Orleans Daily Picayune, "Another Mysterious Murder: Sleeping Grocer Again Victim," May 17, 1912.

———, "Beaten by Burglars," September 20, 1910.

———, "The Black Hand Case," January 10, 1908.

———, "Black Hand Outrage," December 6, 1907.

———, "Black Hand Outrage," December 9, 1907.

———, "Bomb Thrower is Found Guilty," May 22, 1908.

———, "Burglar with Stolen Cleaver Attacks August Coutti [*sic*] Abed," August 14, 1910.

———, "Cleaver Murder Deemed Black Hand . . .," July 2, 1911.

———, "Cleaver Mystery." *New Orleans Daily Picayune*, July 3, 1911, 5.

———, "Cleaver Mystery Still Unsolved . . .," July 4, 1911.

———, "Cleaver Still Mystery," *New Orleans Daily Picayune*, June 30, 1911.

———, "Couple Attacked in Their Bed; Motive Seems Deep Mystery," September 21, 1910.

———, "Cowardly Assassinations," June 29, 1911.

———, "Davi Dies From Cleaver's Wounds . . .," June 29, 1911.

———, "Davi Mystery," July 14, 1911.

———, "Davi's Wife Dreams of Slain Spouse and Digs Up Black Hand Letters," August 3, 1911.

———, "Fiendish Cleaver Abroad Again, and Joseph Davi Will Die From Blow," June 28, 1911.

———, "Governor Offers $500 Reward for Conviction Davi Murderers," July 1, 1911.

———, "Hair Dresser Durel Found Murdered," July 10, 1908.

———, "Is the Axe-Man Type of Jekyll-Hyde Concept?" August 13, 1918.

———, "Marrerro Takes Monfre," April 16, 1908.

———, "Mme. Durel Only Bidder," September 8, 1908.

———, "Money of Durel Found . . .," July 11, 1908.

———, "Monfre Convicted in Quick Time," July 25, 1908.

———, "Monfre on Trial for Dynamiting," July 24, 1908.

———, "Monfre Still Fights," December 12, 1908.

———, "Mrs. Davi Moved," July 6, 1911.

———, "Mrs. Durel Hurries Home . . .," July 14, 1908.

———, "Mrs. Durel's Death," December 10, 1908.

———, "Mrs. Lowe Removed to Besemer Home," July 15, 1918.

———, "Mrs. Sciambra Succumbs . . .," May 27, 1912.

———, "Mrs. Sciambra's Crisis," May 19, 1912.

———, "Not the Negress," July 20, 1908.

———, "Old Man Pepitone Gets Twenty Years," August 10, 1910.

———, "Petrich and Monfre Sentenced By Court," August 22, 1908.

———, "Pizzo, a Davi Murder Suspect . . .," August 5, 1911.

———, "Rissetto and Wife Have Affectionate Meeting in Hospital." September 27, 1910.

———, "Rissetto Attack Remains Mystery, with Wife Slowly Sinking," September 22, 1910.

————, "Rissetto Dead," November 25, 1912.

————, "Rissetto Mystery," September 23, 1910.

————, "Rissetto Suspects," September 24, 1910.

————, "Several Arrests Made," December 7, 1907.

————, "Wife Will Live," May 18, 1912.

New Orleans Police Department. Report of Homicide: Joseph Davi. June 28, 1911. New Orleans Public Library, Louisiana Division.

————. Report of Homicide: Anthony J. Sciambra. May 16, 1912. New Orleans Public Library, Louisiana Division.

————. Report of Homicide: Mrs. Anthony J. Sciambra. May 26, 1912. New Orleans Public Library, Louisiana Division.

————. Report of Homicide: Mr. and Mrs. Joseph Maggio. May 23, 1918. New Orleans Public Library, Louisiana Division.

————. Report of Homicide: Harriet Anna Loew [*sic*]. September 16, 1918. New Orleans Public Library, Louisiana Division.

————. Report of Homicide: Joseph Romino [*sic*]. August 10, 1918. New Orleans Public Library, Louisiana Division.

————. Report of Homicide: Mike Pipetone [*sic*]. October 27, 1919. New Orleans Public Library, Louisiana Division.

New Orleans Times-Picayune, "Algiers and Gretna Daily News Budget," July11, 1916.

————, "Another Hatchet Mystery; Man and Wife Near Death," June 28, 1918.

————, "Beaten with Bar, Grocer May Die of His Injuries," October 27, 1919.

————, "Besemer Aids Detectives in Probing Own Mystery," July 4, 1918.

————, "Bloody Clothing Found on Scene of Maggio Crime," May 25, 1918.

————, "Brother's Razor Involves Him in Double Killing," May 24, 1918.

————, "Concussion Caused by Laumann Attack," August 5, 1919.

———, "Deaths: Pipitone-Albano," August 25, 1940.

———, "The Durel Murder," July 15, 1908.

———, "Elder Jordano is Accused in Gretna Axman Tragedy," March 18, 1919.

———, "Girl of 19 is Attacked by Mysterious Axman," August 4, 1919.

———, "Gretna Italians Latest Victims of Axe Murderer," March 10, 1919.

———, "Gross Brutality Charged Against an Angry Father," September 13, 1919.

———, "Mystery!" July 3, 1918.

———, "Mystery Shrouds Murderous Attack on Uptown Grocer," December 23, 1917.

———, "Neighbor Named by Victims Held For Ax Assaults," March 15, 1919.

———, "Pepitone Murder Due to Vendetta, Theory of Police," October 28, 1919.

———, "Police Believe Ax-Man May Be Active in City," August 6, 1918.

———, "Police Puzzled by Many Angles in Hatchet Case," June 30, 1918.

———, "Police Still Without Clue to Slayers of Pepitone," October 29, 1919.

———, "Police Superintendent Believes Ax Murders Are Work of One Man," March 16, 1919.

———, "Victim of Ax-Man Now Happy Mother." August 7, 1918.

———, "Who'll Be Next Is the Question Italians Asking," August 11, 1918.

———, "Wounded Woman Expected to Give Clue to Axman," March 11, 1919.

Newton, Michael. *The Encyclopedia of Unsolved Crimes*. New York: Facts on File, 2004.

Ortolano, Karen. E-mail to author. January 10, 2005.

Reid, Ed. *Mafia*. New York: Random House, 1952.

Tallant, Robert. *Ready to Hang*. New York: Harper and Bros., 1952.

Birmingham Ax Murders

Birmingham News, "Another Merchant and Wife Fall Victims . . .," November 7, 1922.

———, "Arrest Expected in Axe Assault," October 2, 1922.

———, "Axe Victims Here Still Unconscious . . .," January 25, 1923.

———, "Charley Graffeo is 19th Victim in Grocery Attacks," May 29, 1923.

———, "Fingerprints May Release Negroes . . .," January 12, 1922.

———, "Four Are Killed, Two By Axe Fiend . . .," December 21, 1921.

———, "Fourteen Killed in 18 Assaults...," October 23, 1923.

———, "Grocer Assaulted by Negro Thugs," March 6, 1921.

———, "Hammer Victims Expected to Live," June 5, 1922.

———, "Man Hit By Negro Axeman Succumbs," November 8, 1922.

———, "Merchant Bound, Gagged, Robbed, Beaten . . .," December 24, 1919.

———, "No Clues in Dorsky Case." August 12, 1921.

———, "No Clues Left by Belser's Slayers . . .," December 26, 1919.

———, "Police Baffled Over Slaying of Grain Merchant." January 11, 1923.

———, "Robbery Believed Motive in Attack . . .," January 11, 1922.

———, "Second Victim of Axe Assailant is Dead . . .," October 25, 1923.

———, "Storekeeper and Wife Axe Victims . . .," January 24, 1923.

———, "Storekeeper is Knocked in Head and then Robbed," August 17, 1921.

———, "Storekeeper, 60, Victim of Axeman," October 1, 1922.

———, "Storekeeper, Wife and Child Victims of an Axe Assault," July 13, 1921.

———, "Tells of Attack: Klein Assault . . .," January 25, 1923.

———, "Two in Hospital as 'Axeman' With Hammer Returns," June 4, 1922.

———, "Two Near Death in Axe Assault . . .," January 26, 1922.

———, "Vitellaro Attack Twenty-Sixth Ax Case, Unsolved," January 24, 1923.

———, "Vitellaro, Victim…Dies in Hospital," January 30, 1923.

———, "Woman Fatally Injured as Fiend Wields Meat Axe," October 23, 1923.

———, "Woman is Hit in Head and Robbed by Thugs," September 6, 1921.

Kazek, Kelly. *Forgotten Tales of Alabama*. Charleston, S.C.: The History Press, 2010.

Louisville Courier-Journal, "Ax Slayings Stir Hysteria," February 5, 1922.

New York Times, "Axe Murders Reach 20," October 24, 1923.

A Sharp Retort for Professor Turner

Baton Rouge State Times, "Brothers Say Dead Man Did Not Have Enemy," June 8, 1925.

———, "Coroner's Query in Murder Likely to Close Tonight," June 16, 1925.

———, "Crime Horrifies City," June 8, 1925.

———, "Expert Says Printing of Fingers Was Very Successful," June 10, 1925.

———, "Faculty and Students Pay Their Final Tribute to Prof. Turner," June 9, 1925.

———, "Fifth Day Ends With Murder Mystery Little Nearer Final Solution," June 11, 1925.

———, "Fingerprint Expert Busy as Axe Murder Mystery Grows Deeper," June 8, 1925.

———, "Fingerprints May Furnish New Clues in Turner Murder," June 9, 1925.

———, "Lone Fingerprint of Blood May Prove Solution of Murder," June 10, 1925.

————, "Members O. B. Turner's Agronomy Class Are Questioned," June 8, 1925.

————, "Negro Janitor Questioned but Later is Released," June 9, 1925.

————, "Officers Have Reached End in Mystery," June 12, 1925.

————, "Renew Effort Solve Turner Murder Riddle," June 15, 1925.

————, "Solving the Mystery," June 10, 1925.

East, Charles. "Murder at LSU!" *Baton Rouge Morning Advocate Magazine*, March 19, 1950.

Houston Post-Dispatch, "Ax Victim's Books New Murder Clue," June 10, 1925.

————, "Louisiana University Teacher Murdered." June 8, 1925.

————, "Mistaken Identity Latest Ax Theory," June 12, 1925.

————, "University Murder is Still Unsolved," June 9, 1925.

The Servant Girl Annihilator

Austin Daily Statesman, "Alleged Outrages," November 12, 1885.

————, "Another Clew," February 3, 1886.

————, "Another Outrage," March 10, 1885.

————, "Around Austin," February 24, 1885.

————, "Around Austin," March 31, 1885.

————, "Around Austin," May 1, 1885.

————, "Around Austin," May 15, 1885.

————, "Around Austin," May 20, 1885.

————, "Arrest of Hancock," editorial, January 28, 1886.

————, "At It Again," April 30, 1885.

————, "An Atrocious Crime," September 1, 1885.

————, "Austin Affairs." January 26, 1885.

————, "Bad Blacks," March 14, 1885.

————, "Blood! Blood! Blood!" December 25, 1885.

————, "Bloody Work," January 1, 1885.

————, "Bound to Stop It," March 21, 1885.

————, "The Colored People Aroused," September 2, 1885.

————, "The Colored People Moving," September 3, 1885.

————, "A Colossal Star Chamber," February 12, 1886.

————, "County Jail Notes," October 14, 1885.

————, "The Courts," May 29, 1886.

————, "The Courts," May 30, 1886.

————, "The Courts," June 6, 1886.

————, "The Courts," June 23, 1886.

————, "Decisive Action," January 3, 1886.

————, "Devilish Deeds," March 20, 1885.

————, "The Eighth Victim," December 30, 1885.

————, "Examining Trial," May 14, 1885.

————, "The Father Speaks," January 3, 1886.

————, "The Foul Fiends," May 8, 1885.

————, "Gave Bond," June 10, 1886.

————, "Golden Nuggets," July 23, 1885.

————, "Golden Nuggets," September 4, 1885.

————, "Golden Nuggets," September 15, 1885.

————, "Golden Nuggets," September 16, 1885.

————, "A Great Trial," June 19, 1886.

————, "Hancock," January 30, 1886.

————, "Hancock Arrested," January 28, 1886.

————, "The Hancock Case," January 30, 1886.

————, "The Hancock Case," January 31, 1886.

————, "The Hancock Case," February 5, 1886.

————, "The Hancock Case," June 18, 1886.

————, "The Hancock Case," June 22, 1886.

————, "The Hancock Case," editorial, June 23, 1886.

————, "Hancock Horror," December 29, 1885.

————, "Hancock Talks," January 29, 1886.

————, "Home Happenings," January 3, 1885.

————, "Home Happenings," January 8, 1885.

————, "Houston's Detectives," October 3, 1885.

————, "Important Action," December 27, 1885.

————, "Important Arrest," December 30, 1885.

————, "An Inefficient Police," September 2, 1885.

————, "The Inquest Ended," January 6, 1885.

————, "An Inquiry Answered," June 6, 1885.

————, "In the Toils Again," June 5, 1886.

————, "James Phillips Arrested," January 2, 1886.

————, "Let Justice Reign," April 24, 1886.

————, "Local Short Stops," October 10, 1885.

————, "Local Short Stops," December 23, 1885.

————, "Local Short Stops," November 16, 1885.

————, "Local Short Stops," December 30, 1885.

————, "Local Short Stops," April 27, 1886.

————, "Lynch Law," January 22, 1886.

————, "Midnight Outrages," December 28, 1885.

————, "The Monday Morning Tragedy," editorial, September 30, 1885.

————, "More Butchery," May 23, 1885.

————, "More Mischief," May 2, 1885.

————, "The Murders," October 1, 1885.

————, "A Mystery," May 27, 1886.

————, "Nothing New," January 3, 1885.

————, "One More Unfortunate," May 26, 1885.

————, "The Other Side of That Sensational 'Monstrous Outrage,'" October 16, 1885.

————, "Over the City," March 17, 1885.

————, "Over the City," March 19, 1885.

————, "Over the City," March 27, 1885.

————, "Over the City," May 29, 1885.

————, "Over the City," June 11, 1885.

————, "Patty Scott," February 5, 1886.

————, "Phillips," May 28, 1886.

————, "The Phillips Case," February 13, 1886.

————, "The Phillips Case," February 17, 1886.

————, "The Phillips Case," April 28, 1886.

————, "The Phillips Case," May 26, 1886.

————, "The Phillips Case," May 26, 1886.

————, "The Phillips Trial," February 12, 1886.

————, "The Phillips Trial," May 25, 1886.

————, "The Reign of Blood," December 31, 1885.

————, "Reward Offered," December 31, 1885.

————, "San Antonio," January 31, 1886.

————, "Slain Servants," September 29, 1885.

————, "Slain Servants," September 30, 1885.

————, "Still a Mystery," January 2, 1885.

————, "Supposed Murderer Corraled," June 22, 1886.

————, "Taken at Temple," December 27, 1885.

————, "That Mexican," January 1, 1886.

————, "The Town Meeting," editorial, December 26, 1885.

————, "Trial Set," January 20, 1886.

————, "The Verdict," editorial, May 30, 1886.

————, "A Vigilance Committee," March 20, 1885.

————, "Walkabout," December 26, 1885.

————, "A Woman Wounded," June 3, 1885.

————, "Young Phillips," January 26, 1886.

————, "Young Phillips," February 14, 1886.

————, "Young Phillips," February 16, 1886.

Chester (PA) Times, "Outrages Repeated," February 1, 1886.

Fort Worth Daily Gazette, "Beason Dead," March 2, 1888.

————, "Beason Dying," March 1, 1888.

————, "A Startling Story," February 29, 1888.

Louisville Commercial, "Murdered by a Maniac," July 17, 1887.

————, "A Negro's Story," August 5, 1887.

Louisville Courier-Journal, "The Austin, Texas, Fiend," January 1, 1886.

————, "Brained with an Ax," September 30, 1885.

————, "A Brute Lynched," January 22, 1886.

————, "Crime and No Clew," July 20, 1887.

————, "Crime's Carnival," December 26, 1885.

————, "Jack the Ripper," December 15, 1888.

New York Times, "Burglar and Murderer," March 2, 1888.

————, "Three Murders in One Night," December 26, 1885.

San Antonio Daily Light, "Murder and Outrage," January 30, 1886.

————, "To a Focus," February 3, 1886.

Sugden, Philip. *The Complete History of Jack the Ripper.* New York, Carroll and Graf, 1995.

Mr. Flanagan Rings in the New Year
Louisville Courier-Journal, "Attempts to Lynch Flanagan,"
 February 18, 1897.
————, "Came From Tennessee," January 5, 1897.
————, "Death the Sentence," August 1, 1897.
————, "Escaped from Jail," September 16, 1897.
————, "Flanagan Makes Up a Story . . .," January 2, 1897.
————, "Flanagan's Neck Saved," January 10, 1899.
————, "Flanagan's Second Trial," July 26, 1897.
————, "Militia Protects a Murderer," February 19, 1897.
————, "Murderer Cheats the Gallows," March 7, 1900.
————, "Sheriff's Child Seized . . .," October 22, 1899.
————, "Speedy Trial for Flanagan," July 29, 1897.
————, "Three Lay Dead," January 1, 1897.

Blue Floyd's Light Show
Cornett, William T. *Letcher County, Ky.: A Brief History.*
 Prestonsburg: State-Wide Printing Co., 1967.
The Hanging of Floyd Frazier. N.p., 1984.
Louisville Courier-Journal, "Alleged Murderer on Trial,"
 January 24, 1908.
————, "Appeal Taken from a Death Sentence," June 27, 1909.
————, "Attempt to Escape," March 16, 1910.
————, "Breaks Down When Told Court's Decision," January
 31, 1910.
————, "Capture Floyd Frazier," November 20, 1908.
————, "Charged with Murder of Woman," September 13,
 1907.
————, "Crowds Poured into Whitesburg...," April 8, 1910.
————, "Death Penalty in Floyd Frazier Case," April 28, 1909.
————, "Death Watch," April 5, 1910.
————, "Evidence in Frazier Murder Case Completed,"
 April 25, 1909.
————, "Floyd County Jury to Try... Frazier," April 26,
 1908.
————, "Floyd Frazier on Trial," April 29, 1908.
————, "Floyd Frazier Sentenced," May 5, 1909.

————, "Floyd Frazier to be Executed Today," May 19, 1910.

————, "Floyd Frazier's Trial," April 23, 1909.

————, "Frazier Must Hang," May 18, 1910.

————, "Frazier to Hang April 7," March 8, 1910.

————, "Frazier to Hang July 23," May 3, 1908.

————, "Guarded in Jail," January 16, 1908.

————, "Hung Jury in Murder Case," January 28, 1908.

————, "The Last Hanging," April 4, 1910.

————, "Murder Cases on Docket," April 20, 1909.

————, "Murdered and Thrown into Drain," May 24, 1907.

————, "Murderer to Face Trial," April 21, 1908.

————, "Must Hang," January 29, 1910.

————, "Must Hang Thursday," April 6, 1910.

————, "Pays Penalty," May 20, 1910.

————, "Ready for Execution," May 16, 1910.

————, "Respite for Condemned Man," April 7, 1910.

————, "Taken to Pineville Jail," May 2, 1908.

————, "To Make Final Appeal," March 30, 1910.

————, "Under Death Sentence . . .," May 16, 1909.

————, "Want Commutation of Sentence," February 11, 1910.

————, "Would Save His Neck," March 31, 1910.

Henry Delaney's Half-Hour Marriage

Louisville Courier-Journal, "All Admit Their Guilt," April 9, 1893.

————, "Arguing Delaney's Case," November 23, 1894.

————, "Attorneys Each Spoke Half a Day," November 24, 1894.

————, "The Delaney Case," March 23, 1895.

————, "Delaney Gets Another Continuance," July 10, 1895.

————, "Delaney May Go Free," February 14, 1895.

————, "Delaney Released on Bond," September 26, 1894.

————, "Delaney Released on Bond," November 29, 1894.

————, "George Delaney on Trial," March 17, 1896.

————, "George Delaney's Trial," March 19, 1896.

———, "A Girl's Ruin," April 6, 1893.

———, "Henry Delaney Acquitted," March 19, 1895.

———, "Henry Delaney's Trial," March 14, 1895.

———, "In and About Kentucky," April 9, 1896.

———, "In His Own Behalf," March 15, 1895.

———, "Jail Under Guard," April 11, 1893.

———, "The jury in the case of Henry Delaney . . .," November 27, 1894.

———, "Jury Secured for Henry Delaney," March 12, 1895.

———, "The Jury Will Get the Case . . . Today," March 20, 1896.

Kirchner, Dennis. *Sourcebook of Union County History, Volume Two*. N.p., 1988.

———, "Laid Bare," April 8, 1893.

———, "Lewis Land Pardoned," June 19, 1897.

———, "A Mockery of Justice," March 22, 1895.

———, "Modifies His Confession," April 10, 1893.

———, "Murdered Bride's Body Stolen . . .," November 28, 1907.

———, "A New Trial Refused," March 29, 1896.

———, "No Verdict, Hung Jury the Probable Result . . .," March 21, 1896.

———, "Odds and Ends of State News," March 25, 1895.

———, "Other Arrests," April 7, 1893.

———, "A Regular Don Juan," September 6, 1894.

———, "Sequel to a Crime," September 3, 1894.

———, "Six Years in the Pen," March 22, 1896.

———, "A Special Judge," March 20, 1895.

———, "Strong Case Against Delaney," November 22, 1894.

———, "To the Jury Today," March 16, 1895.

———, "A Tragedy Recalled," May 31, 1898.

———, "Trial of George Delaney," March 11, 1896.

———, "The Verdict Unsatisfactory," March 22, 1895.

Psychopathia Sexu-Alice

Bolivar (TN) Bulletin, "Alice Mitchell Dead," April 1, 1898.

———, "Alice Mitchell's Death," April 8, 1898.

Krafft-Ebing, Dr. Richard. *Psychopathia Sexualis*. 12th ed.

1903. Reprint, Brooklyn: Physicians and Surgeons Book Co., 1935.

Louisville Courier-Journal, "After Those Letters." February 14, 1892.

———, "Alice Mitchell Dead," April 1, 1898.

———, "Alice Mitchell Improving," October 1, 1892.

———, "Alice Mitchell Is Insane," July 31, 1892.

———, "Alice Mitchell Played Ball," July 22, 1892.

———, "Alice Mitchell's Insanity," July 19, 1892.

———, "Alice Mitchell's Letters," July 21, 1892.

———, "Alice Mitchell's Story," July 28, 1892.

———, "Anxious to See Her," August 4, 1892.

———, "The Attempted Elopement," July 23, 1892.

———, "Before the Law," February 2, 1892.

———, "Bernhardt Interested," February 17, 1892.

———, "Both Indicted," January 31, 1892.

———, "Drawing Pictures," March 3, 1892.

———, "Fellow Inmates Love Her," March 1, 1893.

———, "For Health's Sake," February 28, 1892.

———, "The Freda Ward Case," September 20, 1892.

———, "From Mother to Child," July 20, 1892.

———, "Getting At the Facts," January 30, 1892.

———, "Habeas Corpus Proceedings," February 12, 1892.

———, "Had a Man Correspondent," February 12, 1892.

———, "Imperative Insanity," July 26, 1892.

———, "Insanity the Plea," January 29, 1892.

———, "In the Same Cell," January 27, 1892.

———, "Like a Tigress," January 26, 1892.

———, "Lillie Johnson Set Free," March 30, 1893.

———, "Lillie Johnson's Story," February 25, 1892.

———, "Made to Unvail [sic]," February 16, 1892.

———, "Miss Mitchell's Defense," February 6, 1892.

———, "Miss Mitchell's Vagaries," February 22, 1892.

———, "Odds and Ends About Women," November 16, 1893.

———, "Placed Where Maniacs Dwell," August 2, 1892.

———, "A Ruling on the Letters," February 23, 1892.

———, "Seem to Be Indifferent," January 28, 1892.

————, "Still Talking Insanity," July 27, 1892.

————, "Taken Under Advisement," February 26, 1892.

————, "Thank Goodness!" February 24, 1892.

————, "Their First Sunday in Jail," February 1, 1892.

————, "There is now no doubt . . .," editorial, February 23, 1892.

————, "The Trial of Alice Mitchell," June 28, 1892.

————, "Tried to Drown Herself," June 9, 1895.

————, "Two Queer Girls," February 11, 1894.

————, "Two Silly Women," May 3, 1899.

————, "Undoubtedly Insane," July 24, 1892.

Memphis Commercial Appeal, "Alice Mitchell died yesterday morning . . .," April 1, 1898.

The Two Mr. Rathbuns

Louisville Courier-Journal, "After Silence of Nine Years," August 6, 1909.

————, "At Work," November 22, 1901.

————, "Beats Barrier," August 7, 1909.

————, "Begins Today. Rathbun Goes to Prison . . .," December 25, 1901.

————, "Both Sides Are Ready For Trial," December 14, 1901.

————, "Broke Down," November 15, 1901.

————, "Can it be true . . .," editorial, December 12, 1901.

————, "Caused Surprise, Report of No Poison Found . . .," December 12, 1901.

————, "Dark Plot to Murder . . .," November 12, 1901.

————, "Dead Body Will Be Started to Louisville Today," November 18, 1901.

————, "Fate . . . Still Undecided," December 23, 1901.

————, "Feels Better," November 16, 1901.

————, "For Murder Rathbun Indicted . . .," November 23, 1901.

————, "Found Dead," November 8, 1901.

————, "In a Vault," November 25, 1901.

————, "In Good Health," November 26, 1901.

————, "Lieut. Rathbun . . .," November 10, 1901.

————, "Last Step," November 24, 1901.

————, "Marries in Memphis," June 19, 1903.

————, "Men for Jurors," December 18, 1901.

————, "More Trouble For . . . Rathbun When Released," December 26, 1903.

————, "Mother of Rathbun Receives His Belongings," January 8, 1902.

————, "Murder?" November 9, 1901.

————, "'My Husband,' Exclaimed Mrs. Talbert . . .," November 27, 1901.

————, "No Poison?" December 11, 1901.

————, "Not So Easy," December 26, 1901.

————, "Parole May Be Given . . .," December 15, 1903.

————, "Prisoners Expect to Be Free Next Christmas," December 26, 1902.

————, "Proof Must Be Offered by Rathbun Himself . . .," November 13,   1901.

————, "Rathbun a Free Man," April 22, 1910.

————, "Rathbun Has Diphtheria," January 12, 1902.

————, "Rathbun is Not Talbert," November 28, 1901.

————, "Reject...Petition for Parole," January 5, 1904.

————, "Start Back," November 21, 1901.

————, "Still Out," December 22, 1901.

————, "Taken Back," November 14, 1901.

————, "Tells More," November 17, 1901.

————, "Thinks May be Husband's," December 3, 1901.

————, "Third Degree," December 24, 1901.

————, "To 'Widow" the Corpse Is to Be Delivered," November 19, 1901.

————, "Trial Begins . . . Today," December 16, 1901.

————, "Uncertain As To the Cause . . .," December 21, 1901.

————, "Used Poison, Says Prosecutor . . . ," December 20, 1901.

————, "Who Was It?" November 11, 1901.

————, "Why Not?" November 20, 1901.

————, "Will Finish His Analysis . . .," December 8, 1901.

Two Shopworn Legal Defenses

Louisville Courier-Journal, "Although there is reputed to be . . . ," editorial, July 4, 1907.

———, "Change of Venue in Judge Loving's Case," May 30, 1907.

———, "Defense Claims Loving Was Insane," June 27, 1907.

———, "Judge Loving's Mistake." Editorial, June 27, 1907.

———, "Judge Makes Drastic Ruling," June 28, 1907.

———, "Judge Strikes Out Unwritten Law," June 29, 1907.

———, "Loving Acquitted of Estes' Murder," June 30, 1907.

———, "More Unwritten Law," editorial, April 25, 1907.

———, "Murder Made Easy," editorial, July 1, 1907.

———, "Shot Him Down," April 24, 1907.

———, "Sobbing, She Tells Story," June 26, 1907.

———, "Unwritten Law is Loving's Defense," June 25, 1907.

———, "The Victims of 'Insanity,'" editorial, May 2, 1907.

———, "The Virginia statesman who proposes . . .," editorial, July 2, 1907.

Rube Burrows Has His Portrait Taken

Louisville Courier-Journal, "Bad Rube Skips Out," September 4, 1889.

———, "The Bandit King," October 10, 1890.

———, "A Bloodless Fight With Burrows," November 1, 1889.

———, "Bold Rube Burrows," September 26, 1889.

———, "Burrows' Captors," October 26, 1890.

———, "Burrows' Captors," December 20, 1890.

———, "The Burrows Gang Suspected," May 31, 1890.

———, "Burrows' Slayer," December 16, 1890.

———, "Burrows Still At Large," October 30, 1889.

———, "Captured by Outlaws," October 29, 1889.

———, "Desperado Rube Burrows," July 19, 1889.

———, "A Desperado's Death," October 9, 1890.

———, "Desperate Rube Burrows," October 27, 1889.

———, "His Last Jump," November 11, 1890.

———, "Is It the Real Rube?" December 26, 1889.

———, "It Was a Fake," November 11, 1889.

————, "Mississippi Prisoners En Route North," December 9, 1890.

————, "On Rube Burrows' Trail," December 15, 1889.

————, "Outlaw Rube Burrows," August 8, 1889.

————, "The Outlaws Escape," October 31, 1889.

————, "The Outlaw's Home," November 7, 1890.

————, "Rewards Paid Over," September 12, 1891.

————, "Rube and His Gang," October 4, 1889.

————, "Rube Burrows," September 5, 1890.

————, "Rube Burrows . . . Captured in Alabama," October 8, 1890.

————, "Rube Burrows Again," March 17, 1890.

————, "Rube Burrows Gets Away," October 28, 1889.

————, "Rube Burrows' Pal," December 28, 1889.

————, "Rube Burrows' Pal," April 12, 1890.

————, "Rube Burrows' Partner Convicted," November 14, 1890.

————, "Rube Burrows, the Outlaw," February 9, 1890.

————, "Rube Burrows' Victim," March 9, 1890.

————, "Rube Burrows' Victim," March 21, 1890.

————, "Rube Holds the Fort," August 1, 1889.

————, "Rube Was Not Killed," August 9, 1889.

————, "Rube's Partner," July 17, 1890.

————, "Rube's Partner," July 28, 1890.

————, "Supposed To Be Burrows," November 15, 1889.

————, "The Trial of Rube Burrows," May 28, 1890.

————, "Troops After Rube," July 31, 1889.

————, "Was He Murdered?" November 9, 1889.

————, "Watching For Burrows," September 13, 1890.

————, "Will Never Take Him Alive," August 2, 1889.

A Farce in More Ways Than One

Chattanooga Times, "The Entire Troupe Leaves the City," September 26, 1899, 5.

————, "A Fair Test of Public Sentiment . . . ," January 12, 1900.

————, "Frank Leiden, Actor, Shot By a Woman," September 23, 1899.

———, "Her Health Failing," September 30, 1899.

———, "The Julia Morrison Case Aftermath," January 14, 1900.

———, "Julia Morrison James a Free Woman," January 11, 1900.

———, "Ladies of City Visit Julia Morrison," September 25, 1899.

———, "The Last Act," January 12, 1900.

———, "Leiden's Murder Will be Investigated by Grand Jury . . .," September 28, 1899.

———, "Miss Morrison Held to Grand Jury," September 27, 1899.

———, "Miss Morrison Indicted for Murder," September 29, 1899.

———, "Trial of Miss Morrison Continued," September 24, 1899.

Louisville Courier-Journal, "Acquittal the Verdict . . .," January 11, 1900.

———, "Actress Indicted for Murder," September 29, 1899.

———, "Actress Julia Morrison Testifies . . .," January 6, 1900.

———, "Argument Begun by Attorneys . . .," January 10, 1900.

———, "An attempt to make a heroine . . .," editorial, October 6, 1899.

———, "Bail Refused," October 5, 1899.

———, "Grand Jury Recalled," September 26, 1899.

———, "Held For Trial," September 27, 1899.

———, "Important Testimony," January 8, 1900.

———, "Influential Women Call . . .," September 25, 1899.

———, "Interest Manifested in Physician's Testimony . . .," January 8, 1900.

———, "Julia Morrison on Trial . . .," January 5, 1900.

———, "Julia Morrison's Case," December 21, 1899.

———, "Medical Experts Testify . . .," January 9, 1900.

———, "Plea of Insanity," January 7, 1900.

———, "Plea of Insanity," editorial, January 12, 1900.

————, "Public Sentiment," January 23, 1900.

————, "Real Tragedy," September 23, 1899.

————, "Self-Defense," October 4, 1899.

Christmas for the Sims Gang

Louisville Courier-Journal, "May Be More Bloodshed." December 29, 1891.

————, "Men and Women Lynched," January 7, 1892.

————, "Neil Sims Reported Surrounded," January 9, 1892.

————, "Shot Down Like Dogs," December 25, 1891.

————, "The Sims Lynching Denied," January 8, 1892.

————, "Sims Surrounded," December 26, 1891.

————, "Two More Strung Up," December 28, 1891.

————, "Wiping Out the Sims Gang," January 19, 1892.

New York Times, "Another of the Sims Gang Lynched," January 19, 1892.

————, "Another Sims Lynched," December 31, 1891.

————, "Bob Sims Lynched," December 27, 1891.

————, "Bob Sims Reappears," December 25, 1891.

————, "Bob Sims War," December 26, 1891.

————, "An Idyll of Alabama," December 30, 1891.

————, "The Sims War," December 29, 1891.

Crime and Punishment on the Fast Track

Florida Times-Union and Citizen [Jacksonville], "Both Tried to Plead Guilty," September 21, 1902.

————, "Bronson Murderers Hanged . . .," October 1, 1902.

————, "Coffins as Baptistries . . .," September 28, 1902.

————, "Day Set for Trial," September 19, 1902.

————, "Died from Shock," September 22, 1902.

————, "Excitement is High," September 6, 1902.

————, "Faircloth Stays at Gainesville," September 9, 1902.

————, "Homicide in Levy County," August 31, 1902.

————, "In Gainesville Jail," September 4, 1902.

————, "The Lewis Murderers Convicted . . .," September 22, 1902.

———, "The sentence of two white men . . .," editorial, September 23, 1902.

———, "Smith . . . Puts His Confession in Writing," September 15, 1902.

———, "White Men Confess . . .," September 13, 1902.

"Double Murder." *Louisville Courier-Journal,* September 13, 1902.

———, "Wonderful Nerve Exhibited . . .," October 1, 1902.

A Murder Ballad

Louisville Courier-Journal, "Almost Escapes Electric Chair by Oversight," August 22, 1911.

———, "Coroner's Jury Returns Verdict of Murder," May 24, 1911.

———, "Deadly Voltage Imparts Strength . . .," August 23, 1911.

———, "Death Penalty Ordered . . .," June 24, 191.

———, "Electric Chair at the Eddyville Prison 'Fixed,'" August 27, 1911.

———, "Gov. Willson Protests," October 1, 1911.

———, "In and Out of Prison," May 21, 1911.

———, "Louisville Murderer Executed . . .," September 29, 1911.

———, "Negro Slayer on Way to Eddyville," August 21, 1911.

———, "Refuses to Enter Plea," May 25, 1911.

———, "Repents of Serving Devil and His Angels," August 24, 1911.

———, "Sennings' Negro Lunch Boy Kills Sweetheart," June 7, 1901.

———, "Sleeps Beside Bodies . . .," May 21, 1911.

———, "Wants Medium to Talk With Women He Slew," June 21, 1911.

———, "Will Die September 28," July 2, 1911.

Louisville Times, "Negro Murders Two; Sleeps Near Bodies," May 20, 1911.

———, "Verdict of Guilty by Coroner's Jury," May 23, 1911.

————, "'Will Wear White Robe in Heaven,'" September 28, 1911.
Newman, John. E-mails to the author. November 23, 2009; December 11, 2009.

The Reprehensible Mr. Powers
Davis, Dorothy. *History of Harrison County, West Virginia.* Clarksburg: American Association of University Women, 1970.
Eastman, Mary, and Mary Bolté. *Dark and Bloodied Ground.* Riverside, CT: Chatham Press, 1973.
Louisville Courier-Journal, "'Bluebeard' Sentenced To Death," December 11, 1931.
————, "'Bluebeard' Sobbingly Constructs His Alibi," December 10, 1931.
————, "Bodies of Woman, Three Children Found," August 29, 1931.
————, "Bodies Sought In Powers' Well," September 1, 1931.
————,"Killer's Trunk Adds To Clews," September 2, 1931.
————, "Man Says He Slew Widow, Three Tots," August 30, 1931.
————, "Powers Confesses and is Hanged," March 19, 1932.
————, "Powers Loses Hope For Life," March 18, 1932.
————, "Wife of Bluebeard Turns Against Him," September 3, 1931.
New York Times, "Admits Killing Four; Fifth Body Found," August 30, 1931.
————, "Family of Four Slain," August 29, 1931.
————, "Mob Surrounds Jail Where Powers is Held," September 20, 1931.
————, "Outwit Mob Seeking Lynching of Powers," September 21, 1931.
————, "Powers Confesses to Fifth Murder," August 31, 1931.
————, "Powers Convicted; He Faces Hanging," December 11, 1931.
————, "Powers is Hanged, Smiles at His End," March 19, 1932.

————, "Powers, Killer of Five, Held Legally Sane," September 1, 1931.

————, "Powers Pointed Out By Slain Woman's Kin," December 9, 1931.

————, "Powers Sentenced to Hang March 18," December 13, 1931.

————, "Powers Sobs Denial of Bluebeard Deed," December 10, 1931.

————, "Powers Unmoved As Death Is Urged," December 8, 1931.

————, "Powers's Wife Detained," September 7, 1931.

————, "Sues Powers for $12,000," September 6, 1931.

Whipple, Sidney B. "Clarksburg in Roman Holiday as Powers Calmly Faces Jury," *Louisville Courier-Journal,* December 8, 1931.

Index